Rosa

32.95
3/55
LA

Maya Resurgence
in Guatemala

MAYA RESURGENCE IN GUATEMALA

Q'EQCHI' EXPERIENCES

Richard Wilson

University of Oklahoma Press : Norman and London

This book is published with the generous assistance of Edith Gaylord Harper.

Library of Congress Cataloging-in-Publication Data

Wilson, Richard, 1964–
    Maya resurgence in Guatemala : Q'eqchi' experiences / Richard Wilson.
    p.   cm.
    Includes bibliographical references and index.
    ISBN 0–8061–2690–6 (alk. paper)
    1. Kekchi Indians—Ethnic identity.   2. Kekchi Indians—Religion.
    3. Kekchi Indians—Government relations.   I. Title.
    F1465.2.K5W57   1995
    305.897'4—dc20   94–36177
                                                              CIP

The paper in this book meets the guidelines for permanence and durability of the Committee on Production Guidelines for Book Longevity of the Council on Library Resources, Inc. ∞

1   2   3   4   5   6   7   8   9   10

For Helene and Kai

CONTENTS

ILLUSTRATIONS

(Note: All illustrations are by the author.)

ACKNOWLEDGMENTS

I owe my greatest thanks to those Q'eqchi's and others who helped me in Alta Verapaz. For security reasons, I cannot name all those who generously gave their time and extended their friendship. B'antiox eere, xineetinq'a xaq.

My greatest intellectual debt is to the late Michael Sallnow, whose unrelenting enthusiasm and sensitive criticism was a constant source of encouragement and stimulation. He was a kind friend and a true scholar, and I, among many others, will miss him a great deal.

This work has also benefited from criticism by Joanna Overing, Olivia Harris, Stephen Hugh-Jones, John Watanabe, David Stoll, Rob Stones, and participants at seminars at the London School of Economics, Cambridge University, the University of Essex, and the University of Manchester. The usual disclaimer applies.

At the University of Oklahoma Press, I would like to thank editor-in-chief John N. Drayton, associate editor Mildred Logan, and two anonymous scholars for their meticulous reading of the manuscript and valuable comments. Jane Kepp's thorough editing work made this a clearer and easier book to read.

Finally, a personal thanks is due to Helene Kvale and my parents for their unstinting support.

Research was funded by a grant-in-aid from the Wenner-Gren Foundation for Anthropological Research and by the Central Research Fund of the University of London.

RICHARD WILSON

London, England

A NOTE ON Q'EQCHI' ORTHOGRAPHY

Throughout this book I use the new unified orthography of Guatemalan Mayan languages promoted by the Academia de las Lenguas Mayas in Guatemala. The Q'eqchi' alphabet has thirty-three letters: a, aa, b', ch, ch', e, ee, h, i, ii, j, k, k', l, m, n, o, oo, p, q, q', r, s, t, t', tz, tz', u, uu, w, x, y, '(glottalized stop).

This orthography is superior to those previously developed because of its simplicity, its decreased dependence on Castilian, and its heightened compatibility with typewriters. Most importantly, it systematizes and standardizes sounds common among all Guatemalan Mayan languages, which hitherto have been written in different ways.

I have employed the new alphabet when writing Mayan words and the names of ethnic groups. I have not, however, changed the spelling of place names. The alphabets are so new and hotly disputed that place names have yet to be revised, although this may come with time. Thus, the ethnic group and language are the "K'iche'," but the department is still spelled "Quiché."

I have not used accents on Q'eqchi' words, all of which are

stressed on the last syllable. The plural in Q'eqchi' is created by adding the suffix/prefix *eb'*, but I have used the English *s* to avoid confusion.

R.W.

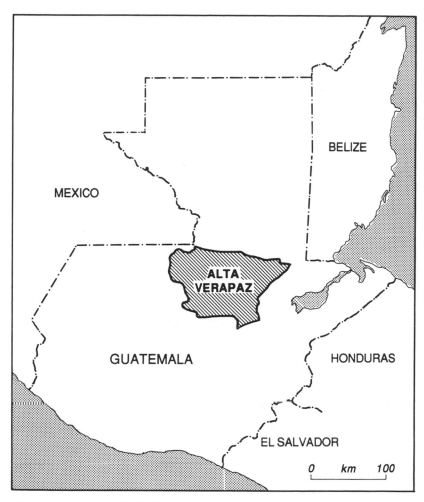

Map 1. Guatemala and Alta Verapaz

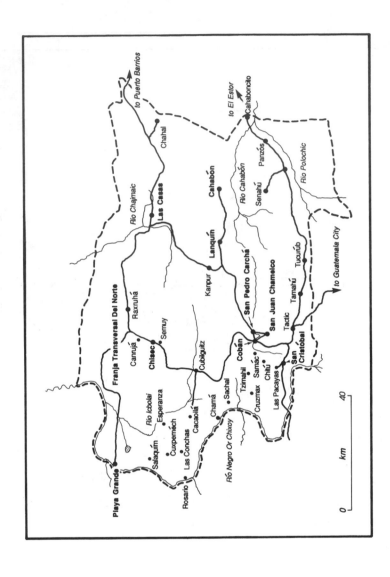

Map 2. Alta Verapaz

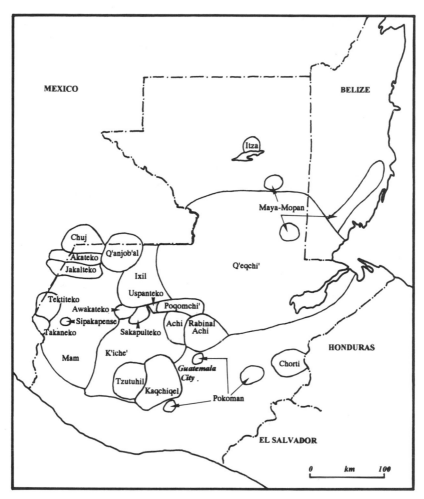

Map 3. Mayan languages of Guatemala

Maya Resurgence
in Guatemala

CONCEPTUALIZING IDENTITY

I originally went to Guatemala in 1987 to study how Catholic base communities were involved in the formation of rural peasant leagues and trade unions. It was a naive plan: the rural trade unions had been virtually wiped out by army repression during the early 1980s, and the few peasant organizations that had survived certainly did not want a conspicuous foreigner traipsing around after them, calling attention to their activities. I ended up doing something completely different.

I had a contact in Alta Verapaz, so I went there and drifted into a semiurban Q'eqchi' community. I persisted for a while in asking about popular organizations, but people were generally reluctant to entertain such topics; they were still dangerous to discuss. During the first few months, it was difficult to get people talking at length about anything. In a "pre-fieldwork seminar" at the London School of Economics, we novices had been advised by Maurice Bloch, "You've got to talk to people about what obsesses them. For instance, if you were to ask the Merina what obsesses them, they would take you to the graveyard." I clearly had not discovered what it was that preoccupied and enthralled the people I was living with.

I had to fall ill to find out how to get people talking. During the dry season, I helped a Q'eqchi' friend dig a well near his house. We dug for two days, deep down into the earth, until we reached the water table at about nine meters. That evening, I felt shaky, weak, and faint. By the next day, I had a soaring temperature and diarrhea and was vomiting every fifteen minutes. The Q'eqchi' family I stayed with was extremely concerned and called over some leaders of the Catholic base group. This grassroots organization within the Church includes about thirty families who meet twice a week to pray and reflect upon the Bible. They divined that the mountain spirit had snatched my spirit while I was down in the well.

I was worried to hear this, but at the same time reassured to know the cause of my sickness. More than anything, I was surprised that these urban Q'eqchi's believed in the traditional earth deities. They had never said anything to me about the tellurian gods, and until that moment they had acted like paragons of orthodox Catholicism. All the same, I appreciated being treated for spirit loss and found that the transition from active anthropologist to passive patient can expose one to the operative symbols of a local culture. I got my spirit back and improved quickly. Afterwards, I started enquiring about the mountain spirits and found them to be a subject upon which many Q'eqchi's could hold forth for hours.

DOING RESEARCH IN Q'EQCHI' COMMUNITIES

During 1987–88, I lived for sixteen months in Q'eqchi' communities in the municipalities of San Pedro Carchá, Cobán, and Cahabón in the department of Alta Verapaz, Guatemala (see maps 1 and 2). I later returned to Cobán for six weeks in 1991.

At first, I lived for a month in one rural village and then eight months in another community on the outskirts of a town. Each of these communities comprised about thirty households and included a variety of occupational groups, from subsistence cultivators to artisans and proletarians. They employed intensive agricultural methods because of demographic pressure on the land. Many members of these communities had access to no more than three to five hectares, and a large number were landless. The members of these communities were regularly exposed to Ladino and national culture through schools, the workplace, and town life in general. Over 50 percent, however, were monolingual Q'eqchi' speakers who understood some Castilian but spoke none.

Using the urban community as my base, I spent the next seven months in about ten remote rural communities, visiting each of them frequently. I could not stay long in any one because of the militarization of the countryside. A prolonged presence was not safe for either the villagers or myself. Rural indigenous villages were traditionally disparate, with each house a long distance from the next. The only physical foci of community life were the graveyard, the village church, and the mountain shrines. This spatial format changed during the war in the early 1980s. In all the rural villages I visited, the houses had been concentrated together by the military into a few hundred square yards. The villages were patrolled by groups of vigilantes drawn from the civilian population and armed by the military.

As it turned out, this multilocale fieldwork method facilitated comparative insights that I would not have gained had I remained in one village. Once I began to travel, I came across a remarkable degree of localized idiosyncracy in knowledge and practice. This enhanced my picture of cultural and religious diversity and allowed me to reach a more nuanced understanding of different experiences of the catechist program and the civil war.

Much of my early fieldwork was spent on intensive language learning, and this was time well invested. For the first five months, I was usually accompanied by someone who could interpret for me, after which I was sufficiently proficient in Q'eqchi' to go it alone. I did not have a basic command of Q'eqchi' until six months into my fieldwork.

The villagers initially categorized me as a young missionary, for after a while I was speaking the local language and attending Catholic services. This label wore off after a few weeks of my doing "normal" activities such as working in the fields, staying up late joking and telling stories, and eating maize and beans. (In the eyes of many rural Q'eqchi's, priests eat only high-status foods such as chicken.) Finally, most came to believe that I was writing a book for my people about their beliefs and way of life. That seemed to them quite a reasonable thing for me to do, because many viewed their spirituality as a source of pride.

During fieldwork, my contact was mainly, but not exclusively, with men. In most contexts, local moralities maintain rigid barriers between non-kin men and married women of childbearing age, but I could talk freely with unmarried girls and postmenopausal women. Elder women provided most of my information on the curing of illnesses, which is the main theme of chapter five.

At first I identified with young male catechists, since they were most likely to be bilingual and closest to the institutional church. The information in chapters five through eight is drawn mostly from these catechists. Slowly, I made stronger contacts with elders, who were generally not prejudiced against me for my earlier orthodox affiliations. Elders generously shared their knowledge and helped me construct a picture of religious tradition, the theme of chapters three through five. I cleared brush and planted and harvested maize with both elders and catechists and so was able to compare their beliefs and practices surrounding production.

I have not named any of my informants or the villages I spent time in, owing to possible ramifications for their security. I have used only informants' first names, and they have all been changed.

TRANSFORMING IDENTITIES

There are two discernible traditions within the literature on Mayan ethnicity and community. Robert Carmack (1990:129) writes that analysts have paid attention either to the form or to the content of ethnicity: either Indian identity is formed in opposition to Spaniards or Ladinos (mestizos), or there is a genuinely nativistic thread of tradition linking modern Mayas with pre-Hispanic society. John Watanabe (1990:183) identifies two similar approaches in the study of Mayan communities, which he refers to as historical contextualism (community as the result of opposition to colonial oppression) and cultural essentialism (community as primordial Mayan survival).

Since Eric Wolf's (1957) paradigmatic comments on the "closed corporate community," cultural essentialism has largely been replaced by historical contextualism. Wolf (1986:326) points out that when he wrote in the 1950s, "anthropologists of the time tended to shortcircuit four centuries of history, to draw a direct line from the pre-Colombian past to the Indian present." Reacting against cultural essentialism, Wolf gave greatest priority to macropolitical and macroeconomic changes. Indigenous cultures could be explained by reference to external regional and global structures, especially colonialism, "rather than in terms of cultural content" (1986:325).[1]

Many years later, the dominant view is still that Mayan culture or community is an artifact of Spanish colonialism, or, in Wolf's (1967:236) words, "a creature of the Spanish Conquest." This fundamentally materialist view has dominated approaches to Catholic (W. Smith 1977) and Protestant (Annis 1987) religions, indigenous identity (Friedlander 1975; Warren

1978), and analyses of state-community relations (C. Smith 1990a). Orthodox Marxists such as the Guatemalan historian Severo Martínez Pelaez (1971) go a step further and argue that just about every aspect of indigenous culture and society was created by Spanish colonial oppression.

These observations have wider import for anthropological approaches to identity, which have been dominated by Fredrik Barth's (1969) boundary perspective. This paradigm emphasizes the relational attributes of categorization, which can be studied by looking at the boundaries between ethnic groups. Barth, and Edmund Leach (1954) before him, asserted that the signs of ethnicity are arbitrary, so they can flux and change. The past has little or no determining effect on cultural signs and is only an ideological construction of the present. In this view, identity is a structure of difference—an organizational vessel that is static even though its elements change. Identity is a form whose cultural content is ultimately arbitrary and undeserving of attention. Thus Barth shares with Wolf a view that the cultural content of identity is a secondary phenomenon and should not be the focus of research. According to Barth (1969:15), "the critical focus of investigation from this point of view becomes the ethnic boundary that defines the group, *not the cultural stuff* that it encloses" (my emphasis). Barth's mentor, Leach (1954:16), took a similar view of culture, writing that it is "the dress" of the social situation, "a product and an accident of history."

Wolf's materialism and Barth's boundary model have been applied to Mayan ethnicity in ways that have emphasized structure and ethnic dualism to the detriment of process and experience.[2] The materialist-relational perspective surfaces in the repeated assertion that Mayan culture is a reflection of Spanish-Ladino culture, having been created through opposition to the Ladino world (see C. Smith 1990a:220). For example, Pierre van den Berghe and Benjamin Colby (1969) use a Barthian approach toward ethnicity in the Ixil Triangle of Quiché. They conclude that indigenous peoples' assimilation of Ladino characteristics does not influence the patterning of social roles or the rigidity of ethnic boundaries. Basically, they assert that the content of identity changes while the boundaries remain the same. Further, the authors argued that Ladino characteristics have come to represent classlike differences within Ixil society itself.

John Hawkins (1984) is a particularly ardent advocate of a relational approach to ethnicity that derives from Ferdinand de Saussure. He also agrees with Lévi-Strauss that meaning is created through binary oppositions and that analyses of culture should focus on abstract forms and not on semantic content. For Hawkins (1984:10), ethnicity in Guatemala is "a system of inverse ideologies." Like most relationalists, Hawkins holds that ethnicity is primarily synchronic, and he argues that Indian culture is inversely derivative of Spanish culture rather than continuous with a Mayan past. Thus he writes that "Indian ideology is a reversal of the structure etched in the Spanish crucible-mold" (1984:23).

The relational approach to identity is the preeminent paradigm of Guatemalan societies not only among U.S. anthropologists but also in sociology, cultural studies, and anthropology in general. Even in books with titles like *History and Ethnicity* (Tonkin, McDonald, and Chapman 1989), one finds a predominantly presentist and relational view. Ethnicity is "a notion only existing in a context of oppositions and relativities." (Tonkin, McDonald, and Chapman 1989:17). Most contributors to that volume study solely how the present creates the past, and not the reverse. One exception is J.D.Y. Peel (1989:198), who points out the functionalist character of explanations that see identity as little more than a product of its "contemporary structural context."

I do not mean to deny the explanatory power of either the materialist or the relational view. Wolf's view has facilitated a powerful analysis of the political economy of ethnicity. Certainly any study should concentrate on community boundaries, which are exactly as Barth conceptualizes them—ultimately unfixed, temporal, and contextually renegotiated. Yet the signs of ethnicity are not just arbitrary "accidents." They are linked to historical meanings, the "cultural stuff" Barth so highhandedly dismissed. It is possible to analyze the historical dimensions of identities without treating them in an essentialist fashion. We must discover how both past and present experiences are implicit in identity and how they enable and limit each other. This book does not attempt to supplant a relational view with a cultural essentialist one; my argument is that both paradigms, relational and essentialist, are limited in scope. In this way, my narrative seeks a contextualized synthesis between structure and process.

There is now more concern in social anthropology with historical transformations of the "cultural stuff" within ethnic boundaries (e.g., Comaroff and Comaroff 1992; Eriksen 1991, 1993; Peel 1989).[3] The problem, it seems, is how to trace the history of the cultural dimension of ethnicity without relapsing into essentialism. John Comaroff and Jean Comaroff (1992:20) offer a programmatic statement that informs this study: "Our historical anthropology begins by eschewing the very possibility of a realist, or essentialist, history. This is not to say that there are no essences or realities in the world. Quite the opposite. But our objective . . . is to show as cogently as possible how they are constructed: how realities become real, how essences become essential, how materialities materialize."

Among writings on the Mayas, several recent contributions have taken a more historical and culturalist view. Kay Warren (1992) examines Kaqchikel notions of the self over time, Robert

Carlsen and Martin Prechtel (1991) sensitively explore the historical dimensions of Atiteco religious symbolism, and Robert M. Hill and John Monaghan (1987) document pre-Columbian continuities in highland community social organization.[4] Against Wolf's historical contextualism, Watanabe has argued effectively that the Maya community he studied constitutes a "problematic social nexus in its own right" (1992:4), with its own "existential sovereignty" (1992:12). He recognizes (1992:58) the dialectical and relational aspects of Chimbal identity, yet he writes that it cannot be reduced to a simple opposition: "The otherness represents the boundary, *not the substance*, of ethnic identity in Guatemala" (1992:106, my emphasis). In getting at that "substance," Watanabe is willing to explore historical cultural continuities through a comparison with Charles Wagley's (1949) previous ethnographic study of the community.

As my monograph demonstrates, change occurs within a constrained and processual framework of meaning. New criteria of identity gravitate around traditional signs of community, even though they may at times express opposite meanings. What the concept of identity needs is a "polythetic definition" (Fardon 1987:170) that explores identity's history of use. Classificatory categories have a complex history that must be investigated; we cannot merely paint a static portrait of each constituent element ("Q'eqchi' language," "Q'eqchi' religion," etc.). Like the floor of an old car, the symbols of identity carry littered traces of their previous occupants. Culture is not a bequest of the past (Peel 1989:199), yet it is no more (and no less) an accident of history than are social structures. There may be discontinuities, ruptures, and slippages, but history constrains and capacitates narratives in such a way that few (if any) aspects of culture are wholly free-floating or unworthy of ethnographic attention.

Benedict Anderson's (1991) ideas about the "imagined community" furnish a more grounded, historical, and discursive approach to identity. Anderson has written mainly about nationalism, yet his approach can just as easily be applied to other types of community.[5] His ideas are particularly valuable in transcending sterile ethnic dualisms and focusing on the role of the state in shaping indigenous identities. The state's role in identity construction is but one of a number of possible relational influences including Catholic and Protestant churches, class organizations, and so forth. Drawing from Michel Foucault, power is construed as multicentered and includes the power to influence the reimagining of identities.

Using Anderson's language, collective identities are formed over time by the action of historical processes on preexisting elements of community and culture; identity is tied to an "imagined community" with a shared past and a common future. A cultural and historical perspective is especially vital to understanding emergent identities because ideas of history and tradition play such an important part in their construction.

For a new imagined community to be established, there must be fundamental changes in prior modes of apprehending the world, which make it possible to "think" the nation (Anderson 1991:22). Anderson argues that the nation arose out of the dissolution of the political power of the sacred imagined community (Christendom) and the demise of the dynastic realm. The events that make up the themes of this book—religious conversions, armed insurrection, and state repression—all transformed previous ways of imagining the community. Yet they created new possibilities for rethinking the community and ethnic group. This book explores how radical "indigenist" catechists recreate Q'eqchi' ethnicity and base their imaginings on the tenets of past sacred communities. Just as, on a worldwide scale, nationalism filled the gaps left by the demise of the dynastic realm and sacred religious community, in Guatemala the demise of the traditional Q'eqchi' community made it possible to think the ethnic group as never before.

In summing up my synthetic approach, I argue that identity can usefully be conceptualized as a process of "constrained refashioning." Imaginings of community and ethnicity are contingent, relational strategies of the present, whose range of expression is framed by the structures and recurring symbols of the past.

THE SYMBOLISM OF IDENTITY

How can a fieldworker actually study historical transformations of identity and culture? I could never phrase in Q'eqchi', much less get an answer to, a question such as, "Uh, how would you say your cultural identity has changed in the last ten years?" But Q'eqchi's have their own idiom for discussing change — the symbolism of the mountain spirits, which are archetypal representations of identities. To begin to understand how different groups of Q'eqchi's perceive the recent changes, I follow their reflective discourse for making and remaking community.

As Max Weber argued, it is not possible to have a universal theory of ethnicity, just a "grounded theory" (Holy 1987:8). A central assumption here is that there is no "objective" basis for ethnic classification because "ethnic boundaries are between whoever people think they are between" (Fardon 1987:176). Ethnicity, then, is an eminently subjective phenomenon. Its coherence is more local and contextual than systemic.

In Q'eqchi' communities, identities are grounded in relation to the mountain cult. Q'eqchi' identities draw upon many dimensions of culture, but none so strongly as religion. This is the case, indeed, throughout the Mayan area, which is one reason why so many authors have focused on religion as a way into a variety of theoretical and substantive issues. For instance,

Carlsen and Prechtel (1991) concentrate on an Atiteco norma-
tive religious construct, *Jaloj K'exoj,* which in one sense means
"Flowering Mountain Earth." It is an archetypal element of local
culture that manifests a significant continuity with pre-Colombian culture. Why should religion be such a pithy idiom of
identity and culture? Richard Fardon (1987:171) offers one
explanation: "Ethnic discriminations are elements of more general classifications which identify relations of similarity and
difference within social universes. As such they are always
'adjacent' to other elements of these classifications which we
choose to treat as non-ethnic. Ethnic idioms draw sustenance
from and plagiarize these other idioms."

Edward Bruner (1984) has drawn attention to a disjunction
between two bodies of anthropological literature, one dealing
with symbolism and the other with ethnicity. He calls this "a
kind of self-induced scholarly schizophrenia" (1984:64). One
of the theoretical ambitions of this book is to bring those two
bodies of literature closer together.

The mountain spirit is a symbolic pocket containing the
history of various local identities. By reaching into it we can
document the twisting path of an identity and what the trip
along that path has meant for the actors. Antonio Gramsci
(1971:419) writes: "The starting point of critical elaboration is
the consciousness of what one really is, and is 'knowing thyself'
as a product of the historical process to date which has depos-
ited in you an infinity of traces, without leaving an inventory."
In Q'eqchi' discourses on the mountain spirits, we can see
Gramsci's "infinity of traces" left by the pre-Colombian period,
the colonial experience, the Catholic church, war, the modern
Guatemalan military, and so on. All of these influences on
Q'eqchi' identities are projected upon and contained within the
collective figure of the mountain spirit. Its meaning is irreduc-
ible and unfixed; it is transformative and ever changing in

relation to historical events and currents. The mountain spirit is a "recurring" symbol that disappears and emerges reinvented in each strategic context.

The mountain spirits are involved in the construction not only of community and ethnic identities but also of gender identities. Ideas of masculinity and femininity and of human health and fertility are intimately bound up with formulations of collective identity. Present sociological thinking places an emphasis on fragmented and multiple identities (e.g., Giddens 1991), but there can be more crossovers and linkages between identities than commonly supposed. I argue that the overlap between gender, fertility, community and ethnic identities results in different gender responses to external attempts to colonize local culture.

Narrating social history by focusing on a core cultural symbol, however, generates its own predicaments. The significance of the mountain spirit is irreconcilably altered by extracting the symbol from its own oral context and recreating it in a written, alien discourse. Fardon (1987:170) has pointed out that "when anthropologists appropriate indigenous terms for the business of comparison, they implicitly alter the practical significance of those terms."

WRITING HISTORIES

Throughout this book, I draw a distinction between the "traditional" religion of the elders and the "orthodox" religion of the catechists. This was the issue that caused me the most angst. In order to assess the changes caused by war and religious conversions, I needed some benchmark against which to compare them, and thus worked with local concepts of "tradition." Chapters three through five of this book assemble an artificial version of this collective past. Some elements of tradition are ongoing practices, whereas others remain murky. I continually had to grapple with competing versions of what was traditional and what was more recent. Subsequent chapters look at how religious conversion and war have altered this version of tradition.

Images of the past were inevitably reworked to some degree in the present context. The people with whom I lived had gone through massive cultural upheavals in the last few decades, which together implied a traumatic break with the past. Some Q'eqchi's embraced the changes, but others gazed back nostalgically. To complicate matters, some of the maverick catechists who once had enthusiastically attacked traditional religious beliefs were now repenting and struggling to reinstate them. I constantly had to ask myself, Whose sense of reality is this, and why might they hold this particular memory of the past? Such distinctions between memory and reality, between traditional and modern are inevitably contingent and embedded in a particular context.

I tried to follow people's own conceptions as much as possible and explain how and when those conceptions conflicted with other interpretations. Mine is not the only possible narrative, and no doubt there are those in Guatemala and elsewhere who will contest it. As this book shows, there no such thing as a single, coherent Q'eqchi' identity. Instead, many social actors, internal and external to Q'eqchi' communities, compete for the right to determine what it is to be Q'eqchi'. This means that there are a plurality of dissenting discourses on history that cannot be worked into one coherent version. This issue can never really be resolved because there is no single, monolithic history, only competing reconstructions of the past, some of which seem more plausible than others.

My account of historical patterns is based upon events and processes (e.g., war, evangelization) that are permeated with the consciousness of those who lived through them. I hope I have fruitfully combined two views of history: a version con-

structed by an analyst standing outside the events and a narrative that begins with the active consciousness of purposive
subjects (see Ingold 1986:74–75).

What follows is a patchwork of my own perspective mixed
with interviews of people in different places who never talk to
one another. It is not a complete master narrative but an
exploratory presentation of a multiplicity of views. The book
follows a number of currents and eddies through the recent
social past—including traditionalism, orthodox Catholicism,
war, and ethnic revivalism—without appealing to a systematized, monolithic "Q'eqchi' culture."

I should make clear that my research was inspired by, but is
not imitative of, the narrative of ethnic revivalists. I became
fascinated by their efforts to construct a new ethnic identity
based on language, to "indigenize" Catholicism, to create self-
sufficient economic practices, and to win more political participation as a Mayan people. My interest in Q'eqchi' history and
identities is very much an interest of the present with immediate practical and moral implications. It was not an interest that I
pursued alone in the field: rather, I was surrounded by conflicting
reconstructions of local narratives on community and the past.

Perhaps it was to be expected that as an anthropologist, I
would fall in with ethnic revivalists, or "indigenists." After all,
we engage in a similar project, the conscious reconstruction of
aspects of Q'eqchi' culture—mine on paper, theirs in real
communities. Both they and I are intellectuals of our societies
with a common interest in identities. Because of this, a central
worry during my writing was how to explore the historical
progressions and discontinuities of being Q'eqchi' without
lapsing into the same essentialism and foundationalism of the
pan-Q'eqchi' activists who had kindled my interest.

In order to explain the development of ethnic revivalism, I
present a sequence of identities—in order of appearance: tradi-

tional community (roughly 1970); Catholic base group (1975); class identity and civil war (1980–85), and ethnic revivalism (1985–present). This sequence is only a description of higher-order tendencies, because these paradigmatic identities still coexist in Q'eqchi' communities. There are no neat fault lines between different identities.

The order of presentation reflects a presentist bias, for history on the ground is reconstructed from various vantage points in the present by different interest groups, with a plurality of collective identities, who compete over an imagined past. The national military, Q'eqchi' traditionalists, and Catholic catechists from different epochs are all working on history and contesting their diverging interpretations. The past, however, is not a complete free-for-all. History and tradition are inevitably reconstructed in the present, but not with total disregard for events. Ethnography is a complex mixture of empirical underpinnings and a writer's fictions (Leach 1989), and yet it always has moral responsibilities emanating from the claims it advances. This statement applies not only to ethnographers but to the revivalists themselves, for if their reformulations are to have any resonance among their audience, they must connect at some level with shared meanings and collective experiences.

Finally, it is important to realize the ethical pitfalls of an outsider's writing the social history of people who have not yet done so for themselves. When Malinowski (1967:150) wrote in his diary during his fieldwork among the Trobrianders, "It is I who will describe them . . . [I who will] create them," he expressed the potentially enormous arrogance of the Zeus-like ethnographer who ushers a people into the globalized world of immortal scholarly texts.

Writing histories and cultures is a relationship of power. In Guatemala and elsewhere, there is a flourishing debate about who has the right to author the past. My view is that anthropologists' accounts are not the definitive versions but can be valuable, specialized bodies of knowledge. Although many aspects of this ethical dilemma are inherently unresolvable, it is possible to attend to certain obligations that make the process of researching and writing one of partnership and open dialogue. Keeping subjects informed during fieldwork and "repatriating" research after writing it up are part of such a commitment. My contribution to Q'eqchi' debates about identity has been conducted in a spirit of dialogue with those concerned, through a number of oral presentations of my work in Q'eqchi' in Cobán and through local publications in Spanish (Wilson 1993b, 1994).

The value of this work for the Q'eqchi' is limited for a number of reasons, including the language used and the tragically high rates of illiteracy in rural communities. Unlike other Mayan groups, Q'eqchi's have not, historically, generated a literary intelligentsia who consciously project a self-awareness of their ethnic identity. Even when this occurs, as it soon will, it remains to be seen whether this cultural elite will participate in the nationalist movement so prevalent in Guatemala. On a national level, there recently has been more dialogue between anthropologists and an emergent Mayan intelligentsia than at any other point in history. These interactions have been to the benefit of both groups, yet they have also thrown into relief the differences in interests between anthropologists and Mayan nationalists. Many Mayan nationalists see the role of foreign anthropologists as one of helping to identify only historical continuities and essential attributes of "Mayanness" (C. Smith 1991; Warren 1992; Watanabe 1995). Yet just as I have counseled against too "accidental" a view of history, so I would advise against one that confines its agenda to the inventing of traditions and naturalizing of transformative social categories.

CHAPTER TWO

ETHNICITY AND A
COLONIZED LANDSCAPE

This chapter provides contextual information on local identities, economy, and gender relations. The first section outlines the distinction between community and ethnic identity and briefly portrays Ladino-Q'eqchi' ethnic relations. The second section outlines class relations in the countryside, paying attention to the structure of the agricultural export economy and to existing forms of community and household production.

COMMUNITY AND ETHNIC IDENTITIES

Throughout this book, I will be working with a distinction between community and ethnic group. I argue that communities are constructed primarily in relation to geographical location, whereas ethnic groups are primarily linguistic classifications. This argument serves as the basis for my claim that processes of war and Catholic conversion have shifted the emphasis of identity from the community toward wider forms of association such as ethnicity and class.

Historically, the Q'eqchi' community has been a more salient basis for identity than has the ethnic group. This is partly because the population of Alta Verapaz is overwhelmingly indigenous. Whatever criteria were used, the National Population Census of 1981 recorded that the department was 89 percent "indigenous." The vast majority of the 361,000 Q'eqchi's today live in the department of Alta Verapaz (Instituto Indigenista Nacional 1985:59). As can be seen from map 3, the Q'eqchi's cover the most extensive area of any Mayan group in Guatemala, and they are the fourth largest subgroup in population.

In the past, a strong pan-Q'eqchi' identity has not existed; people referred to themselves and others as Q'eqchi's (aj Q'eqchi') only when commenting on language ability. The word Q'eqchi' did not originally refer to a group with shared cultural attributes, but to a language. Any person who speaks this Mayan language fluently can be called an aj Q'eqchi'. Members of the neighboring Poqomchi' linguistic group may also be referred to as Q'eqchi' if they speak Q'eqchi'.

Most Q'eqchi's, especially elders, identify themselves as being from a municipality or a certain village. It is an anthropological maxim that the municipality is the basis of indigenous identity in Guatemala (see Tax 1963; Watanabe 1992) and takes precedence over any pan-Mayan identification. Carol Smith (1990a:18) writes that "Indian identity is rooted in community rather than in any general sense of 'Indian-ness'."

The cornerstone of community identity in Alta Verapaz is location—the local geography. There is linguistic evidence that "location" (as in the Castilian estar) is much more important than "being/essence" (the Castilian ser). Indeed, Q'eqchi' does not have a verb for "being/essence," only for "to be located in a place" (waank).

Community identity is imagined in the relationship with the local sacred landscape. Villages are frequently named after an aspect of the sacred landscape, usually a mountain. Surnames are often specific to a locale. Q'eqchi's call themselves aj ral ch'och', or "children of the earth," a term that is also extended to include other indigenous groups. This aspect of identity is the subject of the next three chapters.

Community identity is elaborated in other areas of culture as well as in the landscape. Dialects vary from one microlocale to another. All women wear indigenous dress, but every community puts its unique creative stamp on its clothing. Communities that have not converted to Protestantism have their own patron saints. In some villages, there is an active religious brotherhood (*cofradía*) that is in charge of annual celebrations of the saint. Across Mesoamerica, the *cofradía* was the community institution that served for hundreds of years as a vessel for traditional Mayan beliefs and community values.[1]

Communities are not homogeneous but are the sites of political and religious heterodoxy and economic differentiation. The tendency in earlier anthropological studies of Guatemalan villages was to assume cultural and economic conformity, but John Watanabe's (1992) complex study of the Mam town Santiago Chimaltenango irreversibly put paid to this preconception. He writes (1992:9) that we should regard the community as "a more problematic locus of contingent social cooperation involving diverse—at times divergent—individual interests."

An overt, conscious Q'eqchi' ethnic identity is a relatively new social concept. Past use of the label *Q'eqchi'* as the primary way of identifying a population has chiefly been the act of outsiders. Those who draw maps of "ethnic groups in Guatemala" are doing something most indigenous people have not done historically, and that is make ethnicity the main criterion for classification.

In comparison, Ladino ethnic identity is much more homogeneous, coherently defined, and less subordinate to the concept of community. Because it continually appeals to national and international ideals of *mestizaje*, or "mixed-ness," Ladino identity is self-consciously universal and uniform.

The labels used in ethnic categorizing are contentious and vary according to the speaker. Ladinos call themselves Ladinos, but Q'eqchi's use the label *kaxlan wiing* (chicken men) or *aj Ladiin* (Ladino).[2] The chicken arrived with the Spanish invasion, even preceding it in some areas (Tannenbaum 1943:413). The Q'eqchi' word for chicken, *kaxlan*,[3] is used as a prefix to denote anything foreign. Mayan groups (see Bricker 1981:5) have chosen the chicken as the totem of the Spanish, as opposed to other Spanish imports such as the horse and the cow.

The meanings of terms have not remained fixed and immutable, however. In the colonial period, a Ladino was a Spanish-speaking indigenous person who was landless, belonged to no particular community, and acted as an agent of the landowners (C. Smith 1990a:72). In this usage, a primarily ethnic identification was initially premised upon the denial of community identity and the acquisition of a new class-based identity.

I never came across any concepts of an essence of race (e.g., the blood) that is inherited; apparently there is local agreement with the anthropological maxim that ethnicity is a social, not a physical, concept (see Pitt-Rivers 1973; Wade 1993). From the perspective of outside analysts and the new ethnic revivalists, language is the principal mechanism and criterion for classification into an ethnic group. The native tongue of Ladinos is Castilian, whereas Q'eqchi's speak Q'eqchi' in the home and village. The majority of indigenous people are monolingual; the bilingual education program PRONEBI reckons the percentage is around 90. Castilian is used primarily in the towns or when dealing with government officials. For most rural indigenous Guatemalans, Castilian is the language of power—that of the Ladino government, the army, and the *patrón*. Yet because of their numerical superiority, Q'eqchi's can usually avoid speaking Castilian even in urban areas. Many businesses and stores are owned by Q'eqchi' speakers, and Ladinos from Cobán are frequently conversational in the indigenous language.

Indigenous peoples' knowledge of Castilian is, to an extent, gender dependent; men are more likely to be conversant because of their greater exposure to national institutions such as schools and the army. Indigenous male youths are regularly captured and forced to fulfil military service for two years. Male attendance is higher than that of females in the few schools and literacy programs available. Through wage labor, men also have more contact with Castilian speakers. Women go to the towns as frequently as men, but they are more likely to confine their dealings to those with other Q'eqchi'-speaking women in the markets.

Ethnic distinctions are partly congruent with the distinction between rural and urban. Ladinos are associated with the towns and Q'eqchi's with the countryside. Eighty-two percent of Q'eqchi's live in rural areas (CUNOR 1986). Ladinos live almost exclusively in the towns, although so do a large number of Q'eqchi's. In the rural mountainous regions, there are very few Ladinos, except in particular zones of immigration such as the Northern Transversal Strip. The only Ladinos who make forays into the mountains are plantation owners and foremen, itinerant traders, and middlemen buying cash crops. These Ladinos have to speak the indigenous language well to conduct their affairs.

As elsewhere in Latin America, dress is one of the most significant signs of ethnicity. Ethnic criteria affect female dress more than male clothing, which is determined more by class and occupational categories. Q'eqchi' women have a distinctive traditional dress similar to that of other Mayan groups but with different patterns in the skirt and embroidered blouse. Ladina clothing typically is a print dress, usually made in a Mexican factory. If, in an extremely rare situation, a Q'eqchi' woman were to discard her dress and put on Ladina clothes, she would no longer be considered indigenous.

not so for CPRs - Peter Mexico

Men's clothing is not as immediately defining. Both Ladino and Q'eqchi' males wear factory-made trousers and shirts, but those of Ladinos tend to be more expensive. The difference between the two groups lies not so much in their clothes as in what men on their feet. A large number of indigenous men wear nothing at all, and when they do it is usually a pair of heavily patched rubber boots. Ladinos, on the other hand, tend to wear socks with tennis shoes or leather shoes. Q'eqchi' men from rural areas always wear hats and carry machetes; both are as much a part of their dress as a pair of trousers.

All the preceding attributes of ethnicity are correlated instantly when people define others' or their own ethnicity. At the same time, ethnicity is clearly contextual; there are no absolute boundaries that hold for all situations. As Kay Warren (1992:203–204) puts it, "The construction of polar, mutually exclusive choices—Indian or Ladino—ignores overwhelming evidence that individuals and communities continually rework identities."

With this perspective, it is appropriate to look now at the process of "Ladinoization" by which Q'eqchi's adopt Ladino attributes. Ladinoization is, more than anything, the decision to abandon the community. This occurs most often among land-less proletarians who leave their rural communities and migrate to the towns. Though they may adopt Ladino dress and language and work in Ladino occupations, many still refer to themselves as Q'eqchi's. Alternatively, they can call themselves Ladinos, but other Q'eqchi's and Ladinos may deny them this status because they know that the individual or household comes from an indigenous background. There is no intermediate category of "Ladino-izing Q'eqchi'," or *cholo,* as is used in the Andes. The cultural attributes considered sufficient to make one a Q'eqchi' in the towns may be very different from those in the mountains, where an urban Q'eqchi' may be deemed a Ladino. Ethnic identities, then, can vary according to location and context.

I encountered few cases of apparently permanent Ladinoization. It is, perhaps, the wrong approach to try to explain why Ladinoization does not happen; this somehow presumes that it should. Nevertheless, the relative absence of Ladinoization is in part due to the overwhelming numbers of Q'eqchi's compared to Ladinos. The small size of the towns also obstructs ethnic "passing," for everyone knows everyone else's history. Most Ladinos have only recently came to Alta Verapaz from other parts of the country, and they remain exclusive as a group. Permanent transformations from Q'eqchi' to Ladino identity are difficult. Nor does there seem to be any great incentive for indigenous people to want to become Ladinos, as the linear model of assimilation or "acculturation" theories presumed.[4] Wealthy Q'eqchi's generally have a good understanding of Hispanic culture and language, but they have little reason to forsake their ethnicity. Waldemar Smith (1977) came to the same conclusion for wealthy indigenous peoples in western Guatemala.

Urban Q'eqchi's often assume Ladino attributes not out of a conscious strategy but because they are expected to speak Castilian in the workplace and may not have the financial resources to buy expensive traditional female dress. The creation of an urban, industrial, indigenous working class in Alta Verapaz is so new that it is hard to generalize about the future ethnicity of its members. My speculation is that urban Q'eqchi' workers will take on some of the attributes of national Ladino culture, yet still identify themselves as Q'eqchi'.

Urban and rural Q'eqchi's alike are involved in a continual redefinition of their identity. Ladinoization only happens in a seemingly irrevocable fashion when Q'eqchi's migrate to the capital in search of work. There they must forsake their language, and women often change their dress. If they return to Alta Verapaz, however, they are likely to redefine themselves as Q'eqchi's. Carol Smith (1984:216) writes of the difficulty of Ladinoization in the western highlands, noting that the people most likely to become Ladinos are the few young men who marry out of their communities and never return.

Throughout Latin America, the policies of the state have historically sought to advance the process of Ladinoization as part of a project of "national integration" (see Stutzman 1981). Anti-indigenous legislation characterized the nineteenth century in particular. After independence from Spain, the Guatemalan republican government passed Decree 14, which mandated all parish priests, in conjunction with municipal authorities, to "extinguish, by the most prudent and efficient means possible, the languages of the indigenous peoples" (Estrada Monroy 1974:487). President Justo Rufino Barrios decreed in 1876 that "the indigenous peoples of the aforesaid San Pedro de Sacatepequez of both sexes, are declared to be Ladinos, supposing that, from next year onwards, they use the dress corresponding to the Ladinos" (Mörner 1970:202). The last decree was only suspended in 1935, when the indigenous inhabitants were legally allowed to be indigenous again.

The policies of successive governments have deviated little from the spirit of such decrees. Through laws and the policies of government institutions, the Guatemalan nation-state has continually sought to extinguish indigenous languages and culture. At times, this strategy has involved extreme violence by the state against indigenous communities. During the scorched-earth policies of the Ríos Montt regime (1982–83), the military carried out overt genocide against Mayan peoples. The then defense minister, General Mejía Victores, said, "We must get rid of the words 'indigenous' and 'Indian'" (Minority Rights Group 1989:19).

The central motivation behind education in indigenous areas has been cultural assimilation. For the indigenous child, Guatemalan education is much like that in Judith Friedlander's (1975:147) description of Mexico. She writes that students are taught "how wonderful it is to be a working-class Mestizo, [and] the village students are strongly encouraged to want to conform to this idealized image of the Mexican and to forfeit their own Indian identity."

Even bilingual education, which is a great deal more sensitive toward indigenous languages and cultures than *castellanización* methods (where indigenous children are "Castilianized"), inducts indigenous pupils into fully Castilian classes by the fourth year. According to PRONEBI, in Alta Verapaz in 1988, 40 percent of school-age children attended schools, and 35 percent of them received bilingual education up to the third year of primary education.

In general, however, the Guatemalan state has offered few public services in indigenous areas. Statistics collected in 1986 by the national university located in Cobán (CUNOR) show low levels of state provision of education and health care. Less than 40 percent of children are enrolled in primary school, and at 74 percent, Alta Verapaz has one of the highest illiteracy levels in the country. In the few rural schools that exist, children are taught mostly in Spanish, and the government and school-teachers refer to the entire process of education as *Castellanización*. Teachers constitute the main bearers of modernity in Q'eqchi' villages.

According to the CUNOR study, 45 percent of the population has access to health services, and there is one doctor for every 6,500 inhabitants. In the departmental hospital in Cobán in 1986, more than 5 percent of infants were stillborn, an indication of generally poor health and nutrition (*Anuario Estadístico* 1986:151). Only 12 percent of houses have drinking water; 4 percent have a sewage system. It should be stressed that the preceding services are found almost exclusively in the towns—for example, there are no doctors permanently located in rural areas. The Catholic diocese estimates that only 5 to 10 percent of indigenous communities have access to medical care. The CUNOR document estimates life expectancy to be forty-one years, which is consistent with the national average for rural areas. Health conditions are indeed abysmal. The vast majority of children suffer from malnutrition, and everyone—including me during my fieldwork—suffers at some time from intestinal parasites. Tropical diseases run unchecked, even those that are inexpensive to treat, such as malaria.

To a certain extent, then, rural Q'eqchi's are distant from institutions of the state and national Ladino society. Yet they are by no means as isolated as they once were. Melvin Tumin (1952) applied the paradigm of caste to ethnic relations in Guatemala, a now discredited approach. He proposed that indigenous people and Ladinos had separate value systems, owing to their separate occupations and religious and prestige institutions. This ethnic isolation, wrote Tumin, prevented indigenous people from being aware of their subordinate position. This dualistic model was probably always inappropriate for ethnic relations in Guatemala, yet Tumin was writing at a time when Ladino and indigenous worlds were more segregated than they are today. Nowadays, indigenous people are thoroughly aware of their status and regularly interact with Ladinos in economic activities and in the operations of the state.

It is paradoxical that the state, in its desire to obliterate ethnic identity, has at times strengthened it. The Ladino state and its agents create their own image of "indigenous" and "Q'eqchi'," and thus accentuate ethnic identity more than community identity. The promotion of Ladinoization necessitates the promulgation of its opposed image, and in doing so it expands the basis of association from the community to the wider ethnic group. This issue will take on more importance in the later chapter on civil war.

Indigenous peoples are discriminated against by Ladinos on a number of different levels, and some, though not all, judgments of inferiority are internalized. Rural Q'eqchi's generally subscribe to the ethnic division of labor that confines them to nonprofessional and agricultural occupations, but they do not accept Ladino depictions of them as stupid or dirty. Unlike many other indigenous groups, most Q'eqchi's are proud of their language, religion, and customs. Many overtly disdain Ladinos as people without *na'leb'*, or moral values. A priest among the Poqomchi', a neighboring group, told me, "The Q'eqchi's are very rare in their pride. Look at the Poqomchi's, they are loathe to speak their language, they won't speak it in town and always want me to do the mass in Castilian."

AGRICULTURAL PRODUCTION

This section looks at relations of production, beginning with higher levels of organization—the nation and region—and progressing down to the community and household. Although class is not as important for identity as community and ethnic group, material conditions hold immense importance for understanding the development of the social movements (catechists, revolutionaries, and ethnic revivalists) that have developed in Alta Verapaz. This section also serves as an etic complement to the emic approach to agricultural production adopted in chapters three through five.

NATIONAL AGRICULTURAL PROFILE

The single most important feature of the economic landscape of Alta Verapaz is the unequal distribution of land. The department is not special in this instance. In a now-famous document published in 1982, the U.S. Agency for International Development (USAID) gave Guatemala the dubious honor of having the most unequal land distribution in Latin America. According to USAID, over 78 percent of all farms are under 3.5 hectares and are squeezed onto 10 percent of the country's cultivable land, whereas less than 1 percent of all farms sprawl over 2,500 hectares and occupy 22 percent of all arable land. As James Painter writes (1987:xv): "Virtually all the country's high quality land[s] . . . are owned or controlled by a few hundred Guatemalan families, who for years have treated the country as a limited company."

The country's most fertile lands are used exclusively for export crops such as sugar cane, cotton, coffee and bananas. Agricultural products account for more than 50 percent of total export earnings. The inequality of land distribution and the unstable reliance on export crops constitute a threat to the subsistence needs of the vast majority of indigenous smallholders. The USAID report (1982:6) concluded that in 1979, 88 percent of all farms were too small to meet household food requirements. Hundreds of thousands of smallholders seek seasonal work on the plantations of the Pacific coast.

The agroexport industry employs 53 percent of the labor force (Economist Intelligence Unit 1989a:16). The whole edifice of the Guatemalan export economy is predicated on mostly indigenous smallholders' coming down from the mountainous regions to work for a few months of the year on the plantations. Coffee and cotton plantations rely on over 80 percent temporary labor, and sugar cane is harvested by 89 percent seasonal labor (Cardona 1983:20). Guatemala, then, is a classic example of the *latifundia-minifundia* model (see Barry 1987; Figueroa Ibarra 1980; Flores Alvarado 1977; Paz Cárcamo 1986). In this system, vast export plantations (*latifundia*) with labor-intensive methods depend on a large labor pool of farmers whose smallholdings (*minifundia*) are too small to support subsistence needs. The plantations maintain this land-tenure system in order to benefit from rock-bottom wages that, unlike those of full-fledged wage labor, do not have to take into account the full reproduction of labor power.

AGRARIAN CONDITIONS IN ALTA VERAPAZ

The department covers 8,686 square kilometers and has a population of 522,900. Its physical geography varies enormously from the hot, humid lowlands of the north to the cool southern highlands, which rise to over 2,000 meters. The climate is one of near-continual rain, apart from six to eight dry weeks in April and May; the average annual rainfall in Cobán is 1,864 millimeters (Anuario Estadístico 1986). A fine misty rain called *chipi-chipi* can fall solidly for an interminable two to three weeks during the winter months (so much for my dreams of escaping the English climate).

In Alta Verapaz, coffee and cardamom are the mainstays of the regional economy. The industrial sector is only weakly developed and centered on a few sites such as the ammunition factory in Cobán, the Chixoy hydroelectric plant, silver and uranium mines in the Polochic valley, and the oil fields of the north.

The wide range of production relations makes it difficult to characterize all the dimensions of land and labor relations in the department. Most rural Q'eqchi' households and communities have limited access to sufficient quantities of arable land. The shortage of land for subsistence production necessitates participation in wage labor on the coffee and cardamom plantations. Indigenous communities and agroexport plantations should be seen as integrated into a single system of production—one that exploits Q'eqchi' land and labor. The economy of the indigenous community is not marginal to national production, therefore, as some elements of modernization theory assert. Rather, it is the motor of the Guatemalan economy. Furthermore, the community economy circumscribes the local manifestations of global capital, as well as being subject to the dictates of the international market. Carol Smith (1984) argues that social scientists have given too much weight to global factors influencing local communities. Using a nuanced, microsociological approach, she reverses some of the tenets of dependency theory and shows how the particularities of the western highlands shaped capitalism's development in Guatemala.

Ethnicity does not always follow class lines, but in Alta Verapaz there are not enough poor rural Ladinos or wealthy urban Q'eqchi's to negate a rough correlation between class and ethnicity. Q'eqchi' men are, in the main, poorer subsistence cultivators and rural wage laborers. Class differentiation within Q'eqchi' communities is not pronounced. Ladinos chiefly work in professional or mercantile occupations in urban areas. There are few Ladino smallholders in Alta Verapaz, and they are concentrated in locations that are spatially separated from indigenous communities. The principal landowners of the region are Ladinos, many of whom are descendants of the foreigners who came at the end of the last century with names such as Deiseldorff, Hempstead, and Leal. Class, however, is not a sufficient explanation for all aspects of Q'eqchi' and nonindigenous cultures. The categories overlap, but are not reducible to one another. In terms of people's own self-definitions, class difference is not nearly as salient as ethnic difference, except among those with a past involvement in revolutionary organizations. This situation certainly challenged my initial theoretical framework, since I went to the field as a fairly orthodox materialist, seeing class as a foundational, objective category and ethnicity as a rather derivative cultural epiphenomenon. In the field, I found that the researcher can only bang his or her head for so long against people's contradictory priorities and self-definitions until a more nuanced explanatory narrative has to take shape.

ECONOMIC HISTORY

The unique history of Alta Verapaz provides the template for many present-day economic relations. The myriad expressions of Q'eqchi' communities have been profoundly shaped by the Spanish colonial system and the development of the capitalist agroexport economy.

During the Spanish invasion, indigenous communities were concentrated into *reducciones* and thereby removed from their original lands. In the sixteenth and seventeenth centuries, Spanish landowners quickly assumed possession of the fertile lands along the Pacific coast, but the mountainous terrain of the Verapaces was comparatively bypassed. Colonial and post-colonial reports constantly refer to the recalcitrance of the Q'eqchi's and Lacandones, who periodically abandoned Spanish towns and fled to the forest.

A letter written by the French landowner Rossignon in 1861, before coffee production took over the department, referred to the "dispersion in the mountains" of the Q'eqchi' (Estrada Monroy 1979:380). Rossignon described indigenous life as "essentially nomadic," with "the majority living in their corn fields." Freedom of movement for the Q'eqchi' in these times was possible because landowners did not have great incentives such as export opportunities to cultivate their lands intensively. Rossignon wrote about how indigenous groups "continually invaded private lands." Soon afterwards, new entrepreneurs from northern Europe would take more capitalistic attitudes than their Spanish colonial counterparts toward land ownership and Q'eqchi' labor.

Although the effects of the Spanish invasion on land tenure

and labor relations were sweeping and profound, the development of coffee production in the last half of the nineteenth century had more dramatic ramifications for Q'eqchi' communities. Throughout Latin America, indigenous communities did not suffer dispossession of their lands under colonial rule to the same degree as they did after independence (1821).

In the latter half of the nineteenth century, subsistence practices came under serious threat when it was realized that land hitherto considered marginal was excellent for coffee cultivation. In the mid-nineteenth century, more than 70 percent of the country's best lands were still controlled by some thousand peasant (and mostly indigenous) communities (Cambranes 1985:88). The founders of the Republic of Guatemala were free-market liberals who quickly moved to privatize communal lands. From 1871 to 1883, liberal governments beginning with that of Barrios declared "empty" almost a million acres of land, the majority of which was occupied by indigenous communities (Handy 1984:69).

Indigenous land claims had to be vitiated in order for foreign, especially German, entrepreneurs to begin operations in the country. This was done by a combination of murders, violent coercion, and ideological deception. The new landholders were aided by Catholic priests in Alta Verapaz, as this excerpt from a letter to the president by an indigenous community indicates: "They [the landowners] have made us believe, through sermons delivered by Father Basilio Cordero, that they have received instructions from the Supreme Government to force us to leave our homes" (Cambranes 1985:80).

The majority of the immigrant Germans went to Alta Verapaz, where they built a coffee export empire on the basis of Q'eqchi' land and labor. Two-thirds of the commerce of the region was in the hands of Germans by 1885 (Cambranes 1985:165). Michael McClintock (1985:8) writes, "With their own river route to the coast, planters of the German enclave centred on Cobán in . . . Alta Verapaz, were virtually independent from the rest of the country." From 1870 to 1880, coffee production nearly tripled to 290,000 quintals (over 13 million kilograms) as Guatemala became a leading world producer (Plant 1977:68). In a letter to the president in 1867, the inhabitants of Carchá pleaded, "After having had our houses and farms, which are the fruit of our labor, taken away from us . . . the Commissioner of Panzós has forced us to plant coffee in the mountains where we grow corn. This appears to be nothing more than an attempt to exterminate us" (Cambranes 1985:81).

From the very beginning, then, cash crops were perceived by subsistence cultivators as a direct threat to their economy. In chapters three and four, I will show how this opposition between subsistence and cash cropping has been incorporated into the symbolism of agricultural rituals.

Raul Salvadó (1980:19) writes that by the end of the 1870s, there was no untitled land left in Alta Verapaz. The coffee plantations were vast, and they drew in dispossessed Q'eqchi's as *mozos colonos*, or serfs, and remunerated them with food, usufruct or a salary. In addition to obtaining land for coffee production, landowners were motivated to acquire as much land as possible so as to mobilize indigenous labor. As David McCreery (1976:456) explains, "While they [indigenous communities] retained this [communal land], and the political and social institutions to protect it, an individual member had little incentive to labor for low wages on someone else's coffee plantation."

As foreign landowners dispossessed Q'eqchi' communities of their lands, the government passed legislation to ensure easy control of their labor power. Labor was a more crucial factor in production than land, of which there was plenty. In 1876, President Barrios sent an order to the departmental governors that amounted to a law of forced labor: "May the indigenous peoples of your jurisdiction, provide to the plantation owners of that department that request it, the number of workers necessary, up to fifty or one hundred, according to the importance of the business" (Skinner-Klee 1954:34).

The indigenous work force was to be renewed every two weeks and its wage level arranged between the plantation owner and departmental governor. The majority of Q'eqchi's became *mozos colonos* during this time. Older Q'eqchi's still remember the days of vagrancy laws and debt servitude, which replaced the colonial *mandamiento* system. One group of elders from Cahabón recounted to me how all males had to work on the coffee *fincas* (plantations) from age seven until they were physically incapable. They were usually paid not in cash but with maize and beans. Robert Carmack (1990:129) claims that in the late nineteenth century, "the Verapaz Indians were the most proletarianized within Guatemala."

The relations of production outlined above held true in Alta Verapaz until 1943, when German property was nationalized and tens of thousands of hectares of coffee land were seized by the state. Some land passed into the hands of high officials and local members of the Ladino bourgeoisie. Other plantations became national cooperatives with Q'eqchi' members, but they were managed by a government appointee who often treated the cooperative as a private business and a source of loot.

THE REGIONAL EXPORT ECONOMY

Alta Verapaz is an integrated part of the national agroexport economy and shares with it characteristics such as an unequal land-tenure system and a reliance on export crops. Two percent of the total number of farms occupy 65 percent of the arable land and generate 61 percent of the gross departmental production (CUNOR 1986:92). Military officials are major landowners, especially in the colonization zone of the Northern

Transversal Strip. During military rule in 1983, 60 percent of
Alta Verapaz was reckoned to be military property (Dunkerley
1988:467). Meanwhile, 97 percent of the agricultural properties
jostle for 25 percent of the arable land (CUNOR 1979).

Although this distribution causes a dire shortage of subsistence land for Q'eqchi' villagers, conditions are not as acute as
in other departments in the highlands. Pressure on the land is
still intense, but it has been somewhat diminished by migration
to the vast areas of virgin forest in the north of the department
and in the Petén and Belize (Adams 1965).

Guatemala is now the world's largest producer of cardamom, meeting 60 percent of global requirements and earning
over U.S. $40 million in 1988 (Economist Intelligence Unit
1989b:2). The majority of Guatemala's cardamom is produced
in Alta Verapaz, where it is planted, tended, and harvested by
Q'eqchi' hands. For the exporting Ladino elite that controls
cardamom production, rural Q'eqchi' communities are a vital
labor pool for the cultivation of hugely profitable export crops.

There are a variety of different types of land tenure in Alta
Verapaz and I do not pretend to give here a complete and
thorough examination of them all. There are, however, two
main types of agroexport plantations: traditional coffee estates,
and newer cattle and cardamom plantations.

Many historical coffee plantations are still run on nineteenth-century labor practices that depend on Q'eqchi' laborers, or *mozos colonos*. Conditions vary widely and remu-
neration may take the form of pay, usufruct, or food. In some
instances, the landowner requires that tenants plant three times
as much land for him as for themselves. In the municipality of
Cahabón, Salvadó (1980:25) found that each male *colono* must
work "three days for the landowner for each invested for his
own benefit." In the majority of cases, Q'eqchi' men work
unpaid for an average of ten days per month. This entitles them

to plant the minimum area of subsistence crops necessary to provide for their families. As Marx noted, in usufruct it is always clear which is the labor time of the *mozo* and which pertains to the landowner. On other plantations, workers are paid (usually between U.S. $1 and $1.50 per day) but have no usufruct. Social relations between workers and landlords are characterized by paternalism. The boss is likely to be godfather to most of his indigenous workers as well as the judicial authority and patron of religious events.

Modern cattle and cardamom farms depend on day wage labor (workers are called *voluntarios*, "volunteers") from surrounding communities and beyond. In these cases, the capitalist landowners do not assume responsibility for the reproduction of Q'eqchi' labor power. Labor relations, being more commoditized, are less paternalistic. Wages are marginally higher than on the historic plantations, averaging about U.S. $1.75 per day in 1988.

There are also many types of land tenure in Q'eqchi' communities, including national cooperative ownership, collective ownership, and different forms of smallholder tenure.

The national cooperatives are coffee plantations expropriated from German landowners in 1943. Members have no right to sell land. These cooperatives produce many cash crops using Western agricultural technology. The collectivization of resources means that more capital is available for mechanized transport to markets, fertilizers, insecticides, and advanced strains of seeds. In these cooperatives, 131 households farm 5,865 hectares on average.[5]

Along the border with Quiché, many communities lie on untitled land (*baldío*) belonging to the government land ministry, INTA. These forests are farmed by communities who are petitioning the government for land titles. The number of households on a *baldío* is usually between thirty and forty, and size averages 880 hectares. Ownership is considered collective vis-à-vis the government, although internally, household rights are accrued by clearing a segment of forest. Rights of access may be passed from father to son. The community decides who may or may not join from outside. Usually deep in the mountainous rain forests, these villages are inaccessible by jeep or truck. Poor communications and roads make significant cash-cropping difficult. Traditionally, mobile households produced as shifting cultivators, each house a significant distance from the others. Villages were internally dispersed and had no center other than the graveyard and village *hermita,* or chapel.

Parcelas are smallholder communities created when German plantations were divided into plots. Q'eqchi's also received *parcelas* when the Franja Transversal del Norte road opened up huge expanses of primary forest. Each household owns title to its land, which can be sold. These Q'eqchi's tend to be comparatively better off. Because they own their lands, they can obtain credit to finance intensive cash-cropping methods. On average, 121 households farm a land grant of 3,100 hectares. This represents a mean of roughly 25 hectares per family.[6]

My final type is communities made up of private smallholdings. These are usually in the hinterlands of towns and are made up of mixed-size landholdings. They follow a mixed strategy of subsistence farming and cash crops. Their problems include legal registration of ancestral lands. The size of landholdings is usually smaller than in the *parcelas.*

This brief survey of land-tenure patterns demonstrates that Q'eqchi' communities are by no means homogeneous in their ownership, or lack of it, of their means of production.

HOUSEHOLD AND COMMUNITY PRODUCTION

Subsistence production takes place predominantly at the level of the household. As Richard Wilk (1991) shows for Q'eqchi's in

Belize, the forms of households vary enormously: they may be nuclear or extended and may incorporate single parents of the conjugal unit and spouses of the children.

Relations between the sexes are remarkably similar to those reported for the Andes and are characterized by complementarity (Harris 1978). Men and women are ideologically equal, though the dominance of each is contextual. There is a rigid but interdependent sexual division of labor in agricultural tasks. Ideally, men are responsible for the staple crops, beans and maize, whereas women cultivate the gardens and tend the domestic animals. This ideal, however, is renegotiated in daily behaviour. Catherine Allen (1988:78), among many others, encountered a similar state of affairs in the Andes: "Male and female activities are conceptually distinct but flexible in practice." Thus men and women can do the majority of each other's tasks. There are, however, impermeable boundaries in some agricultural tasks; women are not allowed to plant maize, and men prefer that women plant garden crops. The exclusions against women's crossing sexual boundaries in production are more prevalent than those against men's doing so.

Women play a central role in managing household production (see Ehlers 1990) and are wholly responsible for household consumption. They alone control the processing of food, of which men claim to be utterly ignorant. Men profess not to know how even to make a tortilla, and they value this aspect of women's work highly, saying that they would starve without women. Men recognize and value the female monopoly in the preparation of food, which is seen as an integral part of the whole subsistence process.

Women dominate decision making relating to consumption, although long-term planning involves male input. All labor recruitment outside the family is based upon the provision of food for the work party. Women's control of consumption

means that they must be consulted on important extrahouse-
hold matters, such as those involving labor during planting and
harvesting and the fulfillment of ritual obligations in the saint
brotherhoods and other religious commitments. Female control
of consumption, then, implies an extension of power outside of
the household as well.

Male and female roles in production are perceived as complementary and are accorded equal value. Women are almost
exclusively in charge of agricultural production in the vegetable
gardens and fruit orchards near the houses. A portion of the
goods produced there is taken by women to markets in the
towns and sold. Women are also responsible for the domestic
livestock. Female labor in household agricultural production is
obviously significant. Although men, too, work in the gardens
and care for animals, those tasks are regarded as the domain of
women. Maize and bean production is conventionally portrayed
as the result of male labor only, but women in fact participate in
the weeding and harvesting.

Villagers today depend on a single crop, maize. In most
communities, maize represents up to 90 percent of the diet.
This dependence is partly historic, but it has been accentuated
by the war. Many Q'eqchi's fled their communities and lost a
large percentage of their seeds, especially those for garden
crops. In the slow process of rebuilding the village economy,
displaced communities concentrated almost exclusively on re-
establishing maize crops first. In communities I visited that
were not affected by the war, vegetable garden products were
much more in evidence and constituted a larger percentage of
the diet—about 30 percent.

The comparison of maize production in different communities is made difficult by the altitudinal variation of the local
geography. Two crops are cultivated per year in the lowlands,
but only one in the mountains. The land is richer in the

Women going to market

lowlands and the climate is more suitable, so the highland villages need roughly three times as much land for subsistence. If the average size of a household is six members and each person consumes about 1.4 pounds of maize per day,[7] then a household needs 3,066 pounds of maize per year. A hectare produces some 1,700–2,200 pounds of maize each growing season, depending on the location and quality of the land. In the lowlands, 2.8 hectares were held to be the minimum field size for sustained reproduction of the household, whereas in highland villages, households had to plant 3.5 hectares.

Q'eqchi' households generally plant more than is necessary for mere subsistence requirements.[8] In surveys made in the lowlands, the yearly averages are 4.8 hectares per household for those on land they do not own (rented, untitled, or on a plantation), and 8.5 hectares per household for those with titles to their land (a minority). These figures are higher than those for land necessary for subsistence requirements—roughly 2.8–3.5 hectares.[9] Although it may appear at first glance that most households have sufficient land for both subsistence and cash cropping, one must take into account that land is usually exhausted after two years' cultivation. The ideal fallow time is four to six years. Pressure on the land is much more acute in the highlands than in the lowlands. The experience of most indigenous communities in Alta Verapaz and the rest of the Guatemalan highlands is one of declining fertility and ever-decreasing crop yields.

The average overall time necessary to cultivate a subsistence plot, employing swidden agricultural methods, is eight weeks. Activity is intense during this period. At peak times in the agricultural calendar, cultivators work sixty to seventy hours per week; in the highlands, such peaks can be broken down as follows: clearing (February–March), three to four weeks; burning and planting (April–May), seven days; weeding (June–July), two weeks; and harvesting (September), seven days. Men are responsible for the first two stages of the agricultural process, and women are often involved in the last two.

Q'eqchi's sow an immense number of strains of corn and beans. I alone encountered dozens, seemingly one for each ecological niche.[10] Although this aspect of subsistence agriculture is advanced, the technology used is rudimentary—a machete, a hoe, fire, and a dibble stick for planting. Because of the simplicity of highland swidden implements, migrants have quickly adapted to lowland conditions (Carter 1969:144). Although migration to the northern lowlands has served as a pressure valve for overcrowding in the highlands, there continues to be great pressure on the land. Intensive Western methods using fertilizers and insecticides are often precluded by a lack of credit. Nor are there significant local techniques to restore the fertility of the land. Few efforts are made at conservation and repeated swidden procedures have led to massive deforestation and erosion.

Virtually all villagers plant a mix of subsistence and cash crops, a strategy Wilk (1991) has described in detail for Q'eqchi's in Belize. Indigenous farmers with enough land could plant all their land with corn and beans and be self-sufficient, but instead they choose to cultivate one or more cash crops. This mixed subsistence–cash cropping strategy allows access to local markets and provides a necessary source of cash. Modern Q'eqchi' lifestyles are premised upon access to markets for goods such as clothes, work tools, and radios, but seldom for basic food needs. Conversely, those with enough land could grow solely cash crops, but this seldom, if ever, occurs because villagers fear total reliance on the market. A similar pragmatic blend of opportunistic exploitation of coffee cash-cropping and cautious preservation of the maize-based subsistence economy is documented by Watanabe (1992:138–48) for Santiago Chimaltenango.

The optimum cash crop is one that can be cultivated during the slack season of the corn production cycle. Cardamom is ideal because it is harvested in January and costs little to start. Cardamom was the first export crop to be cultivated on a large scale by Q'eqchi' smallholders, beginning in the 1970s, so villagers still have little depth of experience in producing for the international export market. Coffee, historically grown only for export on the extensive plantations, also began to be cultivated after cardamom proved profitable. Coffee plants, however, are more fragile and demand more labor time and capital investment.

Smallholder cash-cropping is plagued by a dearth of capital and inertia in the face of elastic demand. Coffee requires five years to reach maturity, and cardamom, two, which means that producers are vulnerable to the vagaries of the international market. The large-scale producers, in a situation of declining commodity prices, can afford to destroy coffee groves and plant more profitable crops.

After interviewing farmers in twenty-two highland and lowland communities, I found that households cultivate subsistence crops on an average of 63 percent of their land; the rest is turned over to cash crops. This percentage tends to increase as land resources dwindle, until the minimal levels of subsistence are reached and the percentage becomes 100. The degree of cash-cropping is related to other factors, such as access to credit. For instance, cooperative members tend to have more scope for securing credit and pursuing intensive techniques. Access to roads and navigable rivers also encourages production for export.

Any review of community economics must also include more Chayanovian factors such as reciprocity and collective cooperation. Labor recruitment in Q'eqchi' communities combines elements of both reciprocity and wage labor. The types of intracommunity labor recruitment outlined here refer to independent agrarian communities, and not to populations of *colonos* inside plantations: reciprocal labor, which is unwaged but repaid by labor in kind plus food, and which is used during the planting and harvesting of maize and beans; nominal wage labor (Q2/day)[11] plus food, prevalent during the planting and harvesting of maize and beans; wage labor within the community (Q4/day), which includes all other agricultural labor, such as clearing; wage labor outside the community (Q4–5/day); and unpaid community labor organized by the village authority in special cases such as road building or to help a widow with no male relatives.

Within Q'eqchi' villages, labor recruitment is not generally based on daily wages. The ritually elaborated processes of planting and harvesting staple crops have their own basis for recruitment. They are the main occasions for recruiting outside the household. Planting maize involves more labor exchange than does harvesting it, because planting is a more important religious event. Participation in the reciprocal labor pool for planting and harvesting is an archetypal feature of membership in most Q'eqchi' communities. Autonomous labor pools serve as markers for local identities, fixing the boundaries between "us" and "them." Billie Jean Isbell (1978:67) wrote of the same mechanisms of social enclosure in Chuschi, Peru. All other noncommunity agricultural labor is commoditized, especially any work on the export plantations.

Households tend to be self-sufficient in terms of labor needs. This is because most prefer economic autonomy, and the prevalence of extended families permits it. Traditionally, marriages are uxorilocal for a period of one to two years, and sons-in-law provide an invaluable labor resource.[12] The major bride-service obligation is heavy clearing work at the beginning of the agricultural cycle. In communities where land is held collectively, the act of clearing legitimates claims (not inalienable private ownership) for future years. Bride service has broken down in many areas, but even if sons stay in the house after marriage, all the house members work as a unit, sharing tasks, granaries, and the end product. The women of the household, however, will keep their own gardens, fruit trees, and domestic animals separate from those of other households, for these resources belong only to the conjugal unit.

The majority of Q'eqchi' men engage in day wage labor on

Harvesting maize

the plantations for an average salary of U.S. $1.50 per day plus one meal (in 1988). In a local-level agricultural study in the Polochic Valley, Angel Arce Canahuí (1983:89) found that nearly half of all men interviewed sold their labor power, and wage labor was the greatest source of monetary income. Although levels of participation in the labor market are high, my impression is that men are prejudiced against wage work and avoid it if at all possible. They dislike the authority of the foreman and the long, hard hours of work for low pay. This is what makes cash-cropping attractive: it allows households to earn money to spend in the local markets without having to work under the harsh conditions of the plantations.

Q'eqchi' communities have been integrated into a capitalist

labor market for over a hundred years, initially under forced-labor regulations and later out of economic necessity. Yet other dimensions of the capitalist economy, such as participation in the international commodity market, seemed for a while to be an escape from wage-labor relations. Villagers and even many urban Q'eqchi's actively maintain their positions as both wage laborers and subsistence cultivators. This local strategy echoes Carmen Deere's (1990) elaboration of multiple class relations in Cajamarcan households as a way of ensuring the reproduction of the household. Informants told me they desired access to markets but not complete dependence on them. For both rural and urban Q'eqchi's, it is of great significance to have some land on which to plant maize, because doing so is a vital aspect of indigenous identity, it provides an economic safety net, and it maintains the sacred relationship with the mountain spirits.

Given the picture I have presented in this section, I would have to disagree with Carol Smith (1990a:206), who states that "nothing resembling a peasantry exists in Guatemala"—only rural proletarians and petty commodity producers. Members of the Q'eqchi' communities are, of course, rural workers and cash-croppers, but their main agricultural activity continues to be subsistence-oriented production. They are, thus, a peasantry in a loose sense, but one that is also inextricably involved in capitalist labor and commodity networks.

Cash-cropping among Q'eqchi' villagers increased dramatically in the late 1970s and brought profits to those who had previously only worked for the benefit of the landowners. Development initiatives flourished, as did producer cooperatives. Cash-cropping allowed an escape from traditional relations of subordination to the plantation owners, but it also heralded a new set of relations of exploitation—those of the market and Ladino middlemen. Fast-changing economic and political relations in the countryside during the late 1970s

*Peasant debate

contributed to (but did not wholly determine) the development of revolutionary organizations.

Beginning in about 1981, war devastated the rural economy and halted production for export in many areas. The cash-cropping bubble burst in the mid-1980s, when commodity prices crashed, inducing the reaction against the market that is explored in chapter eight. The boom-and-bust cycle of commodity production is a major factor in shaping each community's stance toward the outside world. During recent boom periods, communities have been more "open," and indigenous identity has incorporated more elements of Ladino culture. During periods of market contraction, communities have tended to become more closed, and indigenous identity has been constructed in opposition to the wider national culture.

CHAPTER THREE

RECLAIMING A COLONIZED LANDSCAPE

This chapter looks at how local communities have traditionally been "imagined" through interactions with the surrounding landscape. Traditional beliefs about agricultural production and human health had their heyday before the mass conversions to orthodox religions in the 1970s. Now they are not so hegemonic, but they continue within a pluralistic cultural milieu. Although the earth cult is not the dominant way in which communities are now imagined, its elements are adhered to by a significant portion of the rural Q'eqchi' population. Because what is related in this chapter is a "living tradition," I describe its elements in the present tense and use past tense only when referring to aspects of tradition that are no longer practiced.

This chapter discusses ritual practices carried out before the planting of corn, when traditionalist men enter caves to make sacrifices to the mountain spirits. The tellurian deities, the *tzuultaq'a*s, play a central role in traditional conceptions of agricultural fertility. *Tzuul* means "mountain," *taq'a* means "valley," and the earth gods encompass the whole of a sacralized landscape. I end the chapter with an assessment of how tradi-

tionalists negotiate community and ethnic identity and assert
their claim to the land through the cult of the tzuultaq'as.

Q'eqchi' rituals of production can only be analyzed in full
with respect to ideas about human reproduction and illnesses,
for the mountain deities are vital figures in the well-being and
fertility of both maize and humans. Chapter five deals with
human pregnancy, illness, and the tzuultaq'as and analyzes
together the themes of production and reproduction.

Informants on the cave sacrifice and planting in general were
primarily men, but I also consulted older women. So far as I
could determine, women believe the traditional knowledge
concerning planting to the same degree as men. Although they
themselves do not carry out many of the rituals, female elders
are seen as valid sources of this type of knowledge within the
community.

THE SYMBOLISM OF PRODUCTION AND
IDENTITY: THE TZUULTAQ'AS

The last chapter gave a straightforward and static account of
ethnic identity—a sort of potted summary. The rest of the book
explores recent historical transformations of local identities.
This narrative unfolds in the local representational medium,
that of the relationship between a community and its landscape.
Eva Hunt (1977:28) argues that one key to understanding a
culture is a "complex, multi-vocal symbol." Just as Hunt chose
the sun as a dominant symbol for illuminating Mesoamerican
cosmologies, I choose the mountain as the best representational
image for understanding the emergence of identities.

The cornerstone of traditional community identity is location—the local geography. John Berger (1979:9) writes in *Pig
Earth* that his French peasant village is "a living portrait of
itself" that is constructed not out of stones but out of words and
legends, and "it is a continuous portrait, work on it never stops."

Among Q'eqchi' traditionalists, the ongoing portrait of the community is a local mountain spirit, a tzuultaq'a. The mountain spirit is a Durkheimian collective representation, a social fact of the cognitive life of the village. As such, the tzuultaq'a figure is a container for all expressions of Q'eqchi' collective imaginings.

As a core image of the community, a tzuultaq'a ties together various cultural domains encompassing human and agricultural fertility, gender, health care, and ethnicity. The tzuultaq'a figure is a focus of sociological tensions and therefore is a good barometer for gauging cultural change, giving us insights into the consequences of Catholic orthodoxy, civil war, and concomitant redefinitions of collective identities.

Duality is an often-cited quality of the Andean landscape (e.g., Isbell 1978; Sallnow 1987), and there is a significant degree of dualism in the figure of the tzuultaq'al as well.[1] It is both mountain and valley, male and female, spirit and matter, singular and multiple, benevolent and vengeful, indigenous and foreign, with a Q'eqchi' name and a Spanish saint's name, linking the heavens and earth. Each tzuultaq'a is both a Maya and a white "boss." Thus the mountain image expresses the contradictory duality of modern Q'eqchi' identities, with their intertwined streams of indigenous and Christian religions.

Traditional Q'eqchi's say that the mountains are living (yo'yo). They have the quality of wiinqilal, or "personhood," a concept that applies only to mountains and people. Those with the quality of wiinqilal have a spirit (xmuhel) —an honor accorded only to people, maize, saints' images, and, sometimes, houses. The tzuultaq'as are spirits that have a human form and live in a "house," the cave, deep inside the mountain. Yet the mountain is also the physical body of a tzuultaq'a. When people scurry about on the mountainside, a tzuultaq'a is disturbed. One informant said, "A tzuultaq'a feels pain when we clear the

brush with machetes and jab the planting sticks into the earth."
The mountain is anthropomorphized, each one having a face,
head, and body and a cave that is said to be either a mouth or a
womb.

Only one tzuultaq'a resides in each mountain; it is called the
owner of that mountain. Each spirit owner of a mountain has a
sex, name, and character. Female spirits tend to inhabit large
mountains with soft contours. When asked why the mountain
Itz'am is a woman, one male elder replied,

"Because she has a large hole."

"A cave?" I asked.

"Yes, female tzuultaq'as have them, and they send the rain,"
he responded.

The mountain Ak'telha' is considered a woman "since she is
over the sea." Her name means, literally, New Arm of Water.
Female mountains, then, are associated with the rain and bodies
of water, whether a spring, river, lake, or sea.

Male tzuultaq'as have sharper contours, more dramatic
peaks, and, frequently, a white cliff face. From their caves, male
tzuultaq'as throw lightning bolts, blast out thunder, and shake
the ground to cause earthquakes. Female tzuultaq'as are no less
destructive than males, but they devastate through deluges and
landslides. Tzuultaq'as are distinctive in being both male and
female: in most indigenous cultures in Latin America, mountains are male.[2]

Tzuultaq'as own the land and everything on its surface.
They are the original owners of corn. People only hold corn on
an extended loan with high interest rates. This is part of the
explanation for sacrifice: it allows access to continued use of
land and corn. Mountain spirits are sometimes called *aj ilol re*,
"she/he who watches over." They are sentinels, guardians of
plants, people, and forest animals, which are held in a corral
inside the mountain. This is why traditionalists do not thank

the hunter who brings home a kill; thanks are due only to the tzuultaq'as. Wild animals are servants of the mountains and can be sent to castigate those who do not fulfill ritual obligations. There is no idea, however, that the mountain guards an animal spirit companion of each person. Animal alter egos, called a *nagual* (Pitt-Rivers 1970) or a *wayhel* (Guiteras Holmes 1961:299), are widespread in the Mayan region. That Q'eqchi's do not also have animal spirits is one example of the immense cultural diversity among Mayas.

Tzuultaq'as are related by affinal or consanguineal ties. For example, San Vicente and Xukaneb' are younger and older brother's, respectively, on opposite sides of the vast highland valley that is the cradle of the Q'eqchi's. The brothers speak to each other, thundering across the three main Q'eqchi' towns. The hierarchy among the mountains expresses past and present power differentials between locales. It is no coincidence that Xukaneb', which dominates the pre-Columbian and colonial capital, Cobán, is king of the mountains. Speculating along this line, one might wonder whether the histories of battles between the mountains narrate pre-Columbian struggles between rival Q'eqchi' lords. Mountain spirits are not, however, integrated into the national governmental bureaucratic structure, as they can be in the Andes (Isbell 1978:151).

Relations between humans and mountain spirits are highly localized. Followers of the earth cult are lost in this respect if they move to another area, because they do not know the names and character of the tzuultaq'as. This is not a generalized earth cult such as that of Pacha Mama in the Andes, the elements of which can be taken from one area to another. The Andean parallel to the tzuultaq'a would be the *wamani*, which is associated with particular features of the landscape. Tzuultaq'as, however, have many characteristics that distinguish them from the *wamani*, as we will see in more detail later.

Villagers interact most with the mountain spirits who dwell in the caves around their communities. It is with this local sacred geography that they have a personal and moral relationship. Traditionalists see their villages as being owned by individual mountains, and villages are often named after the nearest sacred mountain—Sa'kak (In the Fire), Ukulha' (Drink Water), Sa'tzol (In Line), Tusb'il Pek (Arranged Rock). Writing about the Tzeltal, June Nash (1970:19) notes that lineage patronyms are usually the same as the name of the most important sacred hill in the area. Local community identity, then, is closely bound to the cult of the mountain spirits.

The mountain cult is significant in the formation of pan-Q'eqchi' ethnic identity as well, in that traditionalists invoke the names of the "Thirteen Great Tzuultaq'as," the thirteen tallest mountains that circumscribe Q'eqchi' linguistic territory. The number thirteen signifies completeness and unity and is related to both the number of days in the Mayan month and the number of levels in the sky (Villa-Rojas 1978:320, 327).

Rural communities know their tzuultaq'as through the dreams of their elders, male or female. In this way, communities are "dreamed" as much as they are consciously imagined. Dreams are a principal fount of a certain type of traditional politico-religious knowledge in many Mayan societies (see Tedlock 1992). Calixta Guiteras Holmes (1961:149) quotes a Tzotzil elder as saying, "I know everything by my dreams." In the past, elders' interactions with the earth gods buttressed the gerontocratic village authority. The traditional village leaders, or *chinames*, were counseled by the spirits on matters such as setting dates for events and making appointments to religious office. Young men and women can also dream of a tzuultaq'a, but those who do are especially sensitive types—perhaps *aj ilonel*, "she/he-who-sees," who cure illnesses and deliver children. It is in the realm of dreams and their interpretation that there is greatest scope for individual agency in refashioning traditional collective beliefs.

During nocturnal encounters, a tzuultaq'a talks to the dreamer. As one elder stated, "The heart of the mountain speaks." First the spirit says her or his name. Tzuultaq'as appear in human form in dreams, as either men or women, to speak of their needs and desires. Tzuultaq'as demand more food in the form of copious amounts of *pom* (sticky resin from the copal tree, which is burned as incense), candles, *b'oj* (a fermented maize and sugar cane drink), and cacao. Cooked food is accepted only in the form of pure maize, either as ground corn gruel or corn flour cooked in banana leaves (like a tamale). The relationship between people and the mountains is essentially reciprocal. Each must feed the other, not just consume without recompense. An elder expressed this morality in the following way: "We must *mayejak* (sacrifice) and *tz'amaank* (plead permission) because the mountain feels bad when we take what is his/hers." Elders dream about tzuultaq'as frequently before the planting, and these dreams act as a spur and justification for the sacrifice in the caves.

Tzuultaq'as appear in dreams as tall figures, with white skin and hair and, if male, beards. They are robed in white cotton. The mountain gods resemble priests, it is said, since many appear as bearded Europeans. Elders repeatedly told me, "Tzuultaq'as look like the Germans." The Germans, as I mentioned earlier, were the first major landowners in the area. They came to Alta Verapaz after the liberal government reforms of 1871 and bought, stole, and violently seized Q'eqchi' land.

The Q'eqchi's' experience of a plantation economy run by German landlords fundamentally altered the character of the tzuultaq'a. Both the Tzuultaq'as and the Germans are called *patrónes,* or bosses. There are many stories about German landowners who ate their workers, another similarity between them and the mountain spirits. Since both are authority figures and owners of the land, the personas of the mountain spirits and the plantation landlords have merged to a degree. In other parts of Guatemala (Adams 1952:31; Oakes 1951:93; Siegel 1941:67), Mexico (Ingham 1986:105; Villa-Rojas 1978:288–89; Vogt 1969: 302), and most of the Andes (Sallnow 1987:209), mountain spirits appear as rich white people, often plantation owners.

It is fundamental that one sees tzuultaq'as as having been influenced by historical processes. Like community and ethnic identities in general (Warren 1992:203), the mountain symbol is not the product of any single historical period. The mountain spirits are not some fossilized, ahistorical legacy of the pre-Columbian period. Instead, the tzuultaq'a figure has been constructed out of pre-Columbian, colonial, and postcolonial experiences.

Descriptions of fair-skinned tzuultaq'as do not mean that they are perceived solely as nonindigenous. The tzuultaq'as are multifaceted and exhibit myriad aspects at different times. They are also associated with wild "Mayas" who speak the local language and play their drums inside the mountain. In contrast to mountain spirits described for other parts of Latin America, tzuultaq'as never speak Castilian.

Where do these white Mayas come from? This issue will be dealt with throughout this book, but one possible interpretation is that tzuultaq'as were at one time conflated with the *chaks*, the Mayan rain gods. J. Eric S. Thompson (1975:332) noted that tzuultaq'as bear a striking resemblance to *chaks*, and he argued that the *chaks'* rain-making functions were absorbed by the Q'eqchi' mountain spirits. There could be wider precedent in the Mayan area for this interpretation: the white-skinned *'anhel* mountain spirit of the Tzotzil is almost exclusively a rain god, issuing rains from the caves (Guiteras Holmes 1961:290). The Mam earth lords, or *witz,* are associated with snakes, clouds, and lightning, all symbols of the pre-Hispanic Mayan rain gods (Watanabe 1992:75).

The nineteenth-century anthropologist Karl Sapper (1897: 271) wrote that the characteristics of the tall, white-haired rain gods were assimilated along with the Ch'ols, who praised them. This lowland Mayan group was fused with the then highland Q'eqchi's during the sixteenth-century Spanish *reducciones* (relocation into towns). Such historical factors need to be borne in mind when considering who "the Q'eqchi'" are. Over the centuries, they partially assimilated the Maya Mopanes, the Poqomchi', and the Lacandones, and they completely swallowed up the Manché Ch'ols, Acalas, and Xoys (Sapper 1985; Thompson 1932). W.E. Gates (1931) argued that the Q'eqchi' calendar is actually of Ch'ol origin, appropriated during the Old Empire of the Maya, and it does employ what appear to be non-Q'eqchi' names. "Traditional" Q'eqchi' beliefs, then, are not only a legacy of the pre-Columbian past but also a product of the amalgamation of assorted Mayan groups during the colonial period.

In terms of sacrifice, the mountains have become less bloodthirsty over the years. Since the Spanish invasion, the extirpative efforts of foreign missionaries have squelched such practices. Father Delgado, traveling through the Q'eqchi' area in the 1600s, tells us how he encountered sacrificial bloodletting in the caves. Blood was drawn from the tongue, ears, temples, and penis: "Many came from various parts [to submit themselves] to the diabolical cutting, and went off very content. I took away the cutting instrument, I preached against it, and some of them invited me to do the same [whereupon] I hastened to dissuade them from that atrocity and evil" (Thompson 1938:594).

Local oral tradition is rich in stories of mountains that gobble up pilgrims. Usually, only sinners are eaten. Some tzuultaq'as, however, always keep two of their visitors—five may enter but only three leave. Female mountains seem to have been especially devouring, and it is said that the "queen" of the tzuultaq'as, Qana' (our Mother) Itz'am, near Lanquín, regularly consumes people. Itzamna' was the earth-sky god of the Classic Mayan priesthood. According to the Motul dictionary (Thompson 1939:152), *itz* means rain, dew, and milk. In Q'eqchi', *amn* means breast, heart, and soul, and *na'* means mother. The name Itzamna', then, is a semantic complex based on ideas of motherhood and nurturing but fixed upon a female figure that can also be devouring. Tzuultaq'as are both good and evil, nurturing and destructive, in marked contrast with New Testament Christianity, in which good and evil are separated into distinct figures, Christ and Satan.

It must be remarked that the mountains have undergone a fair degree of "Christianizing" over the last 450 years. The process of religious intermixture has been abetted by priests who, recognizing that they could not stamp out the earth cult, tried to Christianize it by locating blessed crucifixes on the cave altars. A Catholic mass was performed in the 1970s inside the cave of the mountain Itz'am, which has been renamed Santa María Itz'am. The king of the mountains, Xukaneb', also attained sainthood by becoming San Pablo Xukaneb'.

The priests' strategy succeeded partly because saints and mountain spirits shared many traits from the outset. Religious syncretism is facilitated by preexisting homologies of features or functions. Catholic saints and mountain spirits occupy a similar discursive position in that they mediate between the land and the sky, the people and their God. They protect crops from bad weather, disease, and insect plagues. In sixteenth-century Spain, for example, the Virgin of Rosario shielded tomato patches from plagues, and Santiago offerred protection to crops from strong winds and hail (Ingham 1986:99).

The way in which traditionalists conceptualize their mountains has been heavily influenced by historical experiences of
the Catholic church. There is an uneasy coexistence between
the Q'eqchi' and Christian identities of the mountain spirit—
part of a wider tension over religious identity that occasionally
breaks out into open defiance. One mountain spirit kept appearing in the dreams of a village's elders to reject his Christian
name, San Vicente, and affirm his original name, Saqtz'iknel.
Saq means white. *Tz'ik* illustrates the sexual duality of traditional Q'eqchi' sacred geography: it means clitoris, penis, and a
certain type of bird. *Nel* signifies "having the property of." All
together: "White Penis/Clitoris/Bird-Ness" instead of San
Vicente.

The important attributes of the tzuultaq'a figure, then, are
its historical nature and its multiplicity of interwoven dualisms
that encompass, without resolution, representations of indigenous and nonindigenous identities. The relationships communities have with their mountain spirits are highly localized and
based on reciprocal obligations. The following sections consider the agricultural rituals performed before planting, the point
of closest interaction between communities and tzuultaq'as.

CHOOSING THE DAY OF PLANTING

> When milpa clearing time comes, the Maya slips
> away like any lover longing to dally with his mis-
> tress. It seems to me that the sex instinct is somehow
> channeled into love and anxious brooding over the
> young maize as it produces its first leaves. —J. Eric
> S. Thompson, *Maya History and Religion*

The cycle of corn production in the highlands begins anew in
February or March with the *k'alek,* or clearing. After the
clearing is finished (March to April), the senior man and woman
of the household select a date for planting, generally one that is

considered ritually auspicious. April 25, for instance, is popular because it is the saint's day of the well-known St. Mark, who is considered particularly effectual in preserving the nascent crop. Choosing his day is quite widespread in rural communities in Latin America. John Ingham (1986:99), writing about a Mexican Nahuatl village, recounts how certain saints are attributed powers of protection over particular crops.

Q'eqchi's also commonly plant on May 3, the day of the Holy Cross. This date coincides with the ending of the ancient eight-day rain ceremony of the Mayas. Thompson (1975:322) wrote that May 3 saw one of the most vital celebrations in the Classic Mayan calendar, a day of community sacrifices of corn, cacao, and turkeys to the rain gods and the earth gods. Nowadays, traditionalists use *pom* resin to fix feathers from their domestic fowl to important mountain crosses in their area. Women usually perform this ritual because they are in charge of domestic animals. They offer candles and *pom* while petitioning "our Father Cross" for the health of their animals and crops. The cross is directly integrated into planting and is a manifestation of the World Tree and "Flowering Mountain Earth" (Carlsen and Prechtel 1991).

The involvement of the cross in agricultural production is found all over Mesoamerica (Ingham 1986:182; Vogt 1976:55). Franz Blom (1956:283), speaking of Mayas in Mexico, wrote, "In all of the indigenous region of Chiapas . . . I have seen a multitude of crosses on ridges and mountains. . . . Never have I seen a Christ figure hanging on one. . . . The Indians always speak of Lord Holy Cross. . . . There is no doubt that the indigenous people have a conception of the cross which is completely distinct from the Christian cross. . . . It is a direct descendent of Yaxche', the tree that provides the water of life."

This description of the cross illustrates a characteristic of traditional Mayan deities—the way in which they blur into one another. The cross is a manifestation of the rain gods and the mountain spirits, and is also the Tree of Life (León-Portilla 1988).

The moon is also linked to agricultural productivity.[3] Some informants planted only during a full moon, when the maize "will come out strong and in abundance." Among the Tzotzil of Chiapas, planting during the waxing moon furnishes the plants with too much fertility, but while the moon is waning there is not enough; the full moon denotes conditions of completeness and balanced fecundity (Guiteras Holmes 1961:35). Balanced fertility is a premise for all actions throughout planting. Like the female mountains, the full moon is said to "send the rain." Fray Diego de Landa (1975:30) recorded such beliefs more than four hundred years ago, and the moon, water, and the Virgin are still linked in various ways by numerous Mayan groups. The Virgin is the companion of the *chaks* for Yucatec Mayas (Villa-Rojas 1978:292). Q'eqchi' elders believe the moon watches over and protects the growing crop, as well as furnishing fertility.

SEXUAL ABSTINENCE AND FASTING

Once the planting date is known, the senior man and woman of the household decide when the period of sexual abstinence will begin. Sexual intercourse is forbidden during this period, which usually lasts for two weeks before the day of planting and two weeks afterward. In order to avoid temptation and "be respectful," men may sleep on the floor under the household altar.

Henri Hubert and Marcel Mauss (1964:21) documented the widespread practice of sexual abstinence and fasting before sacrifice; here I look at the local meanings of these practices. Traditionalists explain sexual abstention in terms of motives that are highly particular to their communities. Sex during the planting season is considered *awas,* a word that has no direct translation but in this instance means taboo. *Awas* is induced by mixing elements that, by their nature, should be apart. *Awas* maintains the boundaries between spheres, fitting well with Mary Douglas's (1966) assessment of the functions of taboos in *Purity and Danger. Awas* is a polysemic concept, and I prefer to unravel its threads slowly in different contexts. For instance, its definition also encompasses the effects of breaking the taboo, because "*awas* comes out" when disease or wild animals destroy the crop. The transgressor may be the one punished for breaking the *awas*/taboo, but more often the punishment is realized in the resulting product of the *awas* action. For example, human transgressions of *awas* taboos during planting lead to a poor crop. In following chapters, we will encounter many instances of *awas* in planting and in human illnesses.

Sex is felt to be *maak,* which can be translated as sin or culpability. Having sex during sowing makes the corn "feel bad." Maize is living (*yo'yo*) and, like the mountain, beans, cacao, and incense, it has *xtioxil,* or "godliness." It must be respected, revered, and praised. Corn is referred to as an "angel." Having a rather phlegmatic urban attitude toward my foodstuffs, I was struck by the way Q'eqchi's could so sentimentally cherish their maize. In everyday conversation, elders in particular would wax lyrical about its virtues: "It is our light, our life, and because of it we are alive." For these reasons, one must follow the maxim *maamuxuk aawib',* or "don't profane yourself," during planting. Sex makes people aggressive and short-tempered and must be avoided because one needs to plant maize with a "good heart." The resulting crop is a direct reflection of the state of one's heart at the time of planting, so purification is a necessary preparation before work.

Sex is also said to be "dirty." Sexual activity is not *awas* because either men or women are deemed inherently impure at any time. Once I asked a friend, "Why don't you have sex during the planting? Are men dirty, women dirty, or is it the act itself?"

He replied, "Oh, women aren't dirty, neither are men, but sex is. You dirty yourself doing it, you profane yourself. The planting is holy [*loq'*], you see. You can't monkey around with the seeds."[4]

The penalties for too much monkey business are high: "Your corn will grow two feet high and give no fruit." The local tzuultaq'a is seen as the agent behind this maize type of *awas*. If people break the sex *awas,* she or he sends wild animals, birds, rats, and mountain pigs to eat the freshly planted seeds. Tzuultaq'as wreak their vengeance when people are careless and disrespectful. They inflict disease and unleash jungle animals that they guard in a corral deep inside the mountain. Among the K'iche', the owl, coyote, and serpent are "messengers of the Earth. Usually their message advises of a death or illness" (Carmack 1979:382).

Implicit in ideas about sexual continence is the identification of the land with women. A female *aj ilonel* (health promoter) stated: "The woman is like the sacred land. They are always receiving the seed of the man and there it is born and there it grows." Because they are alike, the two are mutually exclusive during the planting—that is, a man cannot fertilize a woman while he is fertilizing the land, and vice versa. In the traditional view, women and the land occupy the same semantic space and so must be rigorously separated when either one is receiving male "seeds." It is vitally important to maintain the separation of maize and human fertility at critical stages in the creation process. Being sexually active during planting detracts from a man's ability to cultivate the earth. All of his sexual energy must be directed toward the planting if a bountiful crop is to flourish. This is why young single men are said to produce the best corn crops.

The next story, told to me countless times, even adds an element of adultery to the land-man-woman love triangle: A man had sex with his wife in the weeks before the planting. When he planted, the seeds never germinated. Again he planted but nothing grew. He tried a third time, but at midday he looked behind him and saw that all the seeds were gone. He sat down on a rock and began to cry. Then he heard a voice, that of a tzuultaq'a, which said to him, "I have recovered all your seeds because you showed no respect. Go back to your house now because your wife is making love to another man." And he returned to find the two having sex. It was true: while he was standing (*xaqxo*, also "erect") in the fields, his wife was "doing it" with another man.

This story functions as a Malinowskian moral charter. Its message is that if a man is disrespectful and sex is not well controlled, then while he is "doing it" with the land, his female partner will complement his behavior by doing it with another man. The man is married to the land during the planting, so the woman must be rejected and the marital union temporarily denied.

The metaphor of the land's being like a woman is problematic in that tzuultaq'as are more often than not male. It could be said that a male spirit actively owns a "female" land, but traditional Q'eqchi's do not see it this way. A tzuultaq'a *is* the land, as well as being a spirit inhabiting it. Nor does the "female earth" have a separate name, such as the Andean Pacha Mama, or any conceptual distinction from the individual mountains. The Q'eqchi' landscape can be both male and female at the same time, even if a tzuultaq'a is male. The mountain spirit is called "Our Father Our Mother," regardless of its sex. The sex of the land, then, is contextual. A tzuultaq'a that appears male in dreams and other encounters is feminized when being planted, after which it returns to its masculine status.

The sexual dualism of the mountain spirits has foiled many a Mesoamerican anthropologist. Guiteras Holmes (1961), for one, never reconciled her informants' calling the earth female with the fact that all the mountain spirits (*'anhel*) are male. Nor did she question an informant who called a male *'anhel* "señora" (1961:218). Guiteras Holmes failed to see that the *totilme'il* ("Father-Mother of the Soul") is not a divided deity but an expression of the united, dual gender of the land.

Sexual continence during planting is widespread among Mayas; many neighboring K'iche's and Poqomchi's do the same. The practice of sexual abstinence also occurred in ancient Mayan cultures (Morley 1947:206; Redfield 1941:314). Sexual abstinence during the planting of a staple crop is not Maya-specific but is common throughout the highlands of Latin America. In the Andes, for instance, Irene Silverblatt (1987:37) records that "married men could not sleep with their wives when yams were sown."

Men fast for one to two weeks before sowing, eating nothing but corn, beans, and salt. Sylvanus Morley (1947:207) tells us about ancient Mayan fasting: "They renounced eating meat, using salt and red chile." Fasting and sexual continence are purifying and are a form of personal sacrifice to the mountains. Ritual practice is locally idiosyncratic, and the prohibited *awas* foods tend to vary from community to community. Meat and fruit of all types are usually *awas*, especially bananas, which if consumed will lead to oversized maize stems that will fall over in the breeze. Rice consumption would lead to maggots in the kernels of corn. Here we see another characteristic of certain types of *awas*. The breaking of the taboo affects the end product of the action (in this case, the corn plants) in a way that associates the superficial features of how the taboo was broken with the manner in which it is punished. Both the taboo-transgressing act and the punishment are called *awas*.

REQUESTING PERMISSION

According to the Christian mentality, God has exalted man to have dominion over all creation but

> *according to the autochthonous religion, the gods*
> *are owners of creation and man has only the right to*
> *petition them for permission to use it.* —Father
> Stephen Haeserijn, *Estudio sobre el estado religioso*
> *del indígena de Alta Verapaz*

Before planting each spring, men go to the caves that riddle the
limestone landscape to ask for "permission"[5] from the mountain
spirits. Traditionalists maintain that Q'eqchi's do not own the
land but merely have a renewable usufruct to it. God is the
ultimate creator, but he is far away in the sky. Tzuultaq'as are
God's sentinels here on earth, guarding the fruits of creation
from human abuse. Appealing to them for licence is an indispensable necessity. Without such a request, any agricultural or
hunting activity will be futile.

The cave sacrifice in which permission is asked was traditionally performed as part of a series of rituals by both individual households and the community as a whole. Few villages still
sacrifice collectively, but household offerings in caves are widespread. The community sacrifice demands complete unity as a
prerequisite; any village division, whether political, religious,
or economic, can result in its nonperformance. Revitalizing the
collective sacrifice then becomes problematical.

I participated in just one community vigil and sacrifice
during my time among the Q'eqchi's, partly because they are
now so rare. I arrived at the community chapel in the late
afternoon as some elder men were making beeswax candles.
Others swung in hammocks, lazily lounging and smoking
stubby home-rolled cigars. Elder women organized the food
and drink; they would later come into the chapel to participate.
These male and female elders officiated the events throughout
the evening. The community sacrifice began with an all-night
vigil that every community member attended. The ceremony
started with prayers and the burning of candles and *pom*. Later,

delicate and hypnotic music played on the harp, violin, and guitar led to dancing, not in pairs but individually, and in a calm, reserved fashion. Everything about the event, even the drinking, was moderate and sensitively balanced. The night was punctuated by a midnight meal, which all were served at the same time in single-sex groups segregated by age.

At dawn, some women left to offer candles and *pom*, pray for the crops, and request permission in Catholic chapels in neighboring villages and towns. Most elders, having been in charge of the festivities up to that point, stayed in the village, where they continued praying. Other elders visited the nearest and most accessible caves, while the younger men made arduous trips to distant mountains. They visited one of the Thirteen Great Tzuultaq'as in their travels, because harvests had been poor in recent years.

The petitions to tzuultaq'as, the saints, and God take place about a week before planting. The date varies, but people need to have begun their sexual abstinence seven to nine days before entering any cave, and they cannot enter it after the burning of the fields has begun, two or three days before planting.

Again continence ensures that the men will enter the caves with a "good heart," for if they do not, they may encounter some misfortune. I was told how one very divided community sent a representative from each of the disputing factions to sacrifice in the mountain. The large candle they burned split in half and fell to the floor. The tzuultaq'a had shown his displeasure at the state of their hearts.

The cave sacrifice is performed only on special days in the Mayan calendar. Few Q'eqchi's still know this intricate system of months, but I was told by an experienced *aj ilonel* that only the days *k'atok* (to burn), *q'an* (yellow, ripe), and *aj* (male) were propitious. *Batz'* (monkey), *tz'i'* (dog), and *keme'* (to be weaved) are inauspicious. Once more we see the role of gender symbolism in maize production: "maleness" (aj) is compatible with contact with the supernatural during the planting, whereas the feminine, represented by women's work, weaving, is inauspicious.

Sacrifices are frightening and dangerous undertakings. Before journeying to the cave, the pilgrim must burn a candle and ask for permission from God and the saints at the household altar. Once, before visiting the angry and powerful Saqtz'iknel, I was asked by the elder Lu' to request permission and protection in the foremost temple of traditionalist Q'eqchi's, in Cobán. I did so with a companion, a fourteen-year-old Q'eqchi' boy. Later, on the steep descent to the cave's mouth, the boy fell and tumbled forty feet before being halted by a large tree. Lu' and I scampered down the slope to find him dazed but unhurt. Coiled beside him was a bright green viper, an agent of the tzuultaq'as. Lu' hurriedly hacked it to pieces with a machete. He interpreted this as a sign that the boy had not requested permission "with his whole heart," and the tzuultaq'a knew it.

When visiting the caves, men are often accompanied by one of their young sons, who carries the sacrificial items. He is the aj mayej, or he-who-sacrifices. One father told me, "The boy is an angel like the mountain. He knows nothing. He has no sin." For traditionalists, purity is of the essence in relations with deities. The pilgrims must be "straight in heart" and free of sexual profanity, and the carrier of the gods' food must be without sin. The sacrificial goods themselves must be of the same high quality. Elders do not use store-bought candles if they can help it: "Because they are sold, who knows who has handled them. Maybe they were sat upon." Rather, they use forest beeswax to make their own candles. In Mayan cults of the environment, "wildness" seems to be closer to holiness. Villa-Rojas (1978: 308) documents how the Yucatecs also offer wild ingredients to the yuntzilob, the gods of the forest.

Pilgrims leave their houses in the early morning, planning to reach the cave mouth just as dawn breaks. On arriving, the participants remove items of clothing, in particular the products of Western culture—boots and socks, hats, belts, watches, glasses, bags, and machetes. They explain the necessity of disrobing by saying, "One mustn't go in front of Tzuultaq'a as a rich man." Ritual specialists may don a red bandanna and red cloth belt, the traditional colonial dress that men have now abandoned in secular life.

Once, some other men and I accompanied the elder Kux to a sacrifice, five days before he was due to plant. On arriving at the cave mouth, Kux lit a candle and kissed the rock it rested on three times. He prayed on his own, kneeling, hands clasped. He announced our presence to the resident tzuultaq'a and requested permission to enter.

Some of the caves are vast and are compared with the Catholic cathedral in Cobán. It can take half an hour to reach the "altar," a natural rock formation in the limestone. Caves are wet, cold, and slippery, as one maneuvers between boulders that are not well fixed on their slope. Entering a cave invokes overwhelming emotions of fear and awe. It is a profoundly numinous experience for all concerned. Pilgrims make each movement with great care and reverence. Inside the caves, there is an intuition of the sacred, the feeling that one is in the presence of the holy.

On reaching the altar, Kux lit his largest white candle. He kissed the rock three times and tapped it three times with his small beanbag to alert the tzuultaq'a. The other participants then lit a smaller candle and balanced it on the rock. Some men light thirteen small candles in the sacrifice, one for each of the Thirteen Great Tzuultaq'as. If corn beer is included in the rite, each participant drinks a glass and then the bottle is left on the altar for the mountain spirit to "drink."

Pilgrims place other delectable items on the altar for the consumption of the tzuultaq'a. These may include raw cacao, corn dough baked in leaves (*poch*), corn gruel (*uq'un*), and turkey parts (the legs) or a whole bird. If turkey blood is offered, it is splashed on the altar and walls of the cave or burned on pine torches. All items are autochthonous. Excluded from offerings are all luxury items of outside extraction, such as coffee, cardamom, and store-bought incense.

Last in the ritual, pilgrims burn *pom* to accompany their supplications. They burn pounds of the resin, which gives off a thick, black, aromatic smoke. In the Popol Vuh (Tedlock 1985:116), we learn that *pom*, the "blood" of the sacred copal tree, is a substitute for human blood. *Pom* carries the prayers upward into the mouth of the tzuultaq'a, who consumes the *pom* and the messages with it. *Pom* is *xwa Qaawa'*, the "tortilla of our Father." According to informants, "*pom* calls the spirit [*xmuhel*] of the mountain." *Pom* is the ritual purifier par excellence, sanctifying any space and expunging evil spirits. A proper sacrifice will include a large piece (one to five pounds) of regular white *pom* and small red pieces called *torak'*. *Torak'* is referred to as "pennies" and is given in a specified number, either thirteen, sixteen, or eighteen. One sacrificer spoke about the use of different types of *pom*: "You have to feed God. When we eat stew we include salt, onions, meat, *xayau* [a red dye], squash, and herbs. It's the same when we give food in a cave, there have to be different types of *pom*."

As the tzuultaq'a downs this smoke stew, the pilgrim stands with arms outspread and palms open and "speaks with his heart." (This is definitely not the standard pose struck in Catholic prayer.) The petitions last some ten to fifteen minutes, until the *pom* is all burned. Prayers in the cave are different from those in the church or household. The vocal pitch is higher and more intense and the language is archaic, poetic, rhyming, repetitive, and delivered at blistering speed. I spoke Q'eqchi' reasonably fluently during the last eight months of my field-work, but cave visits would inevitably lead me back to the dictionary, grappling to understand all that was said. Occasionally, a friend would allow me to take along a small tape recorder.

The following is part of a supplication invoked by Kux for his own household. The tract may be long, but I feel it is important to reproduce it here. This prayer bears many similarities to other textualized Mayan prayers (see Bunzel 1952; Nash 1970:93; Tedlock 1985). Yet I have never come across any other examples in the literature of what a Maya says inside a cave during a sacrifice to a tellurian god. I have translated rather literally (pl. = plural; otherwise, singular); for the original Q'eqchi' version, see Appendix A.

O God,[6] O Tzuultaq'a you [pl.] my Father my Mother, here I am underneath your feet and hands, O Father. Forgive my sins. Thank you for I was able to come across how many mountains, how many valleys, how many leagues, how many days. Now I am here in our Father Siyab' [name of mountain], oh thank you for I was able to come all the way here, my Father. In the name of the bigness and sacredness of your power, your personhood, your godliness, your mercy, your love, your holy hardness.

We are here, in this sacred place, and we know who is in front of us, O my Father, we know who is beside me, the one who doesn't die. Thank you for I arrived, O Father. Light sunrise until here in the greatness of your holiness. I am small in your face, Father Tzuultaq'a. You are perfectly huge and ancient.

Thank you for you brought us here to speak with you, to discuss with you, to beg for our help our health our happiness, to offer our sacrifice to you. Here is our holy *pom*, here are our holy candles, here is our white flower [*utz'uj*, euphemism for candle], ooooh God, green *pom* white *pom* yellow *pom*, white wax green wax yellow wax.

We are here in your holy face, your sacred spirit place. A little bit of your tortilla and drink will I give you now. Here, your sacred *pom*, it is holy goodness. Now I am in front of our Mother Moon, our Father Sun, the Red Star [Venus], in front of the Thirteen Mountains, the Thirteen Valleys for the sake of the greatness of our food and water. Eat, my Father, please give it to your feet to your hands to your face. Let us eat.

Here is my debt; whatever size, whatever amount that I burn in front of Tzuultaq'a, with the sixteen pennies. I am paying and burning in the face of our Father our Mother Tzuultaq'a so that you will show us and guide us. Here I am to pay the sacred forest, the sacred jungle. O great God, O Father Tzuultaq'a, please help me. Give your blessing on my corn field. We will soon be planting. I am requesting permission to work in the face of holy Tzuultaq'a where we find our food and water. O Father Siyab', please give my message to our Father God. Please don't send the animals to eat our maize. Have mercy upon me and my children [here he gave his name, that of his wife, and those of his nine children, from oldest to youngest].

We are doing as our ancestors the Mayas did, they who loved our tzuultaq'as. You [pl.] give us our food, our tortillas and drink, our happiness, our chickens, our crops, our animals. Thank you our Mother Itz'am, our Father [*Qaawa',* or Q.] Tulux, Q. Chiaax, Q. Chimam, Q. Xukaneb', Q. Raxon, Q. Raxuntz'unun, Q. Kojaj, Q. SaqiPek, Q. San Vicente, Q. Ixim, Q. Sa'Mastoon, Q. Siyab'.

We are going to go now, my Mother my Father. You received us in your sacred spirit place. Forgive our sins, for we are only men. Guide our path so that there is no suffering, no pain. We will receive it and where we are able to rest, there we will rest as you wish. Thank you.

INTERPRETATIONS OF THE CAVE SACRIFICE

This lyrical passage illuminates a number of important facets of traditional knowledge and ritual practice. First, the prayer repeatedly emphasizes the petitioner's presence and the sacredness of the cave itself. It is the house of God, where one prays in the presence of—standing "in the face of"—the tzuultaq'a. "Tzuultaq'a is there, but can't be seen. If we see him/her, we will die immediately," I was told. The nature of positional holiness was driven home for me at a parish church, when the image of the Virgin Mary was removed for cleaning. Q'eqchi's of the area were accustomed to burning their offerings and praying in front of the Virgin. Although the image was moved, people continued to pray and sacrifice at her spot, but to the blank wall. When I pointed this out to a Q'eqchi' nun, she put her finger right on the issue by commenting, "Yes, the place is more sacred than the image, isn't it?" Sacredness, then, has a strong situational aspect, and it is most crystallized in the caves.

Second, the pilgrim Kux petitioned not only the resident tzuultaq'a but also the other local mountains and distant larger mountains, the Thirteen Great Tzuultaq'as. The act of naming exerts a certain control over the mountains, and the pilgrim reels off all the tzuultaq'as he knows, his supplication spreading across and enclosing the sacred landscape.

In general, offerings are made to define a deferential relationship with authority. They are the basis of a traditional, subsistence-based "moral economy." Q'eqchi's give food and presents to priests, landowners, government officials, and others who stand in a superior position over them. The giver is in the subordinate role but hopes to negotiate the receiver into an obligation to wield his or her power in a beneficial manner. In eating the offering of food, the consumer swallows the hook of responsibility. The offering, then, placates the tzuultaq'as but also contains elements of manipulation and egalitarianism.

Sacrifice establishes and maintains a relationship of reciprocity and balances out the inequalities between deities and people to a degree. In sharing b'oj, the mountain gods and men are in communion and to a certain extent become equals. To eat together is a sign of equality and often kinship. During feasts such as the community sacrifice, the whole village is fed, but in groups of those equal in age and sex. By the same logic, guests in Q'eqchi' households, where nonkin visitors are treated with great respect, eat on their own in front of the altar while the

family remains in the kitchen. (This practice caused me enormous problems until I convinced people to let me eat with them,
because as a prying anthropologist I felt I should be getting
"backstage" in the kitchen.)

By burning up celestial food, the sacrificer keeps his side of
a reciprocal contract to feed a tzuultaq'a. With the "sixteen
pennies" of red *torak'* incense, the debts from last years's harvest
are paid off and the right to a good crop this year is ensured.
Usufruct rights are renewed by paying the landlord his tribute.
Once she/he accepts the sacrifice and eats up its constituents, a
tzuultaq'a is more obliged to grant permission for planting,
bless the crop, protect it from animals, and act as an advocate
before God so that he too watches over the interests of the
farmer. If a calamity does occur, it is a result of the individual's
or community's moral transgressions.

With regard to notions of reciprocity and authority, there are
striking parallels between the tzuultaq'as and Bolivian mountain spirits. Michael Taussig (1980:144) could be writing about
the Q'eqchi's when he says, "By feeding the mountain spirit,
peasant producers ensure that the mountain spirits will feed
them. . . . The ambivalence of the spirit is always present. . . .
But ritual gift exchange can channel this ambivalence into a
favorable outcome."

Reciprocity between people and mountain spirits has a
Faustian edge to it. Wealthy individuals frequently claim to
have a special relationship with a local tzuultaq'a. An elder of
Cobán—one of the richest Q'eqchi's, who owns a pickup truck,
vast tracts of land, and hundreds of head of cattle—claims to
have built his empire beginning with a small patch of land that
produced uncommonly large crops. He maintains that he became wealthy because he alone in his community remained
faithful to the tzuultaq'as: "I go to the cave each year to give *b'oj*
and *pom* and candles. I have huge ears of corn in my fields and I

see the harvests of others getting smaller and smaller. If you do not offer *b'oj* to the tzuultaq'as, the animals will come and eat everything."

There are many stories of devout pilgrims being rewarded with large crops and gifts such as machetes and forest products like beeswax and wild animals. Receiving from tzuultaq'as is not just a matter of self-indulgence on the part of the recipient. Rather, it carries strongly sanctioned moral limitations. An often-repeated story tells of a hunter who faithfully asked permission from tzuultaq'as before he hunted and was consistently rewarded with a kill. One day he encountered a tall, white, bearded man who gave him an hundredweight of salt. The hunter carried it to his house and consumed the salt with his family. The next time he was in the forest, the hunter was given a present of a hundredweight of cacao. On the way back to his house he met a friend on the path and told him how he had come to receive the cacao. The third time, the two went out to hunt together and again were met by the tall, white elder. They were given a sack of cacao each. Whereas the hunter consumed it with his family and friends, his companion took it straight to the market and sold it for a large sum. He never gave thanks to the mountain spirits with a sacrifice. After a while, the two men went out to the forest again. This time, the hunter received a hundredweight of *pom,* but of his friend, the mountain spirit said, "This man is not my friend," and he took him away and ate him.

The second hunter was eaten, it seems, as a punishment for being selfish and commoditizing the gifts of a tzuultaq'a. Elders often say that corn is especially sacred and should not be sold in the market. When corn is sold, it loses part of its *xtioxilal,* or holiness. Elders say that since people recently began to sell cash crops on a large scale, the land does not produce as it did before. There is hunger now in the villages because Q'eqchi's started

growing coffee and cardamom instead of corn. The elders
maintain that the earth should give people sustenance, not hard
cash. In contrast to Taussig's (1980) study of Bolivian tin
miners, the Q'eqchi' history just told explicitly criticizes com-
moditization of staple crop produce, not labor power. The earth
cult can legitimate minor levels of economic stratification based
upon staple crop production, but not the more accentuated
inequality that results from cash-cropping.

Kux's prayer of sacrifice also informs us about the relationship between the deities. Tiox, which I have translated as
"God,"[7] is invoked first, before any tzuultaq'a, demonstrating
one success of evangelization—at least getting the Christian
God mentioned first. There is, however, only a murky separation between God and the tzuultaq'as. Some elders claim that
they are one and the same, others distinguish them from each
other. Traditionalists are generally not too bothered about
whether their beliefs are monotheistic or not. Such obsessions
pertain only to new converts to orthodoxy, Christian missionaries, and anthropologists. At times Tiox and tzuultaq'as seem
interchangeable; they are called Qaawa', "our Father," throughout. Kux addresses the two figures together and then says,
"Here I am underneath your feet," using the second person
singular. He also uses the singular person in the imperative
"please help me" after both Tiox and tzuultaq'as were called
upon. The cave (a tzuultaq'a's house) is referred to by the same
label that would be used for a church (God's house)—santil
muheb'aal, or "saintly spirit place." All the various deities
petitioned in the cave (God, tzuultaq'as, and the sun, moon, and
Venus) are referred to as "our Father our Mother," that is, as a
unified collective of deities. Perhaps they should all be viewed
as a single supernatural entity. I agree with Jon Schackt (1984:
18) when he writes that tzuultaq'as are the "earthly manifestation of a general divinity."

Kux also treats God and the tzuultaq'a as separate—for example, in paragraph five, when the tzuultaq'a is asked to relay the pilgrim's message to God. The mountain deities, who are visible in dreams and in physical form as mountains, act as intermediaries between people and the distant Christian God in the sky. Elders associate tzuultaq'as with Catholic saints in their function as middlemen between heaven and earth. It follows that tzuultaq'as were given saints' names.

The mediating role of the mountain spirit might suggest that God and the tzuultaq'as are separate, but I tend toward the view that they are overlapping and indivisible. When asked how many gods there are, traditionalists had varying replies, from "only one" to "dozens." The issue is a nonissue for them, and they change their answers from time to time. The supernatural is one complex, and the figures within it express only different aspects of the whole. Whether a deity (God, a tzuultaq'a, Venus, the sun, or the moon) appears as detached from or conjoined with the general sacred depends on its context. Yet underlying the divisions is a fundamental unity of the sacred.

This is the approach adopted by many ethnohistorians and archaeologists studying the ancient Maya. Hunt writes of ancient Mesoamerican deities (1977:54–55): "The gods were not totally personified as discrete entities, however. Rather, they were clusters of ideas. . . . God was both the one and the many. Thus the deities were but his multiple personifications." In this view, Mayan groups perceive the deities not as eternally well-defined concepts but as a flux of "symbol clusters" that could coalesce into a defined entity in a certain context and then merge and overlap with other divine images in another milieu. Archaeologists such as Muriel Porter Weaver (1972:234) have concluded from studies of Mayan glyphs that the deities were not discrete entities, each with a single character, but "were both individual and multiple at the same time."

During fieldwork I found it highly problematical to distinguish the divinities of the traditional Q'eqchi' cosmology. I searched in other modern studies of Mayan groups, but other ethnographers have not been able to differentiate the various deities satisfactorily either. I finally arrived at the conclusion that such an attempt is fundamentally flawed. The analysis of Q'eqchi' rituals and histories is greatly facilitated by realizing the intrinsic relatedness of the deities. Julian Pitt-Rivers (1970:193) came to similar conclusions for Mexican Mayan groups: "The notion of God includes all of Divinity and hence the saints, the Ancestor, and the guardians. The distinction between the one and the many, which poses such a problem to theologians who feel the need to be logical, concerns the Indians of Chiapas not at all."

As a heuristic, then, we could say that modern Mayan deities are each a particular expression of the universal sacred and are therefore ultimately indivisible from one another. The idea of a "unified cosmology which integrates Good and Evil" (Pitt-Rivers 1970:202) is remarkably useful, yet has been under-utilized by contemporary ethnographers of Mayas.

CAVE SACRIFICES: ANCESTOR WORSHIP OR ETHNIC RESISTANCE?

In his prayer, Kux refers to God and the tzuultaq'a as "my Mother, my Father," and the collective tzuultaq'as as "our Father our Mother." The "Father-Mother" gods are widespread in Mesoamerica and are part of the cosmogony of nearly all Mayan groups. The *Totilme'il* of the Tzotzil is the primordial "Father-Mother of life" (Guiteras Holmes 1961:292). In the Popol Vuh (Tedlock 1985:72), the sacred book of the K'iche', the creator god is also called the "Mother-Father of life."

Is the cult of the mountain and valley actually a cult of the ancestors, of the dead? Studies among Q'anjob'als (La Farge

1947) and indigenous people of Aguacatán (Brintnall 1979) have shown close association between the ancestors and mountain cults. The ancestors of the Tzeltals live in caves and are honored on May 3, the day of the Holy Cross, itself a symbol of the mountain (J. Nash 1970:19–22). For the Andes, Joseph Bastien (1978), Irene Silverblatt (1987:23) and Michael Taussig (1980:185–90) document the identification between ancestors and mountain spirits.

There also seems to be an association between the mountains and the Mayas, the ancestors of the Q'eqchi'. Tzuultaq'as speak Mayan and don Mayan dress. The pilgrim's petition reproduced earlier called upon the Mayas and referred to them as "our ancestors," *li qaxe'qatoon,* literally "our stem-root." Elders assert that the ancient Mayas truly loved and were in communion with the earth deities. The Mayas could all see into the mountains and converse with their spirits, but now only the *aj ilonel* ("seer," or shaman) has this capacity.

Elder men tell histories about ancient Mayas who continue to live and work inside the mountains. There they walk about in white cotton clothing, with long hair, and move great stones. The mountain Raxuntz'unun (Green Hummingbird) is suspected of being full of Mayas, for drums are heard beating there at night. Mayas are also said to inhabit the dense forest, the domain of the tzuultaq'as. Old men who were forced to work on the road to Panzós in the 1940s tell how Mayas would snatch people at night and devour them. In sum, there is a great deal of overlapping symbolism in traditionalist conceptions of the ancient Mayas and the mountain spirits.

It is problematical, however, to refer to the cult of the tzuultaq'as as a cult of the dead, because there is no overt linking of the dead and the mountains. Q'eqchi' kinship does not involve lineages, nor do communities have an apical ancestor. Whatever is being expressed, it is not a lineage cult of ancestors. Traditionalists are quite orthodox Catholics in their ideas about the dead, who are only significant ritually on November 1, All Saints Day. At this time, food is placed on the household altar for the family dead. When I asked, "Where are the dead?" I would be told, "In the cemetery"—not in the mountain. If I asked, "What are they doing?" the response was always, "Nothing." The dead are buried with the work instruments corresponding to their sex: women with their pots and looms, men with their hoes, machetes, ropes, and cigars. Informants always denied that the dead go to the mountain and work for a tzuultaq'a as *colonos,* or serfs. Few people were preoccupied with issues of death or the fate of the soul, and some reacted to my persistent questioning with, "Look, when you're dead, you're dead!" There was only a vague Christian idea of being raised from the dead on judgment day.

A key to this conundrum can be found in Q'eqchi' language, which employs two past tenses: the *k* prefix is for the remote past and the Mayas, whereas the *x* prefix is used for the recent past and the actions of the more recently dead. This usage expresses a local difference between history (*x*-time) and myth (*k*-time), without any of the usual pejorative connotations ascribed to the term *myth.* There are two different kinds of dead: the remote Mayan ancestors associated with the mountains, and the physical corpse, the recently dead, the Christian ancestors.

J. D. Hill (1988) and Stephen Hugh-Jones (1989) write about similar perceptions of the past and the ancestors among certain South American peoples, for whom there is a present past (the self) and a presocial past (the other). Rituals cross this barrier and draw on the powers of the remote past. Sacrifice is thus an act of mediation, conjoining the worlds of the past and present. For traditionalist Q'eqchi's and countless other peoples around the world, the dead are indispensible to agricultural produc-

tion. The fertility of maize comes from the world of the dead,
the ancient Mayas, who are visited by their descendants in the
cave ritual. These remote ancestors are a perennial source of
legitimacy, power, and fecundity.

The existence of Mayas in caves is a statement more about
identity than about lineage. To understand modern Q'eqchi'
identities in relation to the Mayas, we must go back to the time of
the initial evangelization after the Spanish invasion. The everyday
word for "person" in Q'eqchi' is *kristian*, which is derived from the
Spanish *cristiano*, or Christian. This term replaced the pre-
Columbian word for human being or person, *poyanam*. *Kristian* is
the opposite of the word *xul*, or animal. *Xul* refers to wild and
domestic animals, to unbaptized infants, and, pejoratively, to
rowdy children. In extreme cases of antisocial behavior, an
adult may be called a *xul*. A person, then, is either a Christian or
a beast. I suggest that these polar opposites were encouraged by
earnest priests during the initial evangelization.

During the sixteenth century, Q'eqchi's became "pacified"
before other groups, whom they deemed savages, or "Mayas."
The "Christians" were the Q'eqchi's of the *reducciones* (reduced
towns), those who were baptized and became subservient to the
Spanish king. The "animals" were Mayas, pagans, those who
fled the camps and persisted in leading an independent, unbaptized existence in the forests. As with other stereotypes, the
Mayas are still seen as a single, homogeneous group. There is no
conception of the linguistic and cultural diversity that has
always existed in the Maya region.

It is significant that elders often call the ancient Mayas *Ch'ol
wiinq,* or "men of the Ch'ol tribe," the Ch'ol being the now-
extinguished nomadic group to the north of Q'eqchi' territory.
If the Ch'ol ceased to exist as a distinct ethnic group four
centuries ago, why do they live on with legendary status?
Q'eqchi's and Ch'ols engaged in trading and warring relations

until the Spanish culturally obliterated the Ch'ol by relocating them inside the Q'eqchi' region and forcing them to speak Q'eqchi' (Thompson 1938).[8] The Ch'ol were notoriously difficult to control, continually deserting Spanish *reducciones* for the jungle and raiding Q'eqchi' settlements.

In the end, the Q'eqchi's swallowed up the Ch'ol, incorporating them as a representation of their own wildness. Historically, Q'eqchi's have a conception of the "ultra-indigenous" that they project onto the vanished Ch'ol. The *Ch'ol wiinq* are the "Mayas," the living memory of ancient ancestors. They are what traditional Q'eqchi's see themselves as once having been and, in part, still to be. Traditional identity, then, is created in opposition not only to the nonindigenous but also to the superindigenous. In a similar vein, Robert Redfield and Alfonso Villa-Rojas (1934:331) reported that the Yucatecs also have an image of the "Wild Savages/Mayas," whom they identify with the near-extinct Itzás. The Andean parallel would be the *wayri ch'uncho* dancers at the pilgrimage to the mountain shrine at Qoyllur Rit'i, as described by Michael Sallnow (1987:241).

It is clear, however, that Q'eqchi's would not still be speaking of Mayas in the mountains solely on the basis of cultural legacies from the sixteenth century. Such histories play a role in the construction of modern community identities, not only in opposition to the nonexistent Ch'ol but as distinct from surrounding communities and Ladino plantation owners. In *Shamanism, Colonialism and the Wild Man*, Michael Taussig (1986: 222–5) argues that people of the Putumayo region of Colombia create a zone of power through the "poetics of uncertainty" over the idea of wildness. In Alta Verapaz as in the Putumayo, one way of appropriating an alternative form of power is through interacting with "wild men" and taming their wildness.

Community histories of wild Mayas lay claim to the local landscape and represent a veiled protest to the contested and skewed system of land tenure. Communities, through their idiosyncratic rituals, are saying, "These are *our* mountains, with whom we have had a moral collective relationship over the centuries. They belong to us and our ancestors before us"—even though in the official registry the land may belong to another community, or a Ladino, or the Ladino government. Q'eqchi' communities have met with continuous obstruction to obtaining land rights through the legal process, which leads to an elaboration of those rights in the realm of indigenous religion, the most autonomous and clandestine social activity.

As described in chapter two, Q'eqchi's were dispossessed en masse from their lands after the Spanish invasion and under Liberal party regimes in the 1870s. Many indigenous lands are still untitled, and a large number of villages are petitioning INTA, the government department nominally in charge of land issues. A Catholic legal office opened in November 1987 and within a few years began to represent the land claims of more than 250 Q'eqchi' communities. A staggering number of Q'eqchi' communities are involved in one legal battle or another to obtain land title from the government or defend themselves from encroaching Ladino landlords. Another threat comes from neighboring communities that are also squeezed onto insufficient land. Two communities I knew well had recently fought with machetes over their differences. Q'eqchi's have never to my knowledge collectively struggled for their land on the basis of ethnic affiliation, only as insular communities. As we will see, communities only became united against Ladino landowners by religious and class discourses in the early 1980s.

So long as the Mayas are alive in the mountains, each community's claim to be the rightful owner of the land remains alive too. Elders speak of how Mayas would visit the caves and see and speak to tzuultaq'as face-to-face. That modern Q'eqchi' pilgrims can no longer do this is perhaps a metaphor for their increasing alienation from the land, beginning in the sixteenth century and intensifying after 1871. Sallnow's comments (1991: 152) on Andean pilgrimages are pertinent here, for he asserts that indigenous pilgrimages to mountain shrines are expressions of "chronic cultural schizophrenia." He adds: "To claim and reclaim a colonized sacred landscape for human purposes is to claim and reclaim a compromised cultural identity."

The cult of the mountains surreptitiously and positively affirms Q'eqchi' ethnic identity with respect to Ladinos. Traditionalists recognize that Ladinos have no ritual relationship with the earth. During the cave sacrifice, the pilgrim speaks an ancient, archaic form of Q'eqchi' that is much less littered with Castilian words than is everyday conversation. Forgotten words are renovated. As I have mentioned, the petitioner gives only autochthonous foods to the deities, not items that come from Ladinos, the "Chicken men." Men remove any Western clothes they are wearing and don what they term their "traditional dress." Similarly, pilgrims do not mention Jesus Christ; only in this setting is God's son absent from prayer. Taussig (1980:147) has pointed out that across Latin America, Jesus is not mentioned in petitions to mountain spirits. I could not elicit any comment on this, but my surmise is that Jesus is seen as the unacceptable and "unsyncretized" face of modern orthodox Catholicism. In short, what at first might have looked like a cult of the ancestors is more a matter of traditionalists invoking the ancestors to legitimate claims against their "other," the Ladinos.

Taken as a whole, the earth cult constructs and positively values that which is seen to belong to the community and to be purely Q'eqchi', whether it is in the realm of food, language, dress, or religion. Only in these rituals can one actually speak with the true owners and guardians, the real masters of the land. There is a parallel here with eighteenth-century Arequipa, as documented by Frank Salomon (1987), where the ancestor cults were a focus of resistance to the state. In this part of highland Peru, the mummies in cave shrines were seen as the "true owners" of the land (Salomon 1987:161) and functioned to define the "collective 'self' and 'other' within rigid boundaries" (1987:160).

Mountains play a central role in the construction of community identity and a wider pan-Q'eqchi' ethnicity. If one asks, "Who are you?" a villager is most likely to reply, "A person of such-and-such village," itself more than likely named after the nearest powerful mountain. Idiosyncratic variations in religious practice are employed to make distinctions not only between indigenous and nonindigenous people but also between localized areas. The mountain cult constructs community identity often in opposition to surrounding communities, with whom many villages are locked in dispute over boundaries. Local identity is traditionally stronger than any pan-Q'eqchi' consciousness, but we shall see in the chapter eight how this is changing as the catechists look to the mountain cult to redefine ethnic identity itself.

These comments have wider import for thinking about social classification in Maya communities. Watanabe (1992:77) describes similar classificatory processes in Chimbal that employ analogous religious icons but with different end results from those of Q'eqchi' communities. Chimbal identity is constructed through the opposition of saints (us) to mountain gods, or *witz* (them). Whereas the saints were found in the wild but were domesticated to become well-behaved, reciprocal members of Chimbal, the *witz* stayed in the wild and became asocial, nonreciprocal Ladinos.

CONCLUSIONS

In looking at preparations for planting, we can learn a few things about how fertility is constructed. Productivity and reproduction are on the same level; men reproduce with the land when producing the yearly staple crop. Yet the two are separated by the *awas* taboo on sex; human reproduction (as we will see fully in chapter five) is an area of female hegemony that must be excluded from agricultural production.

Sacrifice is the main mechanism for affirming and renewing individual and communal relationships with the local mountains. Through sacrifice, people feed the gods and in turn are fed. Sacrifice gives notice of intentions, pays off past debts, and ensures the right to plant. The deal is struck and the contract sealed. In traditional knowledge, sacrifice gives up a part of the sacrificer, which is one of the more commonly cited conclusions of Hubert and Mauss (1964:32). During the planting, sacrifice engages tzuultaq'as as the planters' advocates before God and renews fertility by calling upon the powers of the wild Mayas. In a more political sense, sacrifice recreates a community-based system of land tenure to rival that of the Ladinos in their registry offices. Sacrifice inscribes local land tenure, that of the community and individual household, onto the landscape.

Anderson (1991) has characterized "traditional" communities as overly "unimagined" because he construes them as based on face-to-face contact, kinship relations, labor reciprocity, village political organizations, and so on. Dynastic realms and modern nation states, on the other hand, have to be "imagined" because they are too large to be integrated by kinship and face-to-face bonds alone. The mountain cult is the template for imagining the community and constructing Q'eqchi' identities on a number of levels. The relationship between villagers and their nearby mountain spirit anchors community identity. Only a small number of people, the elders, interact with an ultralocalized deity. The elders not only imagine the community, they dream it as well.

It is not an eternally fixed image they hold onto; the villages' tzuultaq'a cult is a template for imagining and reimagining the community. This collective representation has a history—it responds to changes in political economy, as is evident in the portrayal of tzuultaq'as as German landowners. At the same time, the imagining of the mountain spirit shapes the nature of economic and political developments, influencing the ways in which they are perceived and conceptualized.

The local earth cult forms the substrate for higher orders of imagined community. On a larger scale, the Thirteen Great Tzuultaq'as are defining markers of a less well-elaborated pan-Q'eqchi' ethnic identity. The pilgrimages that many Q'eqchi's make to these universal shrines link them together as an imagined religious community. Anderson (1991:53–56) discusses pilgrimage and the formation of imagined identities, and his ideas can be extended to Q'eqchi' pilgrimages to nodal points in a collectively constructed landscape. The architects of a revitalized pan-Q'eqchi' identity, as we will see, use the mountain spirit cult as a cosmological basis for espousing the idea of a Q'eqchi' nation.

CHAPTER FOUR

FERTILIZING THE LAND

The whole community rejoices when we begin to sow our maize. — Rigoberta Menchú, *I, Rigoberta*

This chapter deals with the activities and knowledge surrounding the planting of maize.[1] The planting is a fiesta, an occasion when villagers are cheerful and optimistic. It is the high point in the household's economic and social calendar, when householders exchange reciprocal labor and accrue prestige by rewarding their laborers with food and drink. The banquet cooked for the planters is one of the principal feasts of the year, punctuating the daily fare of tortillas and beans. Until the last ten years, Q'eqchi' villages were dispersed, with households many kilometers from one another, so reunions were rare and special occasions.

During the evening vigil before the planting, the men venerate the corn seeds and maintain strict isolation from women. This gender segregation underlines the separation of maize cultivation and human reproduction. The process of separating the sexes begins with the period of sexual abstinence and fasting and intensifies during the vigil. Maize fertility is seen as resulting solely from the union of male sexuality with the feminized land. The cult of the landscape is, in this way, integral to the construction of gender identity as well as community identities.

This chapter continues the theme of traditionalist sacrifice by looking at different classes of *awas,* or taboos, and eating norms on the day of planting. I argue that *awas* separate the symbolic elements of human reproduction and maize production. They also maintain ethnic boundaries by excluding Ladino foods and material goods and even the Catholic God. The cultural diversity between communities is part of the construction of community identities inside the Q'eqchi' linguistic boundary.

I also continue the process of unraveling the traditionalists' relationship with the land. Rituals and religious knowledge are grounded in everyday actions and thought and are not just the product of a specialized "ideological" discourse. Among the Q'eqchi's, rituals are life-giving activities, inseparable from everyday knowledge of fertility and health. Depending on the context, rituals can be utterly pragmatic in their motivations, performance, and ends. To quote Robert Redfield (1941:238): "They [agricultural rituals] are acts directed more immediately to the practical end: a successful crop." The Durkheimian anthropological tradition, including Radcliffe-Brown and Malinowski, adheres to the distinction between ritual and technical acts, where the former are sacred and symbolic and the latter are mundane and instrumental.[2] This is an improvement over the "mystical primitive" of Levy-Bruhl, but perhaps this cognitive dualism has held too much sway in the anthropology of ritual. It certainly flies in the face of most actors' views of the instrumental nature of ritual acts. In the Mayan area, imposing such binary distinctions necessitates an overinterventionist approach to ethnography.

LABOR RECRUITMENT AND WORK
IN THE PLANTING

Planting creates its own labor pool with special norms of behavior that are infused with moral and religious content. Some of the information relevant to labor induction during planting is contained in chapter two. Field owners primarily recruit their male relatives—consanguineal, affinal, and spiritual, that is, godparents and godchildren. Extending out from their kin, they call upon a network of friends from their own village. Men tend to plant with the same people year after year. For this reason, the host does not pay most of his helpers, "because I will plant/have planted with them this year." Planting and harvesting are the only stages in the agricultural cycle for which labor can be repaid in kind. Labor is also compensated with copious quantities of corn beer, cigars or cigarettes, and food during the twenty-four hour period. At the same time, planting is still considered work, and is part of the production process.

Female recruitment for work in the kitchen is parallel to but autonomous from that of the men. The senior woman of the household is responsible for recruitment and can ask whomever she wants, but in practice the participants usually are elder female relatives of men invited to plant. Spiritual kin (godmothers) feature prominently. Male and female workers, then, are organized in semi-independent reciprocal labor pools. Women also eat well and have excess food to take home but are not paid in cash. Female labor constitutes the basis of the male host's ability to provide the essential gastronomic requirements for his work force. The women make possible the feast and thus the temporary incorporation of other community members into household production. If labor exchange is the basis of the community's moral economy, then it is women who are the basis of reciprocity between households.

Involvement in labor reciprocity is both a defining feature of indigenous identity and a criterion of community membership. No villagers hire day wage labor to plant maize. Unlike other stages of the productive process (such as clearing), planting work is never reimbursed with a full day's wage. As one source stated, "That is what the rich people, the *finqueros* [plantation owners], do. We are poor and work for free for each other." The host is obliged, however, to pay a nominal sum to those whom he will not remunerate with labor in kind. If he does not reimburse them financially, however small the sum, "the holy corn will not give fruit." People's possible resentment at furnishing labor without repayment would damage the crop. As we will see in more detail later, there is a correlation between the inner state of the planters and the future crop.

A household planting the highland average of 3.5 hectares requires between ten and twenty men, but the maximum number invited depends on the host's wealth and breadth of social connections. Many more men are invited than are necessary to complete the task, because one aim is to generate prestige for the host. The owner of the fields spends more money in food and drink than if he were to hire *mozos* at Q4 per day. It is beneficial for the owner to do this for two reasons. First, it is an honor, a sign of closeness and friendship, to be asked to plant with someone. The host's social standing with those invited is enhanced, and relations of *compadrazgo* (the status of godparenthood) are articulated. Second, by inviting a large number of men, the occasion is more a celebration where all can drink and eat and work slowly with no pressure to finish by sundown. Under these conditions, the workers are happy and the crop will be a good one.

The special status of the planting is apparent when compared to other stages in the agricultural calendar. Harvesting is more circumscribed to the household, and only enough workers are recruited as are necessary to get the job done quickly. If the fields are close by, women also harvest, unlike the situation during planting, when they are kept away. This means that one seldom needs to look outside a close network of consanguineal kin and affines. Harvest labor tends to be more commoditized than that for planting: payment is either a nominal wage plus food or a full daily wage.

THE *YO'LEK*, OR VIGIL FOR THE MAIZE SEEDS

The seed is honored because it will be buried in something sacred—the earth. We do it mainly because the seed is something pure, something sacred. For us the word seed is very significant. The candles are lit in every house. —Rigoberta Menchú, *I, Rigoberta*

This section provides a straight ethnographic description with a minimum of comment. Taking place on the night before the planting, the *yo'lek,* or vigil, is performed expressly to ensure that the seeds "are happy in their hearts." If this is attained, they will all sprout and produce healthy corn plants. The corn merits such attention because it is alive and has a spirit. The *iyaj* (seed), whether corn alone or maize mixed with beans, is placed in a basket on the family altar at dusk. A lit candle is stuck in the middle of the seeds, replacing the fading sun. It will burn all night to "watch over" (*yo'lenkil*) the seeds. During the planting vigil, the seeds are "being born" (*yolaak*). They must have light for this because "the seed cannot be born in the darkness." The vigil is a critical time for the seed, and it must be guarded all night. The host stays awake until dawn, sitting next to the altar wrapped in a blanket. If not cared for, the seed may "take fright," lose its spirit, and not germinate.

In some areas, such as Lanquín and Cahabón, the seed is "fed" (*wa'tesiink*) with pieces of flesh or blood from a turkey.

The exegesis of this practice is, "We want the seed to be happy." The blood is also said to "heat" the seed. Other practices carried out to *loq'oniink ru* (venerate or give respect to) the seed include pouring the drink *b'oj* over it. *B'oj* is also a "hot" item. Raw cacao beans, one for each of the Thirteen Great Tzuultaq'as, are mixed with the maize. Cigarettes, one for each man planting, may be stuck upright in the seed. The men smoke these as they leave go out to plant the next morning. In both cases, the seeds and men are in communion, enjoying together the same delicacies of *b'oj*, cacao, and cigarettes. These particulars of the ritual are idiosyncratic, varying at the level of the household, village, and region.

The invited men come at dusk to participate in the vigil. Upon entering the house, they kneel in front of the altar to pray for the forgiveness of their sins and thank the tzuultaq'as and God for delivering them safely to their destination. They congregate on the floor or in hammocks in the room with the altar. The only source of light is the single flickering candle, embedded in the maize seed.

Women work in the kitchen, preparing the festive food and drink. During the course of the evening, they consume food and *b'oj* and smoke cigars. It is a special occasion for them, too. There is no contact between the women and the men from outside the household until after the planting work is finished. Women remain in the kitchen and men stay in their room, where they are completely identified with the corn seed. If a woman enters the room during the vigil, the birth of the seeds will be disturbed and they will not grow properly. The host and his sons mediate between the two rooms.

Elder men sit closest to the household altar. At least one elder from the community is present, performing the function of *testiig* (from the Castilian *testigo*, "witness"). He is the master of ceremonies, the ritual specialist of the occasion. If the host's

father is alive, he is likely to be the *testiig*. Godfathers also play
this role, which involves burning *pom* and leading the prayers
before each meal. The *testiig* makes conversation, ensures that
all present are content, and advises the host on correct ritual
procedure. Functions are divided between the host and the
testiig because the host is "too busy" organizing the distribution
of food, alcohol, and so forth. The host is the ritual specialist
and prayer leader in the fields but not in the house, where he is
displaced by the *testiig*. At home, the host does little more than
serve food and drink in what is conventionally (and at any other
feast) a female role.

The vigils are relaxed affairs in which the men lounge and
chat, drinking mugs of warmed *b'oj* and smoking tobacco. A
local man might play the harp. The music is repetitive and
hypnotic, pleasing to the men and the seed alike. Mexican
ranchera music on the radio and marimba music are inappropriate; they would frighten the nascent corn. The men eat a light
meal of *tz'u'uj*— thin ground corn patties, or tortillas, filled with
ground black beans. *B'oj,* tobacco, and food are distributed in
order of status: those elders nearest the altar first, followed by
younger men and finally boys. No one can commence eating
until invited to do so by the *testiig*. In addition to these
principles of hierarchy, there are some elements of equality. All
drink *b'oj* out of the same one or two cups. *Tz'u'uj* are shared out
of the same baskets, and no one eats until everyone is served.

The *testiig* burns *pom* over the seeds, the altar and saint, and
all those present. He petitions at the altar, giving notice to God,
a local tzuultaq'a, and all the mountain spirits he knows of that
they will plant in the morning. Father Sun, Mother Moon, and
Venus are all invoked. *Pom* carries his message to the deities,
who are pleased by the offering. *Pom* feeds the seed as well and
makes it happy. The resinous incense expunges any evil spirits
from the corn and house.

Elements of Catholic ritual are also in evidence. At the vigil, participants may perform a rosary, kneeling in front of the altar holding their rosary beads and reciting their Hail Marys. Traditionally this prayer was said in Castilian, a language not understood in the almost completely monolingual Q'eqchi' communities.

The men may play games to pass the hours. One popular game is called *dados*. The idea is to rub an ear of corn over the fire and catch the first grain that falls. If it is colored white, the player receives three seeds; if yellow, four; and if black or red, five. The grains are then tossed, and the man whose grain comes closest to a line drawn in the earth wins. A man told me, "We play it to keep from becoming tired, so we can stay up all night." Traditionalists in Cobán thought this was disrespectful to the corn and attributed its practice to immigrants to the hot lowlands of the Polochic Valley.

With or without games, the conversation is jovial and humorous. Men tell jokes, chuckle at word puns, and exchange banter. They boast of their hunting exploits—the killing of jungle animals such as wild fowl and boar, and encounters with dangerous snakes and mountain cats. The greatest awe, however, is reserved not for those who kill but for those who catch wild animals alive and manage to breed them.

Toward the end of the evening, by which time everyone is at least tipsy, the elders begin to recount local history. They tell what happened to men who had sex with their partners during the planting. They discuss dreams and reported encounters with mountain spirits, recounting stories about Mayas seen in the jungle or heard in the mountain. The evening becomes more serious, the young men listening as elders elaborate on their oral history. Their messages are generally conservative and emphasize the punishment of transgressors of the moral code.

At one vigil, I told a story about my friend Kolax, who once mixed Gramaxone (a toxic weed-killer) in with the insect-infested seeds he was about to plant. Kolax had told me, "But my wife did not know that was the bag of seeds for planting and made tortillas out of them. We all ate them but we did not die, so that stuff is no good. I stopped using it." The men hooted with laughter, but the elders used the story as a springboard to moralize against the use of chemicals in agriculture. They repeated that fertilizers ruin the soil—being "too hot, it burns the earth."

The vigil winds down informally after midnight as men who live close by return to their houses. Those taking part in the planting are not specifically included in the taboo on sexual abstinence, only the owner of the fields. Yet because all the men in a community plant during roughly the same two-week period, most are abstaining anyway.

The remaining men fall asleep one by one in front of the altar. Some bring their own hammocks or woven mats to sleep on. If not, the host provides one, ensuring that all are comfortable. Two or three might share a blanket. Everyone sleeps except the host, who keeps vigil with the candle that silhouettes the shapeless forms on the floor.

INTERPRETING THE VIGIL

Motivations for performing the vigil are rooted in local history, which reiterates that Q'eqchi's are not the owners of the land. In order to cultivate it, they must request permission from a tzuultaq'a. Their hold over maize is equally tenuous. In ancient times, only the king of the mountains, Lord Xukaneb', possessed corn seeds. He gave them to Saqlek (Whitespoon) for safekeeping while he struggled with K'ixmes (Thornbroom), who had kidnapped Xukaneb''s daughter, Sujk'im (Basketgrass). The usurper K'ixmes won out. Saqlek, in a fit of pique because he was Sujk'im's admiring suitor, decided to withhold the corn. There followed famine and war between the mountains, which ended with Saqlek reduced to rubble and Xukaneb' with his corn back.[3]

The story continues with "the Mayas" winning Xukaneb''s favor through petitions and sacrifices. In his cave, Xukaneb' then gave five types of corn to the Mayas. Yet Xukaneb' is jealous with his corn. The mountain's trust in people lasts only so long as they treat the corn with respect. If they abuse the maize—for example, by handling it while they indulge in profane actions such as sex or defecation—the mountain spirit will intervene. As a man explained, "If a person rejects corn, if they leave it lying on the ground, a tzuultaq'a will recover it." Taking corn for granted, even in everyday interactions, means forfeiting a fragile right of ownership.

People have the inalienable right to cultivate all crops other than maize. Only corn was delivered at a later time by the chief mountain god to Q'eqchi's, making them, in a sense, more like the gods. Corn itself has "godliness" (tioxil) and so is treated with praise and reverence. Before touching corn, especially when eating tortillas, elders blow on their hands, making an "ush-ush" sound, to "bless" (xk'eb'al xtioxil) the maize.

Some writers contend that ritual recapitulates and reenacts creation myths, a view that seems to fit here (Hocart 1970:66; Witherspoon 1977:44). Although the preceding history is not cosmogonical, it describes the beginning of society, with maize as the staple food and a central element of traditional knowledge and symbolic practice. Part of the meaning of the maize vigil, then, is found in history. This meaning is not just ritual knowledge, however; everyday dealings with maize are similarly shaped. If it exists at all, there is only a gossamer boundary between "secular" and "ritual" behavior toward maize, for both are based on the same premises and contain analogous elements. The vigil emerges not out of a "ritual" or

"nonrational" (or "non-cognitive" for Bloch [1986]) mental
state, but out of a background of quotidian meanings and
histories.

The vigil for the corn seed can be compared to another
ritual: the wake for a dead person, also called a *yo'lek*. Apart
from the corn vigil, a wake is the only other time an object is
placed in front of the family altar and "watched over" during the
night. Both the seeds and the corpse are buried the next day in
the earth. During the "grab crop" ritual detailed in the next
section, the petitioner explicitly tells the tzuultaq'as that he is
going to bury (*muquk*) the seeds. *Muquk* means both "to hide"
and to inter a corpse. Robert Carlsen and Martin Prechtel
(1991:28) write that Atitecos of Santiago Atitlán also refer to
interring (*muk*) maize seeds, which are referred to as "little
skulls." They stress the importance of the symbolism of death
and regeneration in agricultural and human fertility and note
that ethnographies of the Mayas have not explored this cultural
dimension thoroughly.

In both vigils, the participants pray rosaries and consume
only corn- and bean-based foods. The traditional drink for the
death *yo'lek* is *uq'un* (maize drink) with salty beans in it. The
games of chance played in the corn vigil are characteristic of
wakes all over the world (see Bloch and Parry 1982:10). The
corn vigil is undertaken with the same cool, measured, and
balanced attitude as that of the Yucatec death vigil described by
Alfonso Villa-Rojas (1978:426). The vigil, then, is associated
with both human and staple-crop life processes. That both
maize and the dead are the objects of vigils draws another
connection between the ancestors and agricultural fertility.

THE *CHAPOK K'AL*, OR "GRAB CROP" RITUAL

The women are up before the men, rising at 4:00 A.M. They grind
corn, clean and cook the turkeys, and generally prepare the food

for the day. Soon afterwards, the owner of the fields gathers his belongings and, without eating, sets off to his fields. He aims to arrive before the sun breaks. It is important that the *chapok k'al* be performed at a certain conjuncture of the celestial bodies — before the sun rises, but while the moon and the morning star still shine in the sky.

Before entering his field, the farmer cuts a small green sapling. He fashions a cross and places it in the center of the field. Villa-Rojas (1978:278) wrote that Yucatecs place a cross in the field before clearing and burning brush. For them, "wherever the cross is, there also are the eyes of God."

Q'eqchi' traditionalists do not refer to the object directly as a cross (*krus*) but euphemistically as a "sign" (*reetalil*). In this context, naming an object directly unleashes its power. Fearing loss of control over a potentially malevolent power means that one must avoid calling a cross a cross. In Cahabón, a cross does not feature at all; rather, an "altar" is built from two poles connected by an arching branch, facing the rising sun.

The cross, as a manifestation of the mountain spirit, is the locus of the sacrifice. The petitioner lights a large white candle in front of the cross and pours *b'oj* on the ground. He places bean-filled tortillas (*tz'u'uj*) and tamales (*poch*) beside the cross. In Cahabón, the practice of *wa'tesiink li k'al* ("feed the crop") continues. In it, the sacrificer digs a shallow hole in front of the altar and buries raw meat in the earth. Turkey parts are offered — the heart, intestines, and small pieces of the legs and breast. This is how the gods are fed; tzuultaq'as are given a tiny taste of each part of the turkey. The parts represent the whole, which is consumed by the planters back in the house at the end of the day. Gods and humans are thus in communion, eating of the same fowl. As Zinacantecos say, "Men eat what the gods eat" (Vogt 1976:1). Humans eat large portions of meat, the gods very small ones. They consume the same turkey, but the gods eat first.

The sacrificer burns *pom* in an incense holder, swinging it in the four cardinal directions and toward the sun, Venus, and the moon. Different quantities of *pom* are used. As one elder explained, "I use eleven pieces, one for each god I pray to. Some large, some small as tzuultaq'as are accustomed." One petitioner I accompanied stood facing the rising sun with *pom* smoke swirling around him and prayed:

> O you my God you my Father, forgive my sins, thank you for giving us another day under your feet under your hands. You are perfectly great compared to me and too great is your mercy, you my Father, my Mother. You our Father Sun, our Mother Moon, our Father Venus, receive this sacrifice. I am here to ask for my permission. I am about to bury. I am about to plant on this holy day. We are about to work in the face of the holy tzuultaq'a where we find our food and water. Please give your blessing on my crop. Make my crop grow. Give it water. Watch over it so nothing happens to it. I will petition you so that which I plant will belong to me, not to the mountain cat or to the mountain pig. Don't send the animals to eat my crop, guard them so they don't come here. This I am asking of you Father Xukaneb, Father Kojaj, Mother Ak'tela', Father Chitu, Father Woloq', Father Mucaño, Father Sa'pok, Father K'ixmes [all names of mountains]. Hear and accept my petition.

(See Appendix B for the Q'eqchi' version of this prayer.) In addition, the farmer may pray an orthodox Catholic prayer such as the Lord's Prayer.

Having finished praying, the farmer will perform the *chapok k'al,* or "to grab the crop." With a single plunge of his planting pole, he opens a hole about five inches deep in front of the cross or altar and drops three, four, six, or seven seeds into it. People of different communities customarily sow different numbers. The hole is then covered with earth. He repeats this four more times within a few feet of the cross in the four cardinal directions. He places a lit candle by each one of the five groups of planted seeds. A candle may be located in each of the four corners of the field, "to form a corral so the animals can't get in." Part of the meaning of this ritual is containment and classification, defining the borders of cultivated fields versus wild forest.

The "grab crop" rite is practiced with other crops such as chile, beans, cacao, and peanuts, all of which are planted solely by men. It is not carried out for garden crops cultivated near the house, including yucca, manioc, cassava, and bananas. These are seen to be the responsibility of women. The sexual division of labor means that crops have a gender association determined according to who plants the crop.

ANALYZING THE GRAB CROP RITUAL

Try as I could, I never heard any exegesis of the meaning of "grabbing the crop." Even the most knowledgeable and forthcoming men would simply restate the details of the ritual and go no further. This is the most obscure ritual I ever came across, so my interpretations are based less on emic exegesis than on my trying to find echoes of meaning in other Q'eqchi' and Mayan rituals and histories.

I believe the act of preemptive planting in the four cardinal directions serves as a metaphor for planting the whole crop "in the face of" the tzuultaq'as. In five plunges of the planting pole, the whole crop is signified, encompassed, and "grabbed." Evon Vogt (1976:58) makes a relevant observation that field rituals "are small-scale models of a quincuncial cosmogony."

The symbolism of the grab crop ritual could be an expression of pre-Columbian cosmologies. The four cardinal directions hark back to the *chak*s, the Mayan rain gods. In the previous chapter, I suggested that some of the features and functions of the Q'eqchi' mountain spirits overlapped with those of the *chak*s. Redfield and Villa-Rojas (1934:339) write that the Yucatec Mayas perform agricultural rites in the four cardinal directions, which are called the four *balam,* or rain gods.

The grab crop ritual displays clearly the relations between people and the gods. Celestial deities feature prominently, along with the mountain gods. The rising sun is petitioned and offered burning *pom.* The moon goddess, one of the few female elements in the planting, assists with her powers of fertility. Traditionalist versions of history inform us about how the sky gods relate to the tellurian deities. In one version told to me (see Appendix C), tzuultaq'as are kings and queens and reign over their daughter, the moon, and their son-in-law, the sun, though not always with success. Mountains control the climate and movements of the celestial bodies, uniting heaven and earth. Both the sun and the moon are subservient to the mandates of the mountains.

Eva Hunt (1977) has made an exhaustive study of the symbolism of the sun deity in Mesoamerica (see also Aveni 1992; Sosa 1986). Here I shall focus only on the relevance of solar symbolism for the Q'eqchi' mountain cult. In the story I just referred to, the sun descends to earth in the form of a hummingbird. Raxuntz'unun, or Green Hummingbird, a male mountain, is one of the Thirteen Great Tzuultaq'as. Further solar imagery is present in that the tzuultaq'a kills the moon with his "smoking mirror," a fire-making device of both Mayan and Aztec sun gods. The Aztec sun god's name, Tezcatlipoca, means Smoking Mirror (Benson Gyles and Sayer 1980:59).

Writers on the Mayas such as J. Eric S. Thompson (1954: 227–28) have presumed the sun cult to have been the primary aspect of the religion. Perhaps this was the case for the priests in the ceremonial centers such as Chichén Itzá and Tikal, but for the peasants, especially in peripheral highland areas, the sun was a lesser figure. Michael Sallnow (1987:36–38) makes the point that celestial markers are more useful for empires in the

integration of disparate peoples than are local shrines, which
are spatially limited. John Sosa (1986:196) suggests that ancient Mayan priest-rulers tried to impersonate celestial deities
in an attempt to legitimate their divine right to rule. Perhaps
Mayan imperialism, like that of the Inka state, expanded ideologically by a process of "celestialization."

To my knowledge, the *chapok k'al* is the only collective rite
in which Q'eqchi' traditionalists petition the sun. He is the big
"candle" that gives growing heat to the newborn seeds. Heat
symbolism, a central metaphor of fertility, permeates the planting preparations. The candle used in the vigil causes the seeds to
be born. Throughout, the men drink fermented *b'oj,* a drink that
is seen to "make people hot." *B'oj* and blood, both hot, are
poured over the corn. Men smoke cigarettes or cigars as they
plant. *Pom* incense is burned at all stages of the planting.
Q'eqchi' traditional ideas clearly link solar imagery and agricultural fertility, as is also the case in other Mayan groups.
Carlsen and Prechtel (1991:30) note that Atitecos use the same
word, *xlexa,* to refer to the dawning of the sun, human birth,
and the sprouting of maize seeds from the earth.

Qana' Po, our Mother the Moon, is more essential to fertility
than the sun. Expressly identified with women, she is the
goddess of definitive female skills—weaving and medicine,
especially that which involves children (see chapter five). The
symbolism of female mountains overlaps with that of the moon.
The mountain Ak'telha (New Arm of Water) is one of the few
female tzuultaq'as and is associated with the sea, as is the moon.
The moon is linked with bodies of water and rain; for the
ancient Mayas, she was the goddess of floods. Time was created
by the moon's division into thirteen parts (that is, thirteen
moons or months in the Mayan calendar) after she was killed
and fell into the sea, causing a flood of blood. Though at times
associated with the Virgin Mary, the moon is bawdy and

sexually promiscuous. Seed, human or vegetable, planted during a certain stage of the moon can produce healthy, strong offspring. The moon's role is to help the plants grow, not to protect them from animals. She owns nothing, so her permission is not needed to use the land.

Why is the moon included in this ritual when she is so identified with "femaleness," which is *awas* for most of the time? Perhaps this can be explained by the strong association between children and maize, and their relative *awas,* which are explored in the next chapter. The moon is an active agent in both human and agricultural fertility, straddling the two related spheres.

During the planting, traditionalists are open to petitioning all the gods they feel can help them, from the Christian God and saints to the sun, moon, and mountain spirits. Men offer *pom* as they pray for protection and fertility. A.M. Hocart (1970:245) states that the motivation for ritual is not so much the need to propitiate fearsome powers as it is the practical need to ensure life. These motives need not be mutually exclusive; rituals can include both elements. In their prayers, traditionalists ask for what is necessary to ensure survival. When asked, "Why do you do the rituals?" they invariably reply, "Because we want to eat." Offerings and gift exchange with the tzuultaq'as helps create the fertility of the field, but it means being in contact with some awesome and dangerous powers of procreation. One of the best explanations for sacrifice came from an elder man named José, who told me,

> The mountains give us our sustenance so that we will eat and live. It is not ours to give to ourselves, the mountains give it to us. That's why we make requests and supplications to the mountains. Those who don't petition won't receive their sustenance. They won't have maize or chickens or turkeys. No. They will have to buy their food. Bought food. That's what happens to people of bad

character. Making an offering—it is sharing. Sharing food with
the mountain. You are giving the mountain back its due, even if
your offering is small. Even the most poor people, who just clear a
little bit.

Feeding the gods seals a contract and upholds a relationship
of reciprocity, echoing Hubert and Mauss (1964:100), who
wrote of the "contractual element to all sacrifice." The breakdown of reciprocity results in destruction and ruin. This idea is
underlined in the history of Xukaneb' and his seeds. Saqlek
denied reciprocity by keeping the seeds, leading to famine and
war. Reciprocity is present in a range of interactions but is most
marked in relations with the gods and in planting. Yet it need
not be assumed, as Taussig (1980) has done, that reciprocity is
the central social linchpin of all indigenous economics and
culture.

This analysis applies well to sacrifices to the mountain
spirits, but not to other recipients of offerings, such as the corn
and the planting pole. The earth receives sacrifices because it
has power (*wankilal,* literally "presence"), personhood (*wiinqilal*), and godliness (*tioxil*). Wiinqilal is morally neutral; *tioxil*
is always positive and benign; *wankilal* is both benevolent and
malevolent. The corn has only *tioxil*—only good. The planting
pole has only *wankilal* and must be given offerings so that its
benevolence is enhanced and its malevolence minimized. Ancient wooden crosses are also fed with blood, as are saints'
images. Crosses, saints, and wood have a spirit (*mu*) and
wankilal, and therefore an ambivalent power to be propitiated
and harnessed to ensure life.

Only powerful and feared spirits are honored by being fed
(*wa'tesiink*). In the ritual initiation of a newly built house,
turkey blood is splashed on the walls and earth by a young son
to prevent the house from eating the children or domestic
animals. This sacrificial blood is a substitute (*reqaj*) for the

flesh of the children, the "little animals," of the household.
Children are associated with domestic animals in the feeding-
of-the-house ritual and, as we shall see, with jungle animals on
the day of the planting. In the same way that feeding the house
and the earth sanctions human reproduction, feeding the seed
and the earth in the grab crop ritual sanctions maize production. Traditionalist Q'eqchi' sacrifice draws upon multilayered
meanings that vary according to each context.

THE DAY OF THE PLANTING

By the time the owner has returned from the grab crop ritual,
the other men have risen and washed and are awaiting his
arrival. The sons and *testiig* serve each man a glass of warm *b'oj*.
The same food that the planters will eat steams on the altar,
feeding (*wa'tesiink*) the saint's image. To accord respect, the
saint must be served before all others. The *testiig* burns *pom* and
makes a short prayer to the saint; St. Peter, St. Mark, the Virgin,
and the Black Christ of Esquipulas are favorite images. He
incenses the whole altar and the seeds on it. The people are then
"pommed" and the *testiig* walks around the house, inside and
outside, with the *pom* burning. All are unified by being
wrapped in the same pall of incense.

The ten to twenty men receive breakfast, which consists
completely of corn and bean products and cacao to drink. They
use no plates (even if the household has some); the food is eaten
in the traditional way, with one's hands, off of leaves. The men
do not start to eat until the *testiig* grants permission by saying
wa'inko ("Let's eat!") or *qab'aanuhaq* ("Let's do it"). He will
repeat this periodically during the meal, and those present will
reply, "We are eating!" or, when they have finished, "We have
done it."

As at all meals, there is little discussion; breakfast is nearly
silent. Although the spread is bountiful, the men eat frugally.

Their fast is not fully broken until the planting has been finished. In Cahabón, breakfast is not eaten until midday, as is the case with chile planting in Cobán. Yet maize planters in Cobán must eat something before work in order for the seeds to germinate. The state of the planters during the day is crucial: "If you have a bad heart, a tzuultaq'a will send the animals to eat everything. If you are happy, nothing will happen." Empty stomachs cause unhappiness, which has a detrimental effect on the crop.

All eat together, seated, in the same room. It is considered *awas* to eat standing on the day of the planting. This *awas* manifests itself when the stalks grow tall but produce no ears of corn. Coffee drinking, too, is *awas* on the morning of the planting. In this case, the ears grow full of earth or coffee, not kernels of corn. These two *awas* are widespread, but most of the types of *awas* are idiosyncratic and particular to each community.

In Cobán, it is *awas* to say thank you (*b'antiox*) during the day; this prompts tzuultaq'as to send animals to consume the crop. I could never get an explanation for this, and people in one lowland area thought it absurd. Other types of *awas* are more universal. Eating bread at breakfast is *awas* because the corn ears will come out spongy and pulpy like the bread. While one sits in the house, it is *awas* to look through the slats in the bamboo or balsa-wood walls, because then "the *satana* [a black bird] will find the seeds." A widespread *awas* concerns controlling children severely. The strictest limitations are placed on children on the morning of the planting. They too must be seated while eating and must stay inside or close to the house all day. They cannot play or make any noise. If any of these rules are broken, the wild animals and birds will eat the crop. The children's movements are almost as controlled as those of the domestic animals, which are tied up on planting day.

After breakfast, the planters are given another glass of *b'oj*.

The server passes the cup around in hierarchical order, waiting for each person to down it in one drink before he refills the glass for the next person. Each planter has brought his woven bag, which is filled by the owner in front of the altar, using a *sek'* (half-gourd) to ladle out the seeds. Only he can do this. The *testiig* then burns *pom* and petitions the household saint's image, and all leave.

On arriving at the fields, the men seek a sapling and, using machetes, cut it to a length of about six feet with a pointed end. This is the *aawkleb'*, or planting tool, which is used to open a hole in the turf into which six or seven seeds are dropped. The planters line up along the edge of the field and make sweeps across it while the owner or an elder maintains the boundary between planted and unplanted land. The work contrasts with usual agricultural labor, which is fast paced and efficient and allows for no consumption of alcohol or cigarettes. Planting, on the other hand, is light work in a relaxed atmosphere. Planters smoke cigars or cigarettes provided by the owner. They quench their thirst with *b'oj* or cacao. The men must be content and cheerful if the corn is to come out well, for the crop is partly the result of their internal state. This identification with the corn is common among Mayan groups. Guiteras Holmes (1961:43) writes, "Those who plant must be happy in order to ensure the good outcome of their work." The men's personal boundaries become more permeable during the planting, extending out to include the year's corn crop.

Ideally, the planters are silent while laboring. One man explained, "We don't laugh, make a racket or play during the planting. It is holy. The corn will take fright, the seed is an angel." Others maintained that if the workers spoke or laughed, they would attract wild animals. When elder and married men plant, the atmosphere is sober and quiet.

After a few jugs of *b'oj*, however, this ideal silence can break down, leading to jokes and riotous laughter, especially on the part of the young men. Word puns with sexual innuendos are favorites. For example, a young man was levering a rock to roll it down the slope and was told, *taakanab'* ("Leave it alone") by another. The former rhymed his cheeky reply: *ma laawanab'*? ("What, your older sister?"). Most jokes are more licentious and have to do with comparing the size of one's penis to that of the planting pole, or with the fact that one is throwing one's "seed" about. There is an overt association between the planting activity and human sexuality. Married men tend to disparage such behavior as disrespectful. Young men are "superfertile" and unmarried, so their ability to inseminate the earth is at its zenith. By breaching the elders' sober ideal, they are expressing both what is latent in the planting act and their different generational attitudes towards sexuality.

Planters avoid many different *awas* while working. Again, these vary according to community. Prevalent *awas* in Cobán are as follows: It is *awas* to whistle or chew while working. One must not urinate or defecate near the field during the day. Once a seed touches the ground, it is *awas* to touch it with anything other than the planting pole. An *awas*, if trespassed, will attract ravenous wild animals. There is a series of *awas* that have to do with the use and misuse of the planting pole, an instrument with power (*wankilal*), to be fed with burning *pom*. It is *awas* to sit on the planting pole, as it is to leave it standing, stuck into the earth. I will interpret these *awas* in a later section.

After the day's work, all return to the host's house. The men wash and are seated for the most solemn event of the day. Like all feasts, the meal is segregated by gender. Everyday meals are quiet because one is supposed to appreciate the food, not jabber. Those such as the anthropologist who persist in chatting during a meal are reminded of so-and-so who choked on his food while talking.

The atmosphere at the planting feast is especially heavy and pregnant. The men are silent and eat shyly, as if embarrassed or guilty. This sentiment is not overtly or verbally expressed but is, rather, an emotion I intuited. The most important questions in fieldwork are those one feels should not be asked, and I could never formulate the type of question about this sentiment deserving of an illuminating answer. It is difficult to describe the unstated but dense and pervasive atmosphere of contrition and remorse that surrounds the planting meal. Neither a daily meal nor a festive feast is characterized by such heavy feelings of shame. This guilt may derive from a feeling that the men have just had "sex" with the earth and fertilized it, and have now returned to their wives and the household.

The *testiig* sets the pace of the meal, which is painfully slow, and all follow him, repeating his every action. He begins by dipping tortillas piece by piece into the soup. Only when he picks up the bowl and noisily sups the broth do the men do the same. The meat is eaten last and with great reserve. The conformity is complete; when the *testiig* finishes, all others must stop as well, whether they have eaten their fill or not. Each man eats only about a third of his substantial portion of meat. The rest is wrapped up in leaves and taken home to his wife and children. This is the *xel*, which "carries the happiness of the planting home to the family of the planter, so that they are happy too." The first thing the man's wife will do when he returns is demand her *xel*. The children await it eagerly, knowing that this time they can expect choice cuts, not just the usual fare of feet, head, and giblets.

After the meal, the men wipe their hands on the fresh, fragrant pine needles that blanket the floor on any sacred occasion. When the feast is over, the boundaries and formalities of the ritualized planting process dissolve. The women, especially the elder ones, emerge from the kitchen and chat with the

men. The conversation is relaxed and informal, and all share a
cup of corn beer together. The men are served first, and then the
women, according to age. Men may then wander into the
kitchen, talk to their wives, and mingle freely, tired but relaxed.
To borrow Victor Turner's terminology, the rigid structure of the
vigil, planting, and meal is broken by the antistructure of the
ensuing sociality.

GENDER AND FERTILITY IN PRODUCTION

The sexes are segregated throughout the planting, beginning
with the sexual abstinence that starts two weeks before planting
day. The separation becomes more severe after the seeds have
been shucked from the cobs. From then on, maize is allowed to
reside only in the presence of men. Women may not go near the
seeds. Similarly, men from outside the household cannot enter
the kitchen, the domain of the women. While the men plant in
the fields, not even a young girl is allowed to bring them their
lunch.

The men identify themselves with the seeds, guarding over
their "birth" and introduction to the soil. They feed the seed like
expectant mothers and play it harp music to make it happy. This
is definitely a male birthing process, with plenty of sexual
imagery. A lit candle is stuck into the seeds, a highly masculine
metaphor. The etymology of the word phallus is interesting
here, meaning "shining" or "bright" (Jung 1989:ix).

Like the seed, the planting stick is honored because it has
power and is fed with *pom*. It must be respected and therefore
not sat upon. The joking during the planting, with its constant
references to the sexual act, reveals what is already implicit:
that the planting stick and corn seeds are analogous to the male
penis and semen. The land is likened to women in its function,
although this does not mean that the land is always female. More
often than not, the mountain spirits are male. As noted earlier,

male tzuultaq'as have a bisexual potential and are temporarily "feminized" during the act of planting. Likewise, the host assumes a female role in the house by serving the food and drink. It is precisely the men's exclusion of the female that forces the male host to be feminized. This identifies the host with the land he plants, another temporary redrawing of personal boundaries.

Gender is a major organizing principle in Q'eqchi' production. The division of labor along gender lines means that some crops are associated with maleness and some with femaleness, depending on who plants them. Traditionalist men exclude women and take partial credit, along with the deities, for the production of the staple corn crop. Maize and beans can only be planted by men. During this stage in the agricultural cycle, men eat only the products of these two crops. Fruits and garden vegetables, which can be planted by women, are *awas;* their consumption would mix elements from two different (but intertwined) spheres of symbolic association, leading to the ruin of the crop. Meat is also *awas* because domestic animal production is perceived as part of the female domain.

This is not to say that only men can cultivate corn and beans nor that women have airtight exclusivity over domestic animals, gardens, and fruit groves. Impermeable sexual boundaries exist solely during the act of sowing—an act of conception through fertilization of the land. Fertilization is the crucial act, surrounded by taboos, but once a crop is planted, both sexes participate in its cultivation. For instance, women do their share of weeding after the corn has three months' growing time. They also harvest corn and beans in September. The ritual environment prevailing during a crop's development is unimportant because its destiny is inherent, already written into its original constitution during sowing. The maize crop's development is a product of the state of the household and the planters at the time of planting. There are no prayers, rituals, or taboos directed toward the maturing crop, even if rainfall is insufficient or the crop is plagued by pests or disease.

What is clear is that the men want to assume responsibility for maize crop fertility. The ideology of the rituals states clearly that the fertility of staple crops comes from a combination of the feminized land and masculine sexuality. Only men, maleness (e.g., "male" foods), and bisexual mountains are associated with the germination of the staple crop. Women and "female" foods are barred from the scene.

The exalting of masculine productive fertility finds a resonance in language as well. It is significant that the word for father is *wa'*, which also means "eat it" because *wa'* is the root of the verb *wa'ak,* "to eat." *Wa* is the general term for food and specifically means tortilla. This usage points to an act of symbolic appropriation by the father of the role of provider and feeder. Q'eqchi's call the "owner" of a clearing the *aj e,* which literally means the "Mr. Mouth" of that piece of land. This meaning highlights men's oral attachment to the land, which is manifested in their eating its produce and speaking to it in caves. Combining these linguistic data with information from the rituals described, I believe that Q'eqchi's conceptualize an oral connection to the land that is mediated through an archetypal Father.

AWAS IN THE PLANTING

How can we make sense of the various types of *awas* encountered in the planting so far? The term *awas* has a multiplicity of meanings that are contingent upon their context. In my interpretation, there are two different types of *awas:* one that leads to an abnormality in the physical features of the corn plant, and another that infuriates the tzuultaq'as, who send their animals to eat the crop. In addition, the concept of *awas* encompasses the punishment or outcome of an offensive action as well as the action itself.

In some *awas,* the features or symptoms of the punishment are analogous to an element of the action that is considered *awas.* All of these types of *awas* are food related, so this class will be termed "food *awas.*" For example, eating bananas leads to maize plants that are too tall, like banana trees, and will fall over. By breaching the *awas* against drinking coffee, the *awas* that "comes out" is corn ears like coffee—they are full of earth or coffee itself. In this case, the *awas* is part of the plant's makeup, peverting its development. It is expressly stated that tzuultaq'as are not the agents of this type of *awas.*

The second class of *awas* is not food related, nor are specific features of the taboo activity expressed in the ruinous outcome. Tzuultaq'as are explicitly held to be the moral arbiters, so I refer to this class of *awas* as "mountain *awas.*" Mountain *awas* derive not from the constitution of the planted corn but from an infraction of the tzuultaq'as' moral code. The principle is clearly stated in this *awas:* human fertility must be kept separate from plant fertility. If sexual abstinence is broken, the mountain spirit is offended and either recovers the seeds or sends the animals guarded in his or her corral to consume them. Most of the *awas* on the day of planting are of this second class. Saying thank you, chewing or whistling while planting, defecating or urinating, and misusing the planting stick are all actions that lead wild animals to eat the crop.

Awas on the planting day could be classified according to two types present before planting, one of which is a taboo on certain types of food, the other a taboo on sexual activity. In the food *awas,* the resultant corn resembles the forbidden food in a negative manner. Mountain *awas* are related not to food but usually to sex. Breaches of them incur the wrath of tzuultaq'as, who mandate the jungle animals.

TABLE 1
Food *Awas* and Mountain *Awas*

FOOD *AWAS*	MOUNTAIN *AWAS*
Food related.	Nonfood type.
Causal agent: not clear.	Causal agent: tzuultaq'a.
Punishment: change in inherent constitution of plant.	Punishment: animals sent to devour crop.
BEFORE PLANTING:	BEFORE PLANTING:
Eating anything other than maize or bean products.	Sexual activity between the household heads.
ON PLANTING DAY:	ON PLANTING DAY:
Eating nonmaize/bean products.	Male-female spatial proximity.
Eating while standing.	Saying thank you.
Drinking coffee.	Spying through the slats of the house wall.
Eating bread.	Leaving the children free to roam.
	Chewing while planting.
	Whistling while planting.
	Defecating/urinating near field.
	Sitting on planting pole.
	Leaving planting pole standing, especially downward.

There are two meanings of *awas*: prohibited activity, and the form that the punishment of taboo transgression takes. These two meanings are linked, because the punishment *awas* always fit the crime *awas*; that is, food *awas* lead to one type of disastrous outcome, mountain *awas* to another. A food *awas* is intrinsic, inherent to the plant, and the association between taboo and ensuing corn illness is literal. The tragedy of a mountain *awas* lies in an external source, the tzuultaq'a residing in the mountain. Mountain *awas* concern a variety of human actions and exhibit less literal connections between crime and punishment than do food *awas,* although there could well be some cultural associations of which I am unaware.

A degree of ambiguity exists between these two categories. Some mountain *awas* on the day of planting are activities unrelated to the human sexual act. Moreover, mountain *awas* can be punished in a way that exhibits associations with the taboo-transgressing act, which is what would be expected in food *awas.* It could be, for example, that leaving the children (often called "little animals") loose is like leaving the domestic animals loose on the sown seeds. Spying through the slats of the house is similar to the *satana* bird's spying the maize seeds in their shallow holes.

Another difficulty with my line of interpretation is that *awas* foods before the planting are different from some of those on planting day itself. On the morning of the planting, coffee and bread are suddenly *awas,* whereas they were not before. Female-linked foods are taboo before the planting, but neither wheat nor coffee is associated with femaleness (as bananas are), since neither is usually planted by women. Smallholders increasingly grow hectares of coffee groves, which are most likely to be planted and tended by men. Bread is brought in from outside the community, and only travelled Q'eqchi's have seen wheat. Many villagers are unsure of bread's composition. They do know, however, that bread was introduced and is made by Ladinos. Perhaps this is where we can find the rationale for the taboo on bread and coffee.

Bread is made only by urbanites, often using imported flour. It is called *kaxlan wa,* or "chicken tortillas" — another instance of Q'eqchi' use of the foreign fowl to denote anything nonindigenous. Similarly, coffee production was until recently completely in the hands of Ladinos or foreigners. Coffee was available only in a town shop or at the local plantation. Coffee was the first export crop introduced into Alta Verapaz, and its displacement of subsistence crops nearly exterminated whole Q'eqchi' communities. Because coffee was planted at the expense of maize, it is considered inauspicious to consume the competing export crop during this critical phase in staple crop production. The two food taboos on bread and coffee are not about defining and separating spheres of gender symbolism; rather, they are about creating and reaffirming community and ethnic identities in opposition to those of the chicken men. Q'eqchi's often use the bread/tortilla distinction to talk about the rural/urban, Ladino/Q'eqchi' divide. They say, "Ladinos couldn't live just on tortillas like us," and "Corn is what makes us Q'eqchi's strong to carry heavy loads."[4]

In both the cave *mayejak* are in planting, traditionalists avoid goods that historically have been produced exclusively by urban Ladinos. During the cave visits, boots, hats, belts, and watches are prohibited. In the planting, bread and coffee are marked. The *awas* on *b'antiox,* "thank you," may also be explained in this light. Literally, *b'antiox* means "because of God." If we assume that *Tiox* derives from the Castilian *Dios,* then *b'antiox* may be avoided for the same reasons that Jesus Christ is not mentioned in a cave. Q'eqchi's exclude selected Christian elements when performing the most important acts in their relationships with traditional deities. It is significant that saying *b'antiox* is perceived as outraging the tzuultaq'as personally. There is a similar taboo on saying *b'antiox* to the hunter who returns with a kill, for thanks are due only to tzuultaq'as. In the planting, the same principle applies: one must not go around thanking the Christian God because his local representative (and occasional rival) may become incensed and recover the corn seed.

Finally, *awas* work on many levels and do not serve only to classify community, ethnic, and gender boundaries. *Awas* can have a functional and coercive role; the "eating sitting together" *awas,* for example, clearly unites the planters. The symbolism of feasting is of major importance in the creation of social ties and prestige in Q'eqchi' communities. Unity is not just desirable, it is a precondition for crop growth. Its importance means that its elements are raised to the status of law, the infringement of which has dire consequences.

CONCLUSIONS

Sacrifices to tzuultaq'as give notice of intent and gain the right of usufruct. They cajole a tzuultaq'a into keeping his/her animals at bay and providing fertility for the sprouting maize. Tzuultaq'as give sustenance and expect their pay, cash in advance. Because they own nothing, the sun and moon cannot negotiate rights to the land but can only enhance the land's fertility. Objects such as corn, planting sticks, crosses, and, to an extent, saints' images receive offerings because of the degrees of power or holiness they have.

Fertility comes from coupling masculine sexuality with the bisexual land. Human reproduction and staple crop production are maintained apart by *awas* taboos. As I argue in more detail later, these two realms share the same symbolism of fertility, which draws from a pool of ideas about hot and cold. Anticipating the next chapter, I will say here that human reproduction and maize production are both processes that involve controlled development of heat levels. Before the planting, when men are fasting and the conjugal couple maintains sexual abstinence, the prevalent state is cold and sterile. This changes to a condition of controlled heat during the planting, when the land is fertilized. Abstinence and fasting continue, but hot elements are introduced—*b'oj,* cigarettes, candles, and blood. A balanced, warm state is the ideal, so work is undertaken at a measured pace. Too much heat could frighten the corn's spirit. Once fertilization takes place, the land is gestating, so strong heat is required. To this end, the sexes intermingle and the fasting is broken with a feast full of hot items. In the next chapter, I will show how this agricultural productivity is related to human fertility.

Finally, the planting serves as a forum for expressing and creating collective identities. This chapter was extraordinarily demanding to write, because all along I had to allow for the variety of ritual practices and beliefs from one area to another. In Cobán it is done this way, but in Lanquín they do it differently, and in the Polochic Valley they think both ways are absurd, and so on. The reader may judge that I have paid too much attention to picayune ethnographic details. Yet including an extensive diversity of beliefs and practices has significance. The idiosyncracies operate at the level of the household, community, and region, and this structure of difference marks identity at each ascending level. Every community has a shared discourse on the earth cult that distinguishes it from neighboring communities. This parallels a reciprocal labor pool organized around the ritualized planting of corn. Each community expresses its own nuances and variations on the general themes of *awas* taboos, ritual details, prayers, and histories. Most of the time, these are directed at a mountain that owns only that community.

The earth cult also classifies wider ethnic distinctions. This attitude toward the corn and the mountains is specific to traditionalist Q'eqchi's; they know that their knowledge and actions define them in relation to the Ladinos. Only indigenous music is played on the night of the vigil, not mestizo imports from Mexico. The planting taboos exclude signs of the nonindigenous, whether in the realm of food, clothes, or deities. It is *awas* to eat Ladino foods such as coffee and bread and to eat them like a Ladino, using plates and cutlery. The boundary between Q'eqchi' and foreign deities is redrawn during the planting. The mountain spirits assert their primacy, displacing Jesus and God. In the planting, the villagers not only renew the fertility that keeps them alive but also restate their own sense of identity.

CHAPTER FIVE

CURING HUMAN ILLNESSES

For Q'eqchi's, the mountain spirit is important not just in imagining the community and the ethnic group and in defining gender boundaries but also in ideas about human health and fertility. The collective image of the community is active within the boundaries of the person and holds the power of life and death over the community's members.

Ideas of human and maize fertility and well-being are uniquely bound up together. Human reproduction and agricultural production are conceptualized according to the same principles. This correlation is most evident in the sphere of illness, where maize and humans are susceptible to the same two paradigms of disease. The two main types of human sickness are *awas* and spirit loss. Human *awas* illnesses are specifically those of pregnancy and infancy, and they exhibit similar features to the food *awas* during planting. Spirit loss results in a different type of ailment; it is analogous to the mountain *awas* in corn, which stems from a breakdown in relations with the tzuultaq'as. Both types of illness in humans must be understood in the wider context of ideas about hot and cold and about fertility in general.

Illnesses in humans are analogous to the two categories of maize-crop malaise. Human *awas,* like food *awas* in corn, has to do with an inherent malformation of the victim's constitution, the causal agent of which is unknown or not clearly identified. Mountain *awas* in corn and spirit-loss illnesses in humans are caused by tzuultaq'as when the victim has broken the moral code. There are two analogous pairs of binary oppositions:

> In maize crops,   Food *awas:* Mountain *awas*
> In human illnesses,   *Awas:* Spirit loss

The information for this chapter is derived largely from older female informants. Men know the details of health care, but mothers are more likely to be involved in the rites described. Just as men predominate in staple crop production and associated ritual knowledge, women assume the primary role in affairs of human reproduction and health maintenance. Still, men are not segregated from health care in the same way that women are excluded during the planting. Men participate in health matters as *aj ilonel,* or diviners, literally "seers."

Men tend to predominate as *aj ilonel* and women as *aj xokonel,* or midwives, literally "she/he-who-receives."[1] Yet both women and men can perform the vital community services of the *aj ilonel.* Female seers treat the illness of *awas* and call lost spirits back to their owners. They collect and prescribe medicines, both natural and pharmaceutical. Treatments are usually a mixture of prayer, physical manipulation, medicines, and a change in diet. The *aj ilonel* may also be the local obstetrician, the *aj xokonel.* Male seers perform the same functions as their female counterparts but may have a wider range of duties — such as butchering the village's large animals, a prestigious and dangerous task that is rewarded with a part of the animal. The men preside over matters of life and death, whether they relate to humans or animals.

Older seers are often community religious specialists, called upon to officiate life-cycle rituals, saints' festivals, and Catholic ceremonies. Seers are respected members of their areas, and their health practices may extend across a number of communities.

AWAS IN HUMANS

Awas appears in humans as a major category of illness, and as the main type when infants are concerned. *Awas* illnesses are not unique to the Q'eqchi's but also operate among other Mayan groups. K'iche's, for example, told me about *awas,* yet to my knowledge no other ethnographer has written about this type of illness.

There are many different types of *awas,* but most of them exhibit the following attributes: Human fetuses during gestation contract an *awas* illness if their mother is repulsed by an object (usually food), animal or human. The infant will then be born with a physical feature that is likened to one aspect of the offensive food, animal, or person. Infants can only be affected by their environment in this way, while they are in the womb. After parturition, children do not suffer from newly created *awas,* only from those caused before birth. A few *awas* illnesses affect adults, but they are confined to pregnant women.

As with the food *awas* in maize plants, the causal agent of a constitutional change in the affected infant is an offensive object or act whose characteristics are then "inherited." There is no divine retribution from God or the tzuultaq'as involved. Women would guffaw if I suggested that it was a tzuultaq'a who sent a human *awas.* When I would ask, "How does the *awas* illness enter?" the standard reply was "Only God knows." Illnesses are referred to as entering (*oksiink*) the body. Occasionally "evil spirits/winds" would be blamed, but no one was really clear on the issue.

Unlike *awas* in maize, something can be done about the majority of human cases. When it is thought that a child has *awas*, the *rawasinkil* ritual is carried out. *Rawasinkil* means "getting the *awas* out," and the methods employed are homeopathic. The rite serves as both divination and cure, for if the treatment does not work, then another type of *awas* is suspected. The following list describes some of the most common types of *awas* and their respective *rawasinkil*. In all cases, an *aj ilonel* may or may not be present during the *rawasinkil*.

1. **Awas chicharon** (pork skin)
   SYMPTOMS: Infant has a raised, darkened, hairy patch of skin or an infection.
   CAUSE: The pregnant mother was repulsed by a pig or a piece of pork, or she desired to eat pork but was not offered any.
   RAWASINKIL: The mother and child go to a fork in a path during the night while the moon is waning. There are three different methods of removing the *awas*. (1) Mother and child each taste, chew, or lick, but do not swallow, a piece of pork, preferably from a pig that has been killed for the occasion. (2) The pork is rubbed over the affected area. In both of these cases they then throw the pork away without looking to see where it lands and flee back into the house. (3) Alternatively, the offensive substance is burned and the child's head is held over the smoke so that he or she can inhale it. The ashes are then discarded without looking to see where they have fallen. All *rawasinkil* methods are repeated three times, on the first three nights of the moon's last quarter.
2. **Awas kar** (fish)
   SYMPTOMS: A child has weak teeth that splinter easily. They are likened to the teeth of a fish.
   CAUSE: The pregnant mother smelled rotten fish.
   RAWASINKIL: Same as in *awas chicharon*, but burned or singed fish bones are used instead of pork.
3. **Awas o** (avocado)
   SYMPTOMS: A lump forms under the skin, or the skin is discolored and hard, like the peel of an avocado.

CAUSE: The pregnant mother knocked avocados out of their tree and gave them to her family but did not eat any herself because she did not like them.

RAWASINKIL: Same as the previous two, but avocado peel is used.

4. **Awas manteek** (pig's fat)

SYMPTOMS: Skin is greasy or an infection oozes pus.

CAUSE: The pregnant mother was disgusted by eating food that was too greasy.

RAWASINKIL: Same procedure, but using lard.

5. **Awas pix** (tomato)

SYMPTOMS: Red marks or blotches are present on the skin.

CAUSE: The pregnant mother was repulsed by tomatoes, or saw someone eating tomatoes and wanted to partake but was not offered any.

RAWASINKIL: Tomatoes employed.

6. **Awas kees** (cheese)

SYMPTOMS: Child has frothy or dried spittle on mouth.

CAUSE: Pregnant mother ate cheese when she did not want to, or was not given it when she wanted it.

RAWASINKIL: Same as previously, but using burnt cheese, which is rubbed on the mouth. A raw turkey egg may be rubbed on the top of the head "to get rid of the heat."

7. **Awas kalajenak** (drunkard)

SYMPTOMS: A child grows up to be an alcoholic.

CAUSE: The pregnant mother was bothered by the presence of a drunk man.

RAWASINKIL: At a fork in the path, beginning on the first night of the last quarter of the moon, the mother burns the dirty clothes of the drunk man and her child breathes in the fumes. The ashes are discarded in the customary manner, and all flee back to the house. This is repeated on three occasions.

8. **Awas kamenaq** (dead being)

SYMPTOMS: A fetus is born dead or motionless.

CAUSE: The pregnant mother saw the corpse of a human or saw a pig or cow being killed.

RAWASINKIL: None, for the child is dead or will shortly die.

9. **Awas re li po** (moon)

SYMPTOMS: A child is an albino.

CAUSE: The pregnant mother walked at night in the light of the moon without covering her hair. If she carried a candle at the time, this type of *awas* is more likely to manifest itself.

RAWASINKIL: The child and two candles are put inside a large clay jar in the evening when there is no moon (when the moon is "sleeping"). This is done in the house of the patient.

10. *Awas k'il* (flat earthenware pan)

SYMPTOMS: Labor in childbirth is protracted and painful.

CAUSE: The pregnant mother left the *k'il* over the fire with no tortillas cooking on it.

RAWASINKIL: The women present at the birth will heat up a *k'il* over the fire and splash water on it. The delivery is thereby facilitated.

One of the practical effects of *awas* ideas is that pregnant women have tremendous power to demand or reject any type of food according to their desire. Anyone who eats in the presence of a pregnant woman must offer her food. Otherwise, she may desire that food, but if she is unfulfilled, then the food's characteristics might appear as *awas* in the newborn. On the other hand, she may accept food out of politeness but not really want it, in which case *awas* would again be the result. For non-kin, it is best not to eat in the presence of a pregnant woman at all. Rigoberta Menchú, a K'iche', writes (1984:15), "We never eat in front of pregnant women. You can only eat in front of a pregnant woman if you can offer her something as well." Conversely, *awas* can be manipulated to control female behavior, as one man told me: "If a pregnant woman doesn't like a particular food, she must eat it anyway, otherwise *awas* will come out."

Pregnant women actively avoid or complain about any person (usually a man) who is bothering them, because their children may inherit some characteristic of the offensive person, such as drunkenness or a short temper. People, and men in particular, must behave with respect around a pregnant woman. Any explicit discussion of pregnancy makes men very uncomfortable, especially in the presence of the woman concerned.

When I commented to a man, "Oh, I see your wife is pregnant," he shrugged his shoulders and replied, "I dunno."

The pregnant woman must be in a state of *kalkab'il,* which means peace, contentment and optimism. This word is also used to denote the desired ambience of a ritual. When pregnant, the woman is in a marked, sacred condition, because her state is directly identified with the solemn and holy nature of a community religious celebration. Her condition is akin to that of the planters' during sowing, when they must also be content if the crop is to bear fruit.

The pregnant woman is like the land during planting, and therefore both are treated with care and seriousness. Both are *loq',* sacred. Their human environment must be controlled and pacific. Extremes of behavior and irreverence can cause a child to be born with *awas* or the maize crop to fail. In corn and humans, *awas* illnesses create and emanate from a preoccupation with the mother/earth matrix that produces the growing child/plant. Women and the earth differ, however, in that the critical time in the reproduction of children is the gestation period, whereas the moment of fertilization is most important for the production of the maize crop.

Given the overt association between women and the land, we would expect a clear identification between children and corn. The two are the only entities to suffer from *awas* illnesses. Corn gruel is the only supplement to breast-feeding for the first few months and is said to give infants strength. Furthermore, their association is underlined by their symbolic separation by *awas*—by the fact that out of all the different types of food that can appear as *awas* in infants, maize is not among them. Like land and women during the planting, the equation of maize and children means they are kept apart, in this case in the sphere of *awas* illness.

Among other Mayan groups we find an even stronger association between children and corn. Atitecos use the same word, *xlexa* ("his face came out"), to refer to the sprouting of maize seeds and human birth (Carlsen and Prechtel 1991:28). Thompson (1975:343) includes a tract from the seventeenth century describing how the Pokomam physically unite the newborn with maize in a birth ceremony. The umbilical cord is laid lengthwise over the ear of corn and then cut. The corn is dried and the seeds are planted in the name of the child. The harvested corn is repeatedly replanted until it forms a seed bank for the youth's own crop. Guiteras Holmes (1961:108) recorded a similar ritual among the Tzotzil. An ear of corn is sprinkled with blood from the umbilical cord and is planted, the small corn patch being called the "blood of the child." All the household members attentively cultivate this patch, as it forebodes the future of the child. Later, they eat part of the "harvest of blood," symbolically consuming the infant's blood and thereby integrating it into the household.

In sum, production and reproduction are conceptually united. In humans and maize, *awas* affects different parts of the reproductive/productive process in complementary ways. In maize, *awas* taboos are present only during the prefertilization and fertilization (planting) periods. In humans, only the periods of gestation and parturition are surrounded with *awas*. These distinctions point to a basic unity. The creation of people and maize are part of a single system, for human and maize *awas* together encompass the whole process of prefertilization, fertilization, gestation, and birth.

AWAS, HEAT, AND FERTILITY

Let us consider more closely the constituent elements of human *awas*. The most common types are food related. Within this category, we encounter a seemingly random assortment of animals, vegetables, and fruits. Yet there is an internal logic, the key to which is found in ideas about hot (*q'ix*) and cold (*ke*). The two principles *q'ix* and *ke* are used to categorize all foods, types of people, medicines, and illnesses. The word *ke* is used to describe all cold states. *Q'ix* refers to a constitutional state of heat, to the immutable heat value (as opposed to the degree of heat) of an entity. The word *tiq* is employed to speak about variable temperature and the environment, that is, ephemerally hot states. The sun and a hot day are *tiq,* as is a mug of boiled coffee. *Q'ix* is not used in these circumstances; rather, it denotes inherent qualities that do not change.

Ideas of hot and cold are well documented in Mesoamerica, but the meaning of each caloric system varies according to indigenous group and linguistic area (e.g., Ingham 1986; Neuenswander and Souder 1977; Redfield 1941, 1934; Villa-Rojas 1978; Wisdom 1940). Mayan groups are not hermetically sealed, but influence one another. Different ideas about hot and cold have been stressed heavily by some groups and less by others. Among the Q'eqchi's (and, I suspect, many other groups), the hot/cold distinction is more concerned with fertility, sexuality, and balanced health than with power relations. Yet most writers on Mayan groups, such as Vogt (1976:23–34, 206–207), have tended to approach hot and cold distinctions solely as idioms of power and hierarchy. Guiteras Holmes (1961:71) says, "Heat is power," and ignores all evidence that it speaks of fertility as well. Pitt-Rivers (1970:185, 204) also equates heat and power and denies any relationship with fertility. He argues that the concept of heat as spiritual power should not be confused with "heat as female sexuality, which is important in Spanish culture, but normally unknown to the Indians."[2] So far, ethnographers have not interpreted hot and cold distinctions in terms of fertility.

Table 2 lists the calorific qualities of common foodstuffs. The categorization of a few foods may vary according to region,

TABLE 2
HOT AND COLD DISTINCTIONS: FOOD TYPES

Q'ıx/Hот	Ke/Cold
Chicken	Pig and its products
Chicken eggs	Fish and aquatic animals
Beef	Spinach
Cheese	Salt
Turkey	Turkey
Maize cooked as tortillas	Turkey eggs
Coffee	Beans
Chile pepper	Rice
Deer	Avocados
Honey	Duck
Onions	Tomatoes
Garlic	Cacao
Alcoholic drinks, e.g., b'oj	Bananas
Xayau, a red dye	Fruit, e.g., mangoes, oranges, papayas, apples
	Root crops, e.g., potatoes

which is why turkey appears as both hot (eastern regions) and cold (western areas). In some localities, maize in the form of tortillas is considered neutral (that is, neither hot nor cold) and is unique in this respect. This neutrality no doubt arises from the fact that the tortilla is the staple food eaten at all meals and so is considered a balanced meal in itself.

Fertility is seen as being hot and sterility as cold. A menstruating woman is hot, whereas a girl who has yet to menstruate is cold and is made to consume hot foods and herbs if her period is overdue. Infertile couples are instructed to eat hot foods and medicines because they are too cold. A pregnant woman is very hot, especially just before childbirth. This heat is necessary to create the forming child, and pregnant women avoid eating too many cold foods. As can be seen from Table 2, the majority of foods that appear in infant *awas* are deemed cold (numbers 1–5: pork, fish, avocado, pig's fat, and tomato). These types of *awas* are diagnosed as "cold illnesses" by the seer, because, as one told me, "the blood runs faint." A faint pulse means a cold illness, whereas a rapid or powerful pulse indicates a hot illness. During pregnancy, cold food causes a woman to become colder, which chills the embryo and leads to a cold illness in the newborn. The symptoms of such an illness exhibit features of the cold food agent. A principle of *awas* is elucidated here: hot agents cause hot illnesses and coldness triggers a cold illness.

Fertility and gestation are not just about achieving a high heat level and avoiding coldness. Rather, a finely tuned balance must be maintained. That is why some markedly hot foods such as cheese may appear in infant *awas*. Illness arises not only when there is too much coldness but also when there is an imbalance of hot and cold in the body (Table 3). Balance is regulated at each meal by ensuring an adequate mix of hot and cold foods. A person's diet is altered according to the caloric necessities dictated by his or her temporal state. Fertility is also regulated according to these principles. If a woman's menstruation is too heavy, she will drink an extremely cold beverage of bean juice and salt, which is also known to be a contraceptive and abortive drink. A woman who considers herself too fertile will eat cold foods and infusions of cold herbs to avoid unwanted pregnancies.

The caloric quality of a person depends on his or her state at a certain time. The hot/cold distinction is not analogous to the male/female opposition. Vogt's (1976:32–34, 59) assertion that Zinacantecos categorize women as cold and men as hot is suspect, in my view, and probably derived from his overemphasis on power. Q'eqchi' women are not inherently hotter or colder than men. Women do tend to be in a hot state more often because of menstruation and pregnancy, but no one is colder

TABLE 3
HOT AND COLD DISTINCTIONS:
HUMAN ILLNESSES

Q'IX/HOT	KE/COLD
Common cold	Headache
Malaria	Malaria
Burns	Diarrhea
Heavy menstruation	Intestinal parasites
Kidney problems	Paralysis
Fevers	Fright/shock
Cholera	Spirit loss
Extreme anger	Blood loss
Amoebic dysentery, where	Broken bones/cuts
blood is present in the feces	Vomiting
	Tuberculosis
	Rheumatism or cramps

than a woman who has just given birth. An especially hot herb called chicken leaf is prepared for her in an infusion. She eats only hot foods; cold foods like beans and spinach are forbidden to postparturition women. Men can be very hot—for example, when they are angry, drunk, or sexually active. Such men must not approach pregnant women, or else their high heat level will harm the unborn infant and produce an *awas* illness. This also explains why a pregnant woman's exposure to death produces *awas kamenaq,* a dead child. The dearth of heat in a dead person or large animal would lower the heat levels to such an extent that the child will emerge stillborn (that is, too cold).

When people of either sex are not in one of these states and not ill, they have a neutral, balanced caloric value. Because the pregnant woman is the "hot person" par excellence, and the woman who has just delivered her child is the coldest type of person, I suggest that they are the prototypes for all further human divisions into hot and cold.

TABLE 4
HOT AND COLD DISTINCTIONS: HUMAN TYPES

Q'IX/HOT	KE/COLD
Pregnant women	Women after childbirth
Menstruating women	Infertile men or women
Newborn infants	Prepubescent children
Sexually active people	Postmenopausal women
"Angry" people	Old men (over 50)
Drunk people	"Sad" people
"Insane" people	
Foreigners, esp. Germans	
"Powerful" people, e.g., mayors, colonels	

The transition from hot to cold in the process of childbirth is vital for understanding the *awas k'il* during parturition. Comments by Lévi-Strauss (1968:186) on the Cuna shaman's treatment of a difficult childbirth have resonance in traditional Q'eqchi' parturition practices. In both cases, the myths told or actions carried out seek to have an inductive effect by being homologous with the structure of the ailment. Among both the Cunas and the Q'eqchi's, a woman in childbirth is excessively hot. Whereas the Cuna shaman talks his way down "Muu's way," clearing and opening the vagina and uterus for delivery, Q'eqchi' obstetricians heat up a *k'il* (one of a Q'eqchi' woman's main work instruments) and then throw water on it. Because a woman passes from a very hot to a very cold state in the act of giving birth, the actions of the Q'eqchi' obstetricians symbolically preempt the woman's transition when the child is born.

Though hot versus cold distinctions are predominantly concerned with human fertility, they can also communicate power relations. Fertility seems to be the more important dimension because older men and postmenopausal women are considered cold among the Q'eqchi's, yet both groups are powerful members of society. The Tzotzil, who seem to be more concerned with hierarchy, view elders and ancestors as hot. Q'eqchi' traditionalists see indigenous mayors, Ladino officials, and military officers as hot people. Germans, who constituted the majority of the landowning class in the nineteenth century, are also considered hot. It is significant that the tzuultaq'as appear in dreams as tall, white, bearded men and are likened to Germans. It is logical that tzuultaq'as are like Germans; both are owners of the land. Historically, Q'eqchi's have not seen themselves as owners, which is why they must deferentially petition for the right to cultivate the land. In this sense, traditional beliefs implicitly recognize the ethnic division of land ownership as well as challenge them.

The tzuultaq'as control fertility and agricultural production and are hot. The Germans, in their role as landowners and authority figures, are also hot. From an external analyst's perspective, it is tempting to say that there are two types of power in traditional thinking: the cold power of the community elders, which is the power of order, tranquility, and stability, and the hot power of external authorities—the Ladinos, landowners, soldiers, and tzuultaq'as. This hot power is related to the ownership of resources, especially land, and is more violent and ambivalent.

THE *RAWASINKIL*

Rawasinkil, or removal of a child's *awas,* is usually performed by the mother, although she may call upon a seer to carry out the rite. *Rawasinkil* involves extracting the illness, where like is used to remove like in true homeopathic style. Seldom is the whole body of the *awas*-causing animal, vegetable, or fruit used. More often, a part of it is selected that corresponds in appearance to that of the child's disease. For example, fish bones are like a child's teeth and the skin of the pig is like a child's skin. Smoke from the burning of the offensive agent expunges the feature of the agent that is causing the child to suffer. Avocado peel or pork skin, when rubbed across the affected area, extracts the patch of skin that resembles it.

Rawasinkil repeats, but in reverse order, the constituent elements that originally caused the illness. Human *awas* arises either because the mother wants food and does not get it or because she does not want the food but has to eat it. Chewing or licking the food but not swallowing it is like getting food but not actually getting it. Spitting it out is like vomiting up the food that was unwanted but eaten anyway. It is significant that both mother and child have to masticate and spit out the particular food, not just one or the other. By uniting the two in their feigned eating of the food, the conditions of gestation are recreated. During the mother's pregnancy, what the mother ate was also what the child ate (and possibly suffered from).

Because most of the *awas*-causing foods are cold, burning the food and having the child inhale its smoke could be seen as a way of reintroducing it in a heated form, thus cancelling out the damage done by its coldness. Although some hot *awas*-causing foods are burned in this manner, the tendency is for them to be dealt with by the pseudo-eating *rawasinkil* method.

The rite of *rawasinkil* might at first sight look like a sacrifice to the deities such as the tzuultaq'as, providing a substitute for them to consume instead of the child. Yet informants always denied that tzuultaq'as were involved in child *awas* illnesses; people did not perceive any supernatural intervention in this matter. All informants made it abundantly clear that food discarded into the bush during the *rawasinkil* did not serve as an offering to the tzuultaq'as. One said, "No, the hill does not get a substitute [*reqaj*] when a child has *awas*." Sacrifice to the tzuultaq'as is a facet of another main type of Q'eqchi' illnesses, spirit loss.

PLANTING AND HOT AND COLD

Let me now reconsider the planting of maize in light of the local idiom of hot and cold. I should make it clear that my informants did not explicitly provide the following overview of the planting rite; what follows is my own interpretation, but one firmly founded on Q'eqchi' verbal and nonverbal expressions.

As in human gestation, a balance of hot and cold is essential for the production of a healthy crop. Excessive heat is as harmful as too little. That is why elders oppose the use of fertilizers, claiming they burn the earth because they are too hot, too fertile. The strategy employed by men seeks to create a balanced caloric state that tends toward coldness before planting and hotness on the day of planting itself. This pattern was the norm in sixteenth-century Mayan rituals as reported by Fray Diego de Landa (1975:115). Mayan men would observe sexual abstinence, fasting, and sobriety and would paint their bodies black (associated with the west and coldness) before the New Year celebrations. On the celebration day, the body paint changed to red, the color of heat and the sunrise in the east. This was a day of hot activities, of feasting and drunken abandon.

Male sexual abstinence before planting is partly concerned with separating production from reproduction, but it also keeps the planter from becoming too hot. Fasting, or limiting the range of foods eaten, balances heat levels. Men avoid foods with a strong hot or cold marking, such as chile. Ideally, planters consume only beans (cold) and tortillas (hot), thereby maintaining an equilibrium. Fasting implies the avoidance of foods that are planted, cultivated, or raised by women and so linked to femaleness. Rice and bananas, two cold foods that are markedly *awas,* are linked to femaleness; bananas are planted exclusively by women, and rice can be planted by women, whereas maize and beans cannot.

There is no evidence, however, that the hot versus cold categorization of foods is sex linked. Some crops planted more often by men are cold (beans and cacao) and some are hot (chile, coffee, and maize). Crops and animals identified with femaleness are not the only ones that are *awas* before the planting. Some crops planted by men are *awas,* including chile. Women tend to be more responsible for the domestic animals, some of which are cold (pig and duck), others hot (chicken). Maintaining the correct heat balance is perhaps a better explanation for the food *awas* than upholding a sex-linked distinction. With regard to the taboo on sex before planting, both heat and gender differentiations come into play.

Men can enter the caves to ask for permission from the tzuultaq'as only when they are in a relatively cold state induced by fasting and sexual abstinence. Descending into the earth is seen as entering a high heat zone. Any activity that involves going underground, such as digging a well, runs the risk of exposing one to too much heat and causing a fever.

Why cannot women enter the caves? Men say, "If a woman enters a cave, the mountain will lose its power [*wankilal*]." One elder said that if a woman enters a cave, the hill's power would be lost because "it would go cold." It is interesting that the mountain's power is seen to be lesser than the woman's.[3]

If the production of both corn and children require heat, it is likely that women are antithetical to the mountain because they represent a different type of fertility and therefore heat. Contact between the two is likely to cause sterility, to render one cold. What is interesting is that the mountain is made sterile by the woman, not the other way around, suggesting that the heat of human reproduction is more powerful than that of agricultural fertility.

Some types of *awas* in children are unrelated to notions of
hot and cold but serve to mark the boundary between agricultural and human fertility. We have seen how the two spheres
are separated in many instances, and the illness of *awas re li po*
is another case. This *awas* occurs when a pregnant woman is
exposed to the moon, which harms the developing child.
Similarly, the Yucatecs believe that the moon bites the embryo,
causing birthmarks and skin discolorations (Villa-Rojas 1978:
402). Our Mother Moon may be vital to the production of
maize, but she is detrimental to the reproduction of children.
Her role symbolizes the opposition between these two contextually separated but fundamentally united spheres of creativity.

A myth recorded by Carlos Cabarrús (1979:51) legitimates
the separation of women and caves. In the distant past, Q'eqchi's
would leave their children on the cave altar. After they had gone,
a tzuultaq'a would appear and breast-feed the infant (even if the
tzuultaq'a was male) with huge, multiple breasts. One day a
woman hid behind a rock formation and saw what was happening. The tzuultaq'a noticed her and was so offended that the
mountain gods refused to feed the children any more. Women
have had to breast-feed children ever since. In mythical times,
production and reproduction were fused, but because of a
woman's "transgression," the two must now be kept apart.

In looking at the cave sacrifice from the perspective of hot
and cold distinctions, it seems that two valencies of heat exist.
The majority of the items offered to the tzuultaq'as are in the hot
category: *pom,* candles, beeswax, turkey blood, maize products, alcoholic drinks (*b'oj*), pine torches dipped in blood, and
blood itself. By offering these up, men participate in stoking up
the heat of production. They feed the tzuultaq'a with what it
needs—hot food. Without this reciprocity, there is not enough
heat to produce the fields of maize. Agricultural production is
thus a collaboration between people and the gods, using artifi-

cial means to recapitulate the caloric progressions of human reproduction.

During the *yo'lek*, or vigil, the men pass from being colder to being hotter, and the passage is facilitated by the consumption of cigarettes and *b'oj*. The change in the men's state during the vigil is the inverse of women's transition during childbirth: women go from being too hot to needing infusions of hot herbs because they are too cold. Birth is also the transforming event for male planters, because the corn seeds are said to be "born" during the night of the vigil. The men create the essential heat for the birth of the corn by burning *pom* and mixing turkey blood or flesh into the seeds. The heat from their bodies, like that of a pregnant woman, provides the heat for the nascent corn. A candle stuck into the middle of the seeds acts like a miniature sun, warming the corn. Alternatively, the men's passage from a colder to a hotter state parallels that of women when they are inseminated and become pregnant. It could be said that in the vigil and planting, the processes of fertilization, gestation, and birth are all collapsed into the space of twenty-four hours.

On the morning of the planting, the seeds are "buried." I have mentioned how the vigil for the seeds is similar to the vigil for a human corpse. The two differ, however, in that during the seed vigil, the men pass from a colder to a hotter state, whereas death and participation in the death vigil have a cooling influence. Human birth and death are alike in that both involve a transition from a hotter to a colder state. In this sense, the "birth" of the maize seeds is constructed in opposition to human birth and death, yet it uses the same symbolic elements.

Heat symbolism is present throughout the day of the planting. In the grab crop ritual at dawn, *pom* is offered to the tzuultaq'as and the sun. The sun plays its most important ritual role during the planting because its heat is indispensable for the growing crop. Candles are burned and turkey flesh and blood are buried in the earth to stoke up the heat. During the actual planting work, the men drink plenty of *b'oj* but keep a rein on their heat level. They continue to adhere to a heat-balanced diet of maize and beans. Coffee, a hot drink, is excluded from consumption. The planters avoid extreme behavior such as anger and unhappiness, for this would render them too hot. The work pace is even, measured, and reserved—neither so fast that one begins to sweat nor so slow that one becomes cold.

When the planting is complete, the caloric state is overwhelmingly hot. The men sit down to a feast, but before they eat, *pom* is burned around them, the altar, and the food. The soup is made mainly of hot ingredients and is bright red from the use of (hot) *xayau* dye. Chicken or turkey meat (each hot) forms the base, and the soup is seasoned with garlic, onions, and chile, all hot, and salt, which is cold. The planters eat tortillas with the meal, and *b'oj* is consumed throughout. The cooling segregation of the sexes breaks down and they mingle freely.

In the planting of corn, then, there is a general progression from a colder to a hotter state, but all along the tendency toward one pole or the other must not be extreme. An equilibrium is maintained mostly through the choice of foods eaten. There also seem to be two interdependent types of fertile heat that draw upon a common pool of foods and behavior. In the realm of reproduction, we find sexual heat, menstrual heat, and the heat of pregnancy. In agricultural fertility, there are the sun, candles, incense, and blood sacrifice. The hot versus cold division is partly sex linked, in that it is largely derived from female fertility states, and partly not, in that male and female are not solely designated as hot or cold. The heat value of a food does not depend upon which sex planted or tended it.

One of the social functions of this opposition of agricultural and human fertility is to accord credit to the men for making staple crops grow. Humans would starve unless men renewed their contract with the tzuultaq'as and regenerated the fertility of the land with hot offerings. The autonomous sector of maize production presupposes the exclusion of women and things identified with femaleness. Men appear as if they were solely responsible for staple crop fertility, while women have control over human fertility. In mythical discourses, however, men would take credit for this as well. Evidence for this view is provided in an extension of the myth related in Appendix C about the moon's elopement with the sun. Once the moon is killed, the sun discovers her, reconstituted, in a coffin he filled with her blood. Alas, she no longer has a vagina. The sun then uses a deer's antlers to recreate her sexual organs and they continue their sexual relations.

SPIRIT-LOSS ILLNESSES

One major difference between *awas* in maize and *awas* in humans has yet to be dealt with. *Awas* in humans resembles the category I have called food *awas* in maize, because it is unrelated to actions of the tzuultaq'as and is usually caused by foods. In contrast, the category mountain *awas* shares its features with human illnesses precipitated by spirit loss. These do not have foodstuffs as their source but actions that offend a tzuultaq'a, who then grabs a person's spirit (*muhel*). It could be said that humans and maize plants become ill according to the same two principles. In corn, these are both encompassed by the concept of *awas*. In humans, they are bifurcated into the categories of *awas* and spirit loss.

First, let me examine the properties of the *muhel,* or spirit. The root of *muhel* is *mu,* which means shadow. Some writers (Pacheco 1988:97) have said that Q'eqchi's are animistic and ascribe a spirit to all matter, especially aspects of nature. This is erroneous because only certain things are said to have a spirit, such as people, houses, saints' images, maize, bodies of water, and the mountains. For humans, the word *musiq'*, which also means breath or respiration, is used interchangeably with *muhel*. *Musiq'* is a combination of the words *mu*, or spirit, and *iq'*, which signifies air or wind. The *muhel* of a person is indestructible and continues to exist after death. Maize and humans share the propensity to become separated from their spirits. In such an instance they continue to live, but in a state of "dis-ease." If the spirit does not return to its owner, she or he will eventually die.

The loss of a person's *muhel* can be precipitated by a variety of factors, but once it has become dissociated from the body, it is always held by the local tzuultaq'a in a state of limbo. Sometimes the soul is forced to work in the mountain spirit's underground plantation.[4] The most common cause of spirit loss is a person's falling by a river or in the forest, both strongholds of the tzuultaq'as. Natural features such as ridges, caves, springs, and rivers are all manifestations of tzuultaq'as and are therefore danger zones. One never knows when the mountain god is in an avaricious mood. Rivers are referred to as *josq'*, or angry. Caves and other subterranean areas are hot, and visitors to these places run the risk of losing their spirits. In these cases, spirit loss results from being in too close contact with the heat of the earth. Spirit loss very rarely happens in one's house or in the village compound.

After a fall, a person takes fright and can lose a tight grip on his or her spirit. Fear itself causes spirit loss. The spirit may fall on the ground, where it is "recovered" (*xokb'al*) by a tzuultaq'a. Alternatively, a tzuultaq'a may actively "grab" (*xchapb'al*) the spirit from the victim. This act of spirit seizure is sometimes referred to as a mountain spirit's "eating" the person.

Children ahve a particularly tenuous hold on their spirits, and baths in the river are fraught with danger. It is significant that exposure of children to certain types of people can also cause spirit loss. Contact with "hot" people such as pregnant women, Ladinos, drunk men, and foreign anthropologists may spark this illness. Pregnant women especially are kept apart from other women's children. Q'eqchi's say that a child would certainly lose its spirit if it were to wash in the bath water of a pregnant woman. In such instances, spirit loss has to do with being in too close contact with the heat of human fertility. Spirit loss expresses a clear association between human and agricultural fertility: too close contact with the heat of either one leads to the hot illness of spirit loss.

Spirit loss can be the just punishment for the sins (*maak*) of a person, and as such is a strong moral convention. Redfield and Villa-Rojas (1934:128) wrote that a Yucatec Maya's failure to make compensatory offerings to the *yuntzilob* (gods of the bush) was the main cause of sickness. For Q'eqchi's, the intensity of the illness is proportional to the degree of one's sins. The concept of *maak* includes moral transgressions against both other people and the deities. The tzuultaq'as may seize the spirit of a person who maltreats her or his neighbors or maintains an antisocial attitude. For instance, adultery is punished by the tzuultaq'as. In this sense, spirit-loss illnesses are a mechanism of community social control.

Nonfulfillment of obligations to God or the tzuultaq'as may lead to one's spirit's being grabbed. One man explained why he became ill: "Because I forgot about God." He had stopped praying regularly, burning incense, and attending ritual celebrations. In the case of an older man, a tzuultaq'a appeared in a dream, stating that his spirit had been snatched because he had stopped sacrificing. The mountain god's message was blunt: "If you don't feed *me,* then I will eat *you!*" Once the victim's health returned, the tzuultaq'a came to him again, saying, "Now you are better, do not forget to give me my food."

Failure to request permission from tzuultaq'as may also

result in the loss of one's spirit or that of a family member. Children often suffer, it is said, for the sins of their parents. In one case, a man moved with his family to find work in another area. Shortly after settling, one of the man's sons began to suffer from an infection on his head. A seer told him that the illness was a punishment for failing to ask permission from the local tzuultaq'a. The father visited the mountain shrine of the tzuul-taq'a and burned *pom* and candles, naming all the members of his family and asking for permission to reside in the vicinity. The son quickly improved, I was told.

Finally, spirit loss can result from witchcraft. Some seers are also *aj tuul,* or witches, but one does not imply the other. This situation contrasts with that in highland Chiapas, where all witches are also curers, and vice versa (Pitt-Rivers 1970:184). Seers can be paid by a malevolent person to shake loose the spirit of another and cause him to suffer. My information on this issue is thin. Many recognized that witchcraft occasionally happened, but few accused others of being witches. No *aj ilonel* ever affirmed that she or he knew how to curse as well as to cure. My feeling from fieldwork and reading Cabarrús (1979) is that witchcraft is less important for Q'eqchi's than for many other Mayan ethnic groups, especially the Tzeltal and Tzotzil (see Guiteras Holmes 1961; Oakes 1951; Pitt-Rivers 1970; Redfield 1941). This apparent divergence in concepts of witchcraft, however, may be the result of comparing ethnographies from different historical periods.

DIVINATION BY SEERS

In general, spirit-loss illnesses are diagnosed from the external symptoms manifested. The most common manifestation is insanity: "Your brain goes bad." The person shakes, continually falls over backwards, or may have spasmodic backward jerks of the head. The afflicted experience disequilibrium and may bite themselves.

An *aj ilonel* diagnoses spirit loss by taking the patient's pulse. Such "pulsing" practice is common among Mayan groups, (see J. Nash 1970:147). The blood is said to "talk." In spirit loss, the mountain "grabs the blood and plays with it." The blood "takes fright." Spirit loss is apparent when the blood runs "fast and thin," and it is categorized as a hot (*q'ix*) illness.

Community doctors usually visit patients in their homes. I had the opportunity to attend many such treatments, and the following is one visit I recorded in Cahabón. Lu' is the name of the seer, and the patient he is visiting is a woman complaining of stomach pains. Healing practices differ depending on the illness but do not vary greatly according to the sex of the patient.

Lu' comes into the house and kneels at the altar, praying quietly to himself. The father of the household leads him into the kitchen, where the patient is reclining on a bench, wrapped in a blanket. The woman's sister and her two daughters grind maize and cook tortillas over a raised fire. The room is full of smoke. The patient does not greet Lu' but lies motionless, staring at the ceiling.

Lu' stands over her and is silent for a moment. He makes the sign of the cross over himself and says, "In the name of the Father, Son, and Holy Ghost." He crouches and holds the woman's wrist and forearm with both hands, feeling her pulse. He rubs the forearm with his open fingers, then with his fingertips. He touches her temples with his fingertips and then clasps her ankles. Then back to her wrist and arm as he begins his special "prayer," quickly in a sing-song voice, rocking back and forth. During the rhyming phrases, he lightly touches different parts of the patient's body—her knee, midriff, head— and then scratches, absentmindedly, his own head or back. By these actions and his words, the seer identifies his body with that of the patient. That which follows is only a partial transcription of a prayer, some of which was inaudible or said so quickly that I could not understand it.

> Where is the illness? Where did it come from? Where did it go? How does it talk? Maybe over the sea. Maybe in the sky.
> Where does it walk? I will touch it/you.[5] Maybe it is green-cold-sickness [malaria]. Maybe it is malaria. We have maltreated, we have thought badly, we have been jealous. I will touch you/it.
> I pray to the apostles, Peter, Paul [he names them all]. I call to you God because we are under your feet and hands. I will give to you the thirteen blessings of Jesus. Our Father who art in heaven, hallowed be thy name, thy kingdom come, oh Saint Mary, oh Tzuultaq'a in holy heaven. Help me because I am ill. The holy head, the holy arms, the holy legs, the holy feet, and holy neck, the holy stomach. I reject the illness. I, the person [*poyonam*].

He puts his hand over her heart and repeats the first and third verses. He takes her arm again and blows hard on the forearm as he runs his fingers along it. The next movements are each repeated three times. He brushes his hands from her head across her breasts and presses her stomach inward from both sides. He runs his palms on the outside, then the inside of her legs, downward toward her feet. This part of the treatment ends as Lu' says, "In the name of the Father and Son" twice, both times making only half the sign of the cross.

Lu' then lights a ball of *pom* on a piece of broken roof tile made of fired clay, and adds the herb rosemary to the burning resin. The patient leans over the side of the bed, and Lu' kneels beside her. He drapes a large cloth over both their heads and blows *pom* smoke in her face. Clouds of smoke rise from the *pom*. He continues to pray, but I cannot make out the words.

The name of the illness is not openly announced but will be told discreetly to the relatives later. In this case, the woman turned out to be suffering from *tzuul* (literally, "mountain"), the local expression for spirit loss. She would later be taken to the place where she lost her spirit, and the spirit called with *pom*.

After leaving the patient's house, Lu' instructed me, "Those words are strong, the word is the word. You will not tell anyone here what you have written, you won't say those words, only in your land."

It is hard to assess the effectiveness of these divination techniques. It was clear to me that seers do have an ability to move across personal boundaries and "get inside" a patient's psyche. My own illnesses were divined on several occasions, and I experienced an indescribable experience of dissolution and merging of personal boundaries. Seers perceive something of the internal state of a patient, and at times their interventions are beneficial. In one instance, I visited a renowned curer in Cahabón under a false pretense. I complained of a nonexistent stomachache in order to see the elder's famed methods. After carrying out his divination, the crusty old man chuckled and said to me words to the effect, "You are pulling my leg, my friend. There's nothing wrong with you at all."

The status of traditional health care is ambiguous, even among its practitioners. "We treat the ill like this because we are poor, there are no doctors to attend us," said one seer. Though seeming to disparage traditional medicine, seers rate it highly within its sphere of applicability. "Could a doctor cure *tzuul?*" I asked a seer. "No, never. The person would die," he replied, drawing an impermeable distinction between traditional Q'eqchi' and Western medicines. As pointed out by Maud Oakes (1951:156), traditional health care is a platform for indigenous people to distinguish themselves from Ladinos. As a separate and semi-autonomous area of symbolic activity, health care is an important marker of ethnic boundaries.

CALLING THE SPIRIT

Illness among Mesoamerican indigenous groups is much more an issue of spirit loss than of spirit possession. The restoration of a dissociated spirit involves going to the place where the spirit was lost and calling the person's name.[6] A child goes with its mother to the place of loss, and a seer may be present. There are also community members who specialize solely in the performance of this cure. They are the *aj b'oqonel,* or "callers," and the majority are women.

As I mentioned earlier, spirits usually become separated from their owners near a river or spring. At the edge of the water, the caller burns *pom* incense and candles while calling the name of the afflicted. The caller prays to God and the closest tzuultaq'a for the spirit of the patient. She shouts to the spirit, "Arise! Get up! Come! Come to your house and rest! Come and sit on a chair, on the bench!" A substitute (*reqaj*) for the person is left at the edge of the water as an offering to the tzuultaq'as. This is called a *muñeek,* or doll, and it is fashioned from *pom* and beeswax into a human form. The patient's hair and fingernail and toenail clippings are stuck into the doll. After the calling and prayers, the doll is burned. The spirit of the person may return immediately or after a few days. Often it comes back during the night while the person is asleep. A candle burns under the bed of the afflicted as the spirit's return is awaited.

If the spirit is lost in the forest, the practice of spirit restoration can be different. Patient and seer go to the place of spirit departure, but instead of leaving a *pom* doll, they kill a chicken or turkey and rub it over the patient. It is then thrown into the brush with *pom.* As one curer told me, "This is a substitute for the sick man. It is the mountain's compensation. The tzuultaq'as will eat it instead of the man." (cf. Vogt 1976:57).

Then the patient inhales the smoke from a burning plant named *rismal qamama',* or "hair of our grandfather." *Mama'* means grandfather, old one, and mountain. The head elders of a village are referred to as the *mama'.* The plant is also called *rismal tzuultaq'a,* or "hair of the tzuultaq'a." Only seers can find and pick this plant after having made the appropriate prayers to the tzuultaq'as. Just as the mountain spirit eats of the patient, the patient, inhaling the smoke, eats a part of the mountain, its hair. After all the rituals are performed, the tzuultaq'as may still decide not to give up the spirit but to keep it forever to work as a *mozo* inside the mountain.

SPIRIT LOSS IN MAIZE

The corn has a spirit and, like humans, can become separated from it. We have seen how maize is identified with children, and the parallel extends to spirit loss, for both share a propensity to lose their spirits easily. Much of what goes on in planting is an effort to ensure that the newborn maize does not lose its spirit between shucking and sowing.

The preoccupation over maize spirit loss begins before the planting. We saw earlier how spirit loss results from contact with too much heat, whether from human or agricultural fertility. The planter seeks to maintain a balanced but slightly cold body temperature. Eating hot foods and engaging in sexual activity would raise his heat level, and the heat would frighten the corn and provoke the tzuultaq'as to recover it after it has been sown. In the same way, the mountain recovers the spirit that becomes detached when a person stumbles by the river. The tzuultaq'as are the true guardians of maize and human spirits. They therefore have the right to repossess those spirits if moral imperatives are broken or owners do not hold their spirits tightly.

A man risks the loss of "his" corn to a tzuultaq'a if he forgoes making sacrifices or requesting permission before planting. The most common response to my question, "What happens if there is no sacrifice to the tzuultaq'as?" was either "The plants do not grow" or "The tzuultaq'as send the animals to eat the seeds." The denial of ritual obligations can result in the loss of a man's maize crop, as well as the loss of his own spirit or those of his children.

During the planting vigil, men are careful not to do anything that may frighten the corn (such as play marimba music), causing it to lose its spirit. During the evening, the men's heat levels are artificially increased through the consumption of *b'oj* and cigarettes, not activities that directly relate to human fertility, as sex does. Fertility-related heat would frighten the corn's spirit. The heat of human reproduction is too intense for maize production, but because fertility requires heat, men use mechanisms of heat regulation that are milder and more symbolic, and so will not lead to spirit loss in the corn.

Just as there is no cure for *awas* in maize, there does not exist anything like a cure for maize spirit loss. Harvesters can only take preventive precautions. Sacrifice to the tzuultaq'a in her or his cave before the planting is one of these measures.

A week after the harvest of a ripe corn crop, a ritual is performed to call the spirit of the maize to join the ears in the crib.[7] If this is not carried out, then next year's crop will not produce. The corn spirit is called in the field or in the store hut near the field. The owner burns *pom* around the stored maize and calls for its spirit to come. The petitioner exhorts the tzuultaq'a to let go of the spirit of the corn so that it may join its corporeal body. The corn will not be moved to its permanent storage place in the kitchen until it is felt that the spirit has joined the harvested maize. Luis Pacheco (1985:156) records that if Q'eqchi's dream of a child crying in the field, it is because the spirit of the maize remains out there. Elders particularly worry that some grains may have been dropped during transportation and their spirit remains unrecovered. Spirit loss in corn is most likely when it is on its way to be planted or returning back to the house after the harvest.

POWER AND FERTILITY

I would encourage ethnographers to consider ideas of fertility and the sacred landscape more seriously in any explanation of hot and cold distinctions. My analysis of Q'eqchi' illnesses is applicable to many Mesoamerican ethnographies, perhaps indicating a regional pattern of indigenous ideas toward health. In John Ingham's (1986) study of a Mexican Huastec community, the categories of *chipileza* and *susto* show remarkable resemblance to Q'eqchi' ideas of *awas* and spirit loss, respectively. *Chipeleza* (Ingham 1986:72) is concerned with issues of pregnancy and revolves around hot versus cold distinctions, whereas *susto* is spirit loss caused by fear and is cured through a name-calling ritual. Work on the neighboring K'iche' by Helen Neuenswander and Shirley Souder (1977) shows that the distinctions of *m'an* (hot) and *hron* (cold) are very similar to Q'eqchi' categories in their differentiations of foods, people, and illnesses.

In their analysis of Yucatec medicine in Chan Kom, Redfield and Villa-Rojas (1934:160) wrote of hot and cold symbolism: "It would be a misrepresentation to assert any detailed consistency or system or rules governing native thinking on these matters." yet there is a definite logic to Yucatec knowledge that is strikingly similar to that of traditional Q'eqchi' thinking. For Yucatecs, sterility is caused by too many cold foods (Redfield and Villa-Rojas 1934:162). Pregnant women are seen as hot, and must not consume cold foods. Lime juice (cold), for instance, is deemed poison to a woman in childbirth. Women are hot until they give birth, at which point they become cold and must imbibe infusions of hot liquids (1934:181). Sex is seen to offend the *yuntzilob,* the lords of the forest (1934:131). Sex segregation takes place while the men undertake the sacrificial "dinner of the *milpa*" to give thanks for the ripening corn (1934:135). There are many more parallels besides these. To reconsider all the relevant texts according to the principles detailed here would take more thoroughness than space allows, but the point is clear: anthropologists could afford to explore in more detail Mesoamerican ideas about fertility and health that link the landscape deities, maize, and people.

At times, the symbolic nuances of fertility among the Mayan groups have been lost in an overemphasis on power relations and sociological explanations. Indeed, traditional Q'eqchi' ideas show that conceptions of power (specifically, its heat) cannot be understood without understanding fertility and re-generation. For example, the idea of balance in heat levels has moral implications. Not only does a balanced state lead to bountiful crops and many children, but it is also the most desirable state for peace in the community. The traditional leaders inside the villages are cool elders. The agents of extra-communal authority-soldiers, Ladinos, foreigners, and mayors, are hot and dangerous. Heat symbolism is also an idiom for ownership, because those who own the land, the *hacendados* and tzuultaq'as, are hot.

In sum, Mayan representations of power draw upon and are influenced by the symbolism of agricultural production and human reproduction. Writers such as Tilman Evers (1985:47) in the "new social movements" school have recognized how embedded power can be in all dimensions of the social: "Cultural production as well as the whole sphere of reproduction are accepted as political fields."

CONCLUSIONS

Traditional conceptions of production and reproduction are part of a single complex. I have argued that human and agricultural fertility are strongly associated, and both require a finely balanced heat level for perfect fruition. Deviation from this balance, whether the fault of the individual or instigated by the mountain spirit, causes illnesses. Cure involves a return to the neutral, even-keeled state.

Illnesses in humans and maize are based upon two systems that draw on the same ideas about hot and cold, fertility and gender. The first paradigm includes human *awas* and the food *awas* in maize, both of which lead to a malformation in the maize or child that exhibits features of the prohibited food. The second embraces spirit loss in humans and the mountain *awas* in maize. In this type, the tzuultaq'a recovers the spirit out of vengeance or because it has been abandoned in the forest. I do not presume that these categories are completely airtight; there are overlaps and ambiguities. The bipolar opposites of hot and cold are not the primary principles of traditional culture, rationalized in a neat Lévi-Straussian manner. Rather, hot versus cold distinctions are drawn upon in different ways in specific contexts in distinct communities. A general point could be made here about the importance of not reifying indigenous belief systems. It is problematical to speak of a systematized, traditional Q'eqchi' culture, even as an ideal system á la Leach (1954:107), because doing so can obscure diversity at the level of regions, communities, households, and individuals. It is important to accept this Mayan heterogeneity and to explore both its patterned and its pluralistic character (Hays 1990; Scotchmer 1986).

Like the symbolism of agricultural production, that of human reproduction is involved in the construction of collective identities. Only members of specific communities lose their spirits to the mountains to whom they belong. Only they have a moral relationship with the mountains that defines the categories of illnesses they suffer from. The profusion of discourses on illness, such as those on types of *awas,* also serves to recreate different community identities. Traditional community power structures are seen as being staffed by cold elders, whereas external sources of power are hotter and potentially more destructive.

Human fertility is also involved in the traditionalists' imaginings of their ethnic identity. Q'eqchi' women have their own concepts of fertility, which are not shared by Ladino outsiders. The symbolism of reproduction defines itself as autonomous from Western medicine. The paradigms of disease are incommensurable; no antibiotics could cure spirit loss. In the domain of curing, shamans work with an indigenous concept of personhood, one that refers to the Q'eqchi's not as Christians but as pre-Christian *poyonam,* or "people." This use of archaic terms and references to ancient history connect a present sense of identity with past "tradition." In doing so, they construct that same tradition.

Some lucid insights from Anthony Cohen (1985) on identity in the Shetland Islands are appropriate here. Cohen stresses the importance of seeing the symbolic dimension in apparently instrumental behavior. He shows how the unspoken symbolic element of ordinary behavior marks boundaries between different communities. Cohen describes (1985:309) how symbolic expressions of identity are unrecognizable to those on the other side of the boundary: "Were they to be so intelligible they would be redundant. They are symbolic statements designed to perpetuate the boundary, not to demolish it. Their efficacy depends on the outside world being unable either to recognise the boundary at all or to recognise it in the terms in which it is defined by those 'inside'."

This statement resonates with Q'eqchi' traditionalists' symbolic statements, for so much of their boundary marking is beyond the pitch of the outsider's ear, especially the Ladino's. The vast majority of outsiders are unaware of the rich complexity and boundary-marking functions of each community's discourse on agriculture and health care.

The preceding three chapters have examined the most important and frequent areas of Q'eqchi' contact with the tzuultaq'as. Based in the domain of fertility and health, the relationship with the religious topography extends into many domains of the social. The cult of the mountain spirits expresses not only the traditional imagination of the community but also concepts of health, welfare, and fertility of humans and maize. The religious ideas associated with the mountains reach right down inside the spirits of Q'eqchi's themselves, molding their concepts of personhood. This involvement of tzuultaq'as inside the boundaries of the individual psyche is one of the factors that makes the traditional cosmology and sense of community so powerfully emotive. Next we shall see how Catholic orthodoxy and civil war have led to a refashioning of traditional Q'eqchi' conceptions of nature, self, and community.

CHAPTER SIX

CONVERTING TO RELIGIOUS ORTHODOXY

O *God, how painful it is to hear you say that what we thought isn't true, rather there is another truth.*

O God, don't you hear our ancestors tell us that the tzuultaq'a gives us our corn, the water, the rain, the fire? O God, don't you hear that our kin offered pom *and hit their legs [with a branch] at the crossroads? And didn't that get rid of the pain?*

Don't you know that it got rid of our fevers and chills? O God, how hard it is for us to believe what you say—that there is another truth. O God.

O God, how hard it is to believe that there is no tzuultaq'a, that there never was, nor will there ever be, not over there in the sinkhole, nor in the mountain when we hear the thunder and the lightning flashes in the sky. —Q'eqchi' lament, quoted by Agustín Estrada Monroy, my translation

The preceding verse was recorded in the sixteenth century, when the first Dominican priests entered Tezulutlán to evangelize the Q'eqchi's. When the catechist program spread through rural communities in the 1970s, this lament resonated once again in the mountains of Alta Verapaz.

The catechist program that first began in the late 1960s led to innovations at nearly every level of local life. The movement swept through villages, overturning the local gerontocracy and creating a new Q'eqchi' intelligentsia. It transformed technology and economic relations and led to fundamental changes in the community's relationship with its landscape. It caused a revolution in community political structures and reconstructed the way in which communities were imagined. The attack on traditional ways of conceptualizing the community in turn created the possibility of new and wider collective identities.

   The history of Catholicism in Alta Verapaz, the saint brotherhoods, and the evangelicals all influenced the character of the catechist program and are the subjects of the first three sections of this chapter. Subsequent sections look at how the catechists attacked the earth cult and the brotherhoods, introduced a new image of the community, and reformulated community, ethnic, and class identities.

CATHOLIC HISTORY: FROM TEZULUTLÁN TO VERAPAZ

The initial Catholic evangelization of the Q'eqchi's took place under unique circumstances. It was not, as was the case in most of Latin America, preceded by military defeat at the hands of the conquistadors. In 1528, the forces of Sancho de Barahona captured the head Q'eqchi' cacique (local political chief) at Chamá, but he escaped shortly thereafter and returned to his lands. The Spanish forces then tried on three occasions to enter Q'eqchi' territory but were repulsed each time. The Q'eqchi's were aided greatly by the defection of the Tzutuhils, who had fought alongside Barahona, and who showed Q'eqchi' warriors how to foil the Spanish battle strategies. This collaboration enabled the Q'eqchi's to be one of the few indigenous groups in the Americas to rout the Spaniards repeatedly. For this reason, the province of the Q'eqchi's became known as Tezulutlán, the Land of War. Elders in particular are aware of this history, and in recounting it they stress how "we won because we had the tzuultaq'as on our side."

The "peaceful" evangelization of the Q'eqchi's began in 1537, when Fray Bartolomé de las Casas signed an agreement with the Spanish governor of Guatemala. The document ordered that the province of Tezulutlán "be reduced to the obedience of the Lord our God," in the absence of Spanish troops and other conventions of colonial rule such as the *encomienda* system (Juarros 1981:274). (An *encomienda* bestowed upon a conquistador the right to labor tribute from indigenous communities for his personal exploitation.) No Spanish citizens other than priests of the Dominican order were allowed into the region for the first five years. Las Casas envisioned a pacific victory, with the Bible replacing the sword. In his *Apologética* (1909:241), Casas wrote, "[We come] armed only with the Word of God." Although his methods were less bloody, his final aim was the same as that of any conquistador: to convert the recalcitrant pagans into humble, Christian, tribute-paying subjects of the Crown.

The Dominican priest Luís Cancer entered Tezulutlán in December 1537. He traveled with four indigenous Christians from Quiché, singing verses that explained the creation of the world, the fall of Adam, and redemption through Jesus Christ. The songs were accompanied by autochthonous instruments.[1] The role of indigenous allies was vital to the Church's success. Saint-Lú (1968:428–29) writes: "Given the infrequency and brevity of their visits, the Dominicans had to call upon their Indian assistants, as a mediocre second choice. They [the priests] had to depend, for the daily practice, on Indian catechists, who organized ritual cults or taught lessons to children" (my translation).

The most important new convert in this evangelizing process was the Q'eqchi' chief of Chamelco, Aj Pop o Batz'. He
aided in the burning of "idols" and the creation of *reducciones,*
where indigenous groups could be concentrated and controlled
by the priests. Aj Pop o Batz' himself led the war party that
annihilated the Acalás after they murdered an aspiring evangelist, Fray Domingo de Vico.

The sacrament of baptism played an important role in
conversions. To this day Q'eqchi's refer to people in the generic
sense as *kristianeb',* or Christians, and the unbaptized as *xul,* or
animals. The original Q'eqchi' word for person, *poyonam,* disappeared from everyday use. The ideological opposition between
being a person and an animal was probably formed on the basis of
baptism during these first years of the evangelization.

In 1547, the name of the province of Tezulutlán was changed
by the decree of prince regent Felipe II to Verapaz, or "True
Peace" (Remesal 1932:191). The cross succeeded where the
sword had failed to pacify the warlike Q'eqchi's. Within ten
years, Spanish colonial rule was imposed. Q'eqchi's became
subject to tribute and were treated by the Crown like any other
subjugated people in the Americas. Dominican priests came to
manage the local economy, using labor levies and slave labor,
turning the Verapaz into "a peculiar kind of colony" (Wilk
1991:47). The Dominicans used Q'eqchi' slaves on cotton and
cochineal plantations and they ran small textile and craft operations (see King 1974).

The diocese of the Verapaz closed in 1608, owing to declining Q'eqchi' numbers and political clashes between the bishop
and the Dominican priests. Foreign illnesses decimated the
population, which fell to about five thousand (Estrada Monroy
1979:253). Very little is known about the Verapaz during the
following three centuries. It became a remote region, distant
from the ambit of colonial rule.

During the seventeenth and eighteenth centuries, community religion was semi-autonomous from Spanish priests and orthodox Catholicism. Estrada Monroy (1979:354) says of this period, "The ancient ceremonies returned to mix with the Catholic rites and in the mountain huts . . . the family altar became a church where tzuultaq'a and Jesus Christ were the objects of special worship." Estrada's point about religious syncretism is correct, but the ancient ceremonies had not "returned"—they had been there all along. Q'eqchi's were relatively free from orthodox influences and could practice their own blend of autochthonous and foreign religions. Religious life was predominantly community based and centered on agricultural rituals and the civil-religious hierarchy.

The 1870s brought massive upheavals for institutionalized Catholicism, when the liberal president Justo Rufino Barrios came to power. The Catholic church was persecuted and many clergymen left the country. The Dominicans were expelled. Richard Adams (1970:278) writes that the Liberal period in Guatemala was the longest restriction of the Catholic church in the history of Latin America. At the same time, Protestantism was promoted in an effort to cripple Catholic power and extend state control to indigenous communities (Burnett 1989).

The Catholic institutional structure in Alta Verapaz was decimated, and communities were left to their own devices with regard to religious life. Economically, they were deprived of their resources as export plantations expanded. Progressive economic disfranchisement led to indigenous rebellions throughout the colonial and postcolonial periods. In 1803, the Ladinos of Cobán were attacked and their property destroyed. The nonindigenous population narrowly escaped massacre by hiding in the Catholic convent. According to Daniel Contreras (1968:35), the Ladino mayor "would have been killed had it not been for the intervention of the Dominican priests." In 1878, a

Q'eqchi' uprising in Carchá was led by the head of the village *cofradía*, or religious brotherhood. Drawing upon discontent over the loss of ancestral lands, Q'eqchi's attacked local Ladinos in Carchá. The rebels were dispersed by military reinforcements from Cobán, and the survivors fled to the mountains. There were other, smaller uprisings during the nineteenth century, such as one in Cahabón, where the priest was killed by angry villagers armed with machetes.

In each of these incidents, there was a religious dimension to indigenous rebellion: discontent coalesces over religious issues or uses the symbolism of Catholicism. This is a feature of indigenous revolt throughout Latin America, from Taki Onqoy in Peru to the present day. The main revolts in Mesoamerica were the Tzeltal uprising of 1712 and the fifty-year Caste War in the Yucatan in the later nineteenth century. In the first case, two thousand indigenous "soldiers of the Virgin" sacked Catholic churches and murdered Ladinos. In the second, ideological justification came from the "Speaking Cross" in Santa Cruz (Reed 1964; Villa-Rojas 1978). Yucatec Mayas reformed their traditional, independent *cacicazgos* (kingdoms) and routed the Federal troops repeatedly. Maya autonomy on the Yucatán peninsula was crushed militarily at the turn of the century.

In 1935, the diocese of the Verapaces was restored and the Church's institutional structure began to expand. At the time there were only four or five priests to attend some 150,000 people in an area of about 50,000 square kilometers. It was not until the 1960s that the number of clergy increased significantly, when the whole of Guatemala received an influx of European and North American priests. Foreign priests outnumbered domestic by nearly six to one (Adams 1970:289). In 1967, Father Stephen Haeserijn wrote that all the Catholic personnel in Alta Verapaz were foreign; today, they still constitute the majority. Indigenous men have historically been excluded from the clergy, beginning with Las Casas, who opposed the creation of an indigenous priesthood. The first Q'eqchi' priest was locally ordained more than 450 years after the Christian evangelization began.

THE CATHOLIC BROTHERHOODS

Historically, rural Q'eqchi' communities have been defined primarily in the idiom of the sacred, through both the mountain cult and the patron saint cult.

Cofrades are religious brotherhoods, first formed by the Spanish priests in the sixteenth century, that tend the local church and fête its saint image(s). The saint fiesta (usually in midsummer) and the community sacrifice (in spring) are the main events in a community's ritual calendar. Both celebrate images of the community and thus recreate its unity and distinguish it from nearby communities.

The chinam is the head of the cofradía; in Castilian, he is the mayordomo. The priests initiated the brotherhoods in order to better evangelize the indigenous groups, but over time the villagers made them all their own. This system continues with the participation, but not the interference, of the clergy.

The chinam of a cofradía must have the support of his wife, who is also a mayordoma, or office holder. Single men cannot hold an office in the cofradía. Female participation in the civil-religious hierarchy has, in my view, been underemphasized in ethnographies of Mesoamerica. Because the chinam must host a feast, and women control consumption, no cofradía event can be organized without their collaboration.

The religious brotherhoods organize annual fiestas for the village saint, as was originally intended, but they have also become the whole social structure of the community—the forums for judicial and political decisions, economic organization, and religious practices. Manning Nash (1989:103) writes,

"This [cofradía] structure does for Guatemalan Indians what kinship and clanship does for African societies such as the Tallensi, or what social class does for Ladino society."

The cofradía is the religious half of the civil-religious hierarchy, a unified series of ranked posts that are alternately civil and religious. During a man's life, he moves up the ranked hierarchy of offices, each time taking on a greater civic or religious duty. One year he may be mayor, next year in charge of the saint's feast day, and the following year responsible for feeding the mountain spirit. Ultimately, he becomes an elder, responsible for the overall well-being of the community.

Until the 1970s, the cofrades were the central community organizations in all relations with the outside world, and they still play a key role in many Mayan communities (Watanabe 1992). Interpretations of their social function have varied a great deal. Eric Wolf (1957) focused on how the cofrades defended the community from the nation, protecting the boundaries of the "closed corporate community." Authors such as Frank Cancian (1965) and Steve Stern (1987b) have also stressed the integrative role of the cofrades, asserting that they obstruct fragmentation of the community and ethnic group along class lines. Other authors, however, have stressed how cofrades emphasize separateness but accept a wider context of subordination. Henri Favre (1973) and Waldemar Smith (1977) write that the fiesta system stabilizes both the indigenous and Ladino sectors of society and so preserves the status quo. For them, fiestas are a palliative to those at the bottom of an exploitative regional economy, lessening the pain of subordination without challenging its causes.

There is, however, no single "truth" to the political function of cofrades. They do promote community integration by exalting a focal image of the community (the saint), which allows greater unity and defensive closure against the outside world.

The officers of the civil-religious hierarchy express all that is "community," acting for the whole village in relations with Ladino political authorities, the Catholic church, the saints, God, and the mountain spirits. At the same time, *cofrades* can often implement practices that perpetuate subordination, such as recruiting free labor for the Ladino municipality. They isolate and fragment communities and obstruct political action at the level of the class or ethnic group. Yet in the history of indigenous rebellion against Ladino authority, much of it has been organized at the level of the *cofradía* (Bricker 1979), an observation that militates against applying any final "reactionary" label.

During the 1970s, several anthropologists turned their attention to explaining the collapse of the civil-religious hierarchy. W. Smith (1977) studied the effects of cash-cropping and seasonal wage labor on the civil-religious hierarchies in three villages in San Marcos. Smith polemicized against Cancian (1965), arguing that it is the least "Indian" communities (i.e., those that have been most successful economically and most Ladinoized) that maintain the religious brotherhoods, whereas the most Indian (in terms of dress, language, agricultural methods, etc.) are forced by poverty to abandon the fiesta system.

Douglas Brintnall (1979) claimed that in Aguacatán, changing religious affiliations were based on opposing class distinctions. Wealthier, cash-cropping peasants left the *cofradías* in order to release capital for investment in agriculture. They tended to join the Catholic catechist movement (Catholic Action), whereas poorer subsistence cultivators converted to Protestant groups to avoid their *cofradía* obligations. Kay Warren (1978) focused on the effect of the Catholic lay activist movement on ethnic relations. She argued that the "ideology" of Catholic Action obscured indigenous people's perception of the mechanisms of ethnic subordination. Whereas the civil-religious hierarchy maintained a separation of indigenous and Ladino identities, the catechists promote selective Ladinoization as a way of overcoming subordination.

THE EVANGELICALS

The catechist program can be fully understood only in the context of evangelical conversions. I call these groups "evangelicals" because the alternative, Protestants, connotes more historical congregations such as the Lutherans, Mennonites, and Presbyterians. The groups operating in Guatemala tend to be tiny and numerous (now over three hundred), and many have affiliations to North American organizations. For instance, the former military dictator Efraín Ríos Montt (1982–83) was a pastor of Gospel Outreach, a sect based in Eureka, California (Stoll 1988, 1990).

Evangelicals have competed directly with Catholics in Alta Verapaz for more than fifty years now, and they have had a significant influence on the formation of Catholic lay activists (or catechists). The global rise of Protestantism after World War II greatly influenced the reforms of Vatican II and prompted the training of lay activists across Latin America. In Alta Verapaz, the nature of the catechist movement was certainly molded by the surrounding evangelical groups.

I had very little personal contact with evangelicals during my fieldwork. I was, however, able to interview about half a dozen evangelical Q'eqchi's and the pastor of the Nazarene church in Cobán. The situation was so polarized between Catholics and evangelicals that there was little or no organized ecumenicism or middle ground. Even being seen talking to evangelicals was a sign of possible betrayal. I was also acutely aware of my own personal religious status. Although not a practicing Christian, informants perceived me as coming from a powerful Protestant country, the United Kingdom. When (continually) asked if I was a Catholic, I responded, no, I was a lapsed member of the Church of England. Seeking to allay suspicions, I downplayed the importance of this historical religious division and actively attended all manner of Catholic rituals.

Catholics are still the overwhelming majority, but they feel increasingly persecuted, perceiving an onslaught from the evangelicals. This is because of the evangelicals' massive conversion rates in recent years and because Catholics see them to be linked to dominant power sectors, specifically the military, the United States, and, at times, the Guatemalan state.[2]

There has been only one study of Q'eqchi' evangelicals in Alta Verapaz, an unpublished document by Luís Samandú (1987) of the University of Costa Rica, so I have had to rely heavily on some of its conclusions.[3] Samandú states that the Nazarenes are the largest and most potent evangelical group in Alta Verapaz. They have had a presence in the department since 1904 but did not grow much until the 1960s. Their monopoly was broken by the Pentecostals, whose numbers increased quickly. Samandú reports that the Nazarenes, who are nominally Wesleyan, responded with aggressive conversion drives and more charismatic and salvationist styles of meetings. Their numbers grew from 3,010 in 1971 to 8,560 in 1980 (Samandú 1987:6).

Between 1977 and 1987, evangelical churches were doubling their numbers, even tripling in some areas such as Chisec, La Tinta, and Cobán. The zenith of this trajectory seems to have been reached in 1984. At present, most sources agree that at least 20 percent of the department's population is evangelical. Q'eqchi's constitute the overwhelming majority of members. Indeed, evangelicals are not minorities in some areas; Samandú estimates that they constitute 65 percent of the population of Chamelco and 49 percent of Tamahú. This phenomenon is not confined to Alta Verapaz: in all of Guatemala, evangelicals are said to make up 35 percent of the population and are, according to David Stoll (1988:90), "probably a majority of the country's active churchgoers."

Writers such as Samandú have pointed to many factors to explain the meteoric rise of evangelicals in Guatemala. Social marginalization, landlessness, migration, urbanization, violence, the lethargy of Catholic church, and its exclusion of the laity have all been invoked (Falla 1978; Scotchmer 1986; Stoll 1990). State violence is one of the most significant factors; it is no coincidence that conversion rates rocketed in areas that experienced the worst of the violence and peaked in 1984, a year after the highest levels of state repression. During this time the Catholic church was under siege: the army murdered lay activists and obstructed the clergy from administering to their congregations. Many evangelicals, on the other hand, were closely identified with the army and could travel mostly as they pleased (Stoll 1988). Not all of them were on the side of the military, however, and one pastor in Chisec was a guerrilla organizer.

Generalized rural violence, nevertheless, has been somewhat exaggerated as an explanation for evangelical success. Evangelicals could not have taken advantage of their favored position vis-à-vis the military if they had not already laid the basis on which to expand. They had been working in the indigenous languages of the region far longer than the Catholics, who at the time of this writing still use an evangelical translation of the Bible into Q'eqchi'.[4] Historically, evangelicals have also given more responsibility to lay members. According to Sheldon Annis (1987), conversion to evangelical groups is strongly linked to changing occupational roles and economic prospects. Annis argues that in San Antonio Aguas Calientes, Protestantism was closely associated with the transition from subsistence-based agriculture to cash-cropping and artisan occupations, especially weaving.

The evangelicals have had a mixed impact on ethnic identities. When Q'eqchi's convert, some aspects of their identity are preserved and others discarded. Evangelicals positively promote indigenous languages and maintain Q'eqchi' dress. In the symbolic realm, one finds that evangelicals' strongest opposition is reserved for Catholic saints, and Samandú (1987:24) writes of new converts burning their old saints' images in front of the congregation. Traditional beliefs concerning the mountain spirits also "fall under the rubric of paganism" (Samandú 1987:21). I found all evangelical Q'eqchi's quick to denounce traditional agricultural rituals as devil worship. A telling response came from a Ladino Nazarene pastor, who informed me: "We don't get rid of their culture, but we make sure that they don't mix their culture and their salvation."

For the new evangelical convert, abandoning the relationship with the mountain spirits is one of the main symbols of self-identification. To be an evangelical is not to stop being a Q'eqchi', but it does entail shunning certain traditional signs of community and creating new parameters for identity. Community identity is still primarily defined through religion, but the new religion is more universal and linked to assemblies outside the geographic community. Ethnic identity becomes less constructed through community religion and more dependent on language and dress. Ultimately, conversion to an evangelical sect does seem to have a culturally homogenizing effect, rendering Q'eqchi's more like their nonindigenous brethren in matters of faith.

The evangelicals have had an important influence on the structure and doctrine of Catholics in Guatemala. Evangelical missionaries provided an impetus for the incipient catechist program. In the 1960s, small groups of evangelicals trained local leaders in their own language and translated most of the New Testament. Father Pacheco told me how "the evangelicals were useful in waking us Catholics up and making us work harder. When we began the catechist program we had to get our Q'eqchi' Bibles from Mr. Sedat [a North American missionary]. He said to me, 'Finally you Catholics are starting to read the Bible!'"

Protestant missionaries were the first to employ indigenous languages to convert Q'eqchi' members. As one priest commented, "The Nazarenes helped us to open our eyes to do everything in the indigenous language. We slept as they translated." Father Haeserijn (1967:20) once said, "The language is the people," in arguing for the Catholic church to undertake more linguistic work. He quoted an indigenous woman, who said, "If your God was any good, he would know my language."

In 1967, Father Haeserijn, one of the main instigators of the catechist program, argued that the Nazarene church was having success among the villagers, whereas the Catholic "customs are losing their force as a rule of life." Q'eqchi' traditions were, he argued, in a state of "apostasy," and Haeserijn (1967:13–14) admired the way the evangelicals used indigenous pastors, vernacular language, and lay proselytizing to spread their doctrine. Unless "vigorous immediate action" was taken, Q'eqchi's would "reject Catholicism, with its customs, like used clothes which are out of fashion."

The immediate action taken by Catholics was to recognize the success of the evangelicals and adopt some of their structures for their own ends. This meant changing the liturgy and doctrine of Catholic cults, making them more "modern." The structure and Biblical focus of the catechist meetings are similar to those of traditional Protestantism, as is the transference of responsibility to the lay activist. The contents of the sermons stress themes that are normally more associated with

Protestantism, namely, a concern with internal, individual change of character along with a salvationist ethic and a mandate to evangelize.

The content of catechists' religiosity, like the evangelicals', is significantly more focused on Christ. One reason for this is that only the New Testament has been translated by the evangelical Summer Institute of Linguistics. The translation is strikingly spiritually oriented, understating many socially radical passages and channeling Bible studies in a Christocentric and salvation-oriented direction. The emphasis on Christ may also derive from a desire to undercut support for the evangelicals. William Christian (1981:199), writing about sixteenth-century Spain, interprets the tendency toward more Christocentric cults as a defense mechanism against the iconoclasm of advancing Protestantism.

Overall, the formation of catechists and Catholic base communities among the Q'eqchi's amounts to something akin to the Reformation within the Catholic church. The motivation for these projects came from Vatican Council II (1965) and Episcopal conferences at Medellín and Puebla. Phillip Berryman (1980:58) comments that the main consequence of Vatican II was that the Catholic church reconciled itself to the Protestant reform, with its Bible reading and vernacular worship.

THE CATECHISTS: BEGINNINGS

In the 1960s, foreign priests who came to highland Guatemala encountered a Church that performed sporadic rituals for the communities but was not integrated into daily religious life. One priest reported that the bishop advised him, before he began his work in Quiché, "Do the sacraments, but don't try to meddle with the customs of the people." Villagers saw a priest perhaps once a year when he gave a mass in unknown tongues (Latin and Spanish) and baptized a few children. The most meaningful local spiritual practices were performed by traditional village specialists.

The Salesian priest Francisco Pacheco described to me what he found on entering the parish of Carchá in 1967. I am forced to rely solely on Pacheco's memories because he is the only surviving priest from the team responsible for starting the catechist program in Alta Verapaz.

> The priests at the time weren't dynamic. They were elderly and did no language work; they hadn't translated any part of the Bible or liturgy into Q'eqchi'. They just went around the villages and did baptisms and marriages. That's to say they just tried to maintain the same low level of activity. There had been hardly any priests in the parish since the time of liberalism. The religiosity of the people was a mixture of animism and Christianity. A popular religion was what was left. The priests didn't understand any of this. They had no understanding of the culture or language. The Church was on the floor.

Many new priests had been influenced by Vatican II and ideas of "development" at the time. This current swept the western indigenous highlands in the 1960s in the shape of Catholic Action. The formation of catechists began in fits and starts; only in 1975 did the program become coordinated at the level of the whole diocese. In February 1968, the parish of Carchá had its first course to form catechists. The priests requested that each village send two representatives to the course. Father Pacheco says of those who came, "None of them knew a thing about the Bible, nothing." It was truly radical for the Catholic church to hold courses in the Q'eqchi' language. Not since the initial evangelization over three centuries earlier had Catholic religious instruction been in anything but Castilian.

The catechist program fast became the cornerstone of the diocese's efforts, being seen as a reevangelizing of the Q'eqchi's comparable to the first evangelization of the 1530s. Father

Pacheco declared, "So that is how we began the second evangelization, the conversion of the masses. They had such a great desire to
learn the Bible. It became something we could not control. It is
certain that the Holy Spirit was at work among us. There is no
other explanation of the scale and pace of the process."

There are striking similarities between the evangelization
methods of the 1530s and 1970s. By becoming catechists,
indigenous lay Christians played a role they had not enjoyed
since the 1500s. Bishop Flores (1985:2) wrote, "Indigenous lay
people were the first instruments of God to sow the seeds of
faith in our land!" And so it would be in the "second evangelization," with indigenous catechists as the instruments, always
guided by the hand of the hierarchy. The twentieth-century
evangelization was undertaken using all available modern technology. Priests set up two Catholic radio stations to transmit
songs, doctrine, and masses in Q'eqchi'.

The notion of the "second evangelization" became part of the
discourse of the catechist movement itself. By its methods,
community religion was brought closer to the orthodoxy of
Roman Catholicism and under the control of its local institutional representatives. There was a strong feeling among the
clergy that Q'eqchi's, with their worship of the mountain
spirits, were semipagans with a dire need to be Christianized.
Father Pacheco revealed how "when I got here, I was not sure if
the people were monotheists or polytheists; perhaps monotheists with confusions."

The second evangelization went hand-in-hand with the
doctrine of development. One of the original Q'eqchi' instructors of the courses told me:

> We began the courses to raise up the communities, not just with
> the Bible but what was necessary was a vision of development. In
> the beginning, we spoke less of Christianity than we did of
> cooperatives and how to approach development agencies. We

Training course for aspiring catechists

spoke to the villagers about health care, digging wells for drinking water, and mutual aid within the community. We studied bridge and road building and education in the community, especially literacy teaching.

The Church prioritized land issues and advised people on how to register and gain titles to ancestral holdings. In areas of migration such as the Northern Transversal Strip, priests assisted communities in the titling of newly cleared lands. Agronomists were brought in to teach market-oriented agricultural methods such as the use of fertilizers and insecticides. Yet the Church slowly edged catechist courses away from direct involvement in development matters and into a more spiritualist discourse. The developmental dimension of the Church's teachings diminished in importance when, in 1973, the ministry of agriculture built its own training center in Cobán. It took over the Church's teaching on legal and technical matters concerning agriculture. The Catholic diocese and Guatemalan government were in close collaboration on land issues and agricultural "development" during this period.

At the same time, there was more pressure from Benedictine priests to emphasize Biblical teachings in the courses. By 1975, the catechist program had shifted to a primarily Biblical focus. Catechists discussed social doctrine, but development ideas now took second place to spiritual matters. The main content of the courses concerned the Bible and how to run meetings of the Catholic base community. Regarding social questions, the focus of catechists turned to alcoholism; they were imbued with a strong antialcohol ethic. One priest told me how, in the late 1960s and early 1970s, "I couldn't walk two blocks in town without coming across two dozen drunks in the street."

The clergy and Q'eqchi' instructors took on alcoholism as the main social issue in rural communities. Antialcoholism became an obsessive moral crusade. The catechists, many of whom were previously prone to alcohol abuse, became fixated with stamping out alcohol. The Catholic base communities began to take on all the characteristics and functions of Alcoholics Anonymous groups. The rise of evangelical groups, with their own radical positions against alcohol, also influenced the catechists and clergy. The evangelicals were having great success, especially among indigenous women, and one of the main items on their agenda was the excision of all alcohol consumption in the villages.

To summarize, the two initial platforms of the catechist program were to reevangelize the "semipagan" Q'eqchi's and inculcate in them the ideology of development. In the mid-1970s, the emphasis shifted toward more spiritual tenets. The Church did not abandon development projects, but government agencies took over its active didactic role. Catholic courses centered on matters of faith, and the main social consideration became a campaign against alcohol.

REVOLT OF THE YOUNG

To discover why catechists accepted the Church's teachings, and how the new ideas were made concrete, we must look at Q'eqchi' villages themselves. When villagers were asked to send representatives to the catechist courses, the male elders selected young married men who could manage the often long and arduous trip between Cobán and their parish. Women were not chosen because men traditionally monopolized external relations.

The chosen men were usually those with exposure to the outside world through merchant work, military service, or labor migration. Trainee catechists had to speak Castilian in order to read the untranslated Old Testament, participate in the mass, and fend for themselves in town. Like the ability to speak Castilian, literacy was largely confined to men. One simply had to be able to read the Bible to become a catechist.

These men also were more likely to be better off economically than the rest. Internal economic stratification in Q'eqchi' villages was not pronounced during this time, yet it was increasing. The ranks of the catechists included a large proportion of entrepreneurs in the villages—those who supplemented their subsistence agriculture with work as traveling merchants, carpenters, makers of musical instruments, or transporters of goods by boat or mule. Ricardo Falla (1978:10) reported that young, landless merchants formed the bulwark of the catechist program in Quiché.

Ideas of "development" caught on quickly with this group. Already economically mobile and entrepreneurial in outlook, they were open to trying the new cash-cropping methods of the Ladinos and foreigners. Importantly, they possessed capital to invest in the formation of cooperatives and in fertilizers and insecticides. There are parallels with Robert Carmack's (1979:384) description of the process in Quiché: "The merchants who were most oriented towards capitalism often adopted the beliefs of the Ladinos towards the land."

Max Weber's (1930) approach to religious ideas and economic ethics is appropriate here; the catechists represented an emerging status group in their hitherto relatively unstratified communities. They became the principal advocates of a religion that promoted individualistic, market-oriented agriculture over a subsistence-based economy. Economic trends and religious change reinforced one another in a dialectical manner. Studies of both orthodox Catholic and Protestant conversion across highland Guatemala have revealed markedly similar trends. Brintnall's (1979) work on catechists in Aguacatán concluded that the catechists were the first to forsake seasonal labor migration and commence cash-cropping. Annis's (1987) study of Protestantism in a Kaqchikel village shows that the new converts were the first to become "petty capitalists" instead of subsistence-based "milpa technologists." Warren (1978:174) argues that the conversion to the catechists' religion involved a rejection of the ethnic division of labor and an aspiration for economic mobility.

After a few courses, the catechists returned to their villages and began the weekly meeting called the "Word of God" (*Li Raatin li Tiox*). Just the name of the meeting shows how the Bible serves as the central image of the religious community and the pillar of legitimation of catechist authority. Because catechists read the Bible and have studied its mysteries with the priests, they have a more intimate contact with the supernatural than other members of the community. Only those who have been to courses are allowed to preach in the meeting, so they exert complete control over ritual expression. Suddenly, by studying the Bible and attending courses, young men could circumvent the elders' control over sacred knowledge. The villagers shortly became convinced that the community elders' knowledge was inferior to that of the Catholic clergy. It is hard to understand fully why this switch in religious and moral frameworks took place so rapidly. One explanation is that villagers had been primed by the hegemonic discourses of modernity and development emanating from state institutions and the mass media in particular.

Communities elected the most intelligent, confident, and energetic young men to be the first catechists. Their charisma has become more institutionalized now, but in the beginning it was an uncontrolled force, unleashed on the villagers to transform their whole worldview. Each village catechist was like a local version of the charismatic Seneca leader Handsome Lake, who preached a code of patterned religious and cultural reform (Wallace 1961, 1972).

The newfound status of the catechists was bound to create tensions. The elders were indignant about their loss of political and religious authority. One elder grumbled: "The catechists are snotty-nosed kids; we saw them come into this world and grow up and now they are telling us what to do. We built the church and now they tell us how to use it. It is not theirs, it is ours."

The clash between the traditional civil-religious order and the catechists is well documented (Brintnall 1979; Cabarrús 1979; Falla 1978; Warren 1978), and I will outline only its main developments among the Q'eqchi's. In the mid-1970s, as catechists became well established in their communities, there was a veritable revolution in the villages' balance of power. It is obvious why many young men were attracted to the opportunity to become lay activists: it meant immediate access to village authority and prestige, as opposed to a wait of many years. Traditional holders of political power had fulfilled a lifetime of obligations in the *cofradía* and as local representatives to the municipality. Becoming a catechist meant avoiding the financially crippling expenditure in the *cofradía*. The money saved could then serve as capital for cash-cropping. Richard Wilk (1991:170) makes the important point that the conflict between a moral village economy and the market is an old one, and its intensity comes from the fact that it is so historical. The power of male elders is always opposed to the power of modernity, and the balance of power has shifted many times.

The catechists became the main priority of the Church — its representatives in every village. Catechists now monopolize all relations between the parish and the community. The elders, who had previously managed village religious events and liaised with the priests, are utterly marginal. In one case, the elders of a community requested a mass for the planting. The parish priest agreed and money changed hands, but the catechists dissuaded him from carrying out the ritual. They had not been consulted by the elders and decided to boycott the event. Without further consultation with the elders, the priest returned their money and the mass was canceled. On this and a number of occasions, the sympathy of the parish was unequivocally on the side of the catechists.

The elders struggled to regain their position within the Church and in the communities, and this battle was fiercest in the parish of Carchá. A well-known saying of a Salesian priest in Carchá asserted that "the evangelization will not be complete until the last elder is dead." The Salesian order is in charge of the largest (in size and population) parish in the diocese. They have historically promoted a religiosity closer to orthodox Roman Catholicism. They thus find themselves opposed at times to orders with more tolerance for the vernacular, such as the Benedictines and Dominicans.

In 1974, the officials of the *cofrades* escalated their campaign against the Salesians by protesting to the president of the republic and in national newspapers. They accused the priests of destroying indigenous culture. The priests went so far as to build new churches to break the control of the elders. In some areas, violence broke out as elders and catechists faced off with machetes, each group vying for control of the village church.

The clash between young and old men crystallized around two issues, alcohol and the saints' images, both central to the *cofradía* celebrations. The catechists took a radical stance on alcohol consumption, refusing any whatsoever. The catechists linked all concomitant fiesta activities to the "evil water," especially dancing. This stance resembles the customary attacks by Protestant converts elsewhere on dancing in saint fiestas (see Redfield 1950:96).

The catechists' ban on drinking and dancing and their mocking attitude toward the saints' images meant that the whole fiesta system suffered. This antifiesta ethic is not confined only to Q'eqchi' catechists but seems to be widespread in Catholic base communities in Latin America. Galdamez (1986:40), a priest working in base communities in El Salvador, denounced the "strong temptation" of traditional religion. According to him, to participate in processions of patron saints and Mariolatry is "to adore the golden calf."

In the courses, catechists learned that saints' images do not have *tioxilal* (godliness, holiness) as the elders claimed, but were "just bits of wood made by a sinner." One catechist said, "The elders believe that St. Peter is their god more than the God in heaven. They believe more in what's here on earth than what is in the sky." Many catechists rejected hagiolotry completely, and some even embarked on escapades of burning saints' images and other icons (cf. Watanabe 1992:204). In these cases, the village *cofradía* often collapsed.

In other areas, catechists maintained that images should be given respect (*xk'eb'al xloq'al*) but not worshipped (*loqoniink ru*) as gods. This is basically the orthodox distinction, instigated by the iconoclastic Leo III, between *latria* (worship) and *dulia* (adoration). Catechists assumed the running of the local *cofradía* and celebrated the saint each year, but without alcohol, dancing, and the marimba.

A catechist takeover is the norm in the majority of communities, but it is difficult to judge the degree to which *cofrades* were abandoned due to catechist influence alone. A variety of other factors were involved, such as displacement because of political violence and poverty induced by falling cash-crop prices. Whatever the interpretation, the changes to the fiesta system have been considerable. Expenses in new catechist-led *cofrades* tend to be extended over all the members of the base group; no longer does one person bear the whole burden alone. By becoming collectivized, the fiesta system is no longer geared toward individual prestige and obligation and toward serving as an individual male rite of passage.[5]

In the end, the elders were defeated and reconciled themselves to their secondary position. Without the *cofrades*, they no longer have any institutional structure with which to protect their interests. Most elders now participate in the catechist meeting, especially in the ritual function of *aj k'atok*, "he-who-burns" the *pom* and lights the candles. Elders are obstructed from higher positions of responsibility because they have not received courses from the parish and because the vast majority are illiterate and so have no access to the sacred text.

Q'eqchi' experiences of conversion seem quite different from those in Quiché or Huehuetenango, where the advent of Catholic Action led to violent and permanent splits within the indigenous communities. Falla (1978:258) wrote that catechist conversion was not universal but was confined to the class from which the movement sprang. The *cofrades* in Quiché did not suffer the demise of their Q'eqchi' counterparts. They carried on, but without a large section of the community. In many villages, two churches were built to cope with the divided groups. Pierre van den Berghe and Benjamin Colby (1977:146) report how priests administering villages in Quiché had to give two masses, one for the *cofrades* and one for the catechists.

In contrast, Q'eqchi' catechists won their struggle outright. Although dissent exists on the part of some elders, there is not the level of division to be found in K'iche', Mam, or Kaqchikel villages. Q'eqchi' communities tended to convert as a whole, after varying degrees of initial strife. Part of the explanation for this lies in the fact that the diocese of the Verapaces was more sensitive than others to indigenous culture. At least it respected the local language and musical instruments. In Quiché, the liturgy and a large part of the courses for catechists were in Castilian.

The degree of economic and political division already existing in Quiché and Mam villages influenced the extent of religious division. In the rest of the highlands, economic stratification through cash-cropping and the use of modern agricultural techniques were more pronounced than among the Q'eqchi's. Although the catechists could be called an emerging status group, they were not yet a new class. In addition, political parties had a longer history of organizing in the western highlands. In Quiché, catechists became more identified with the Christian Democrats and the elders with the right-wing MLN party. Political affiliations exacerbated religious distinctions and vice versa.

Among the Q'eqchi's, the catechist program was part of a general drift toward greater economic differentiation within the village. Its development ethic promoted cash-cropping and intensive agricultural methods. Its religious ethic freed the individual from redistributive, leveling *cofradía* obligations. As under Calvinism three centuries before, one could now work hard and reinvest the rewards.

In Quiché, the catechist program rode the wave of economic change, whereas in Alta Verapaz it was a spark for it. In Quiché, religious divisions followed economic ones; among the Q'eqchi's it formed the blueprint for them.

This last statement expresses the influence of Weber on my approach to the role of religious ideas in shaping "structural" factors such as economic relations, war, and political change. I do not propose a general determinist theory, however, because the spread of commodity relations, Catholic orthodoxy, and political violence have not determined the changes in religious ideas any more than the ideas themselves set the parameters for how those changes might be perceived and manifested. Instead of a grand theory of "the role of religion in society," I offer only a "grounded theory," that anchors any determining role to religious ideas and practices in their microsocial context.

THE WORD OF GOD: A NEW IMAGE OF COMMUNITY

The structure of The Word of God meeting was conceptualized by foreign clergy, drawing upon experiences of Catholic base communities in the Guatemalan highlands and other Latin American countries.[6] The meeting is therefore a foreign import, but one that incorporates certain aspects of traditional religion while rejecting others.

Unlike the situation during the days of the *cofradía*, the Catholic church now controls many aspects of community religion through the catechist meetings. The diocese sets the readings from the Bible in its Catholic calendar. In this way the clergy control centrally what the faithful read and discuss in their far-flung villages. The hierarchical position of the catechists in their communities also facilitates the transmission of doctrine. This hierarchy runs counter to the egalitarian ethic reported for other Latin American base communities (Boff 1985:10, 157). For example, in Brazil, Bruneau (1980:227) writes that "spokesman are discouraged." In Q'eqchi' rituals, only the qualified speak. The elders were qualified by their age and rank in the civil-religious hierarchy. Now, young catechists are legitimate speakers because of their association with an external institution, the Catholic church.

The base-group meeting uses some previous elements of community culture. The whole meeting transpires in Q'eqchi' —songs, readings, and sermons. The marimba, an integral part of the *cofradía* fiesta, accompanies the songs. Before the cate-chists, each community had its prayer specialists for ritual occasions and *cofradía* celebrations. These were the *aj tij*— elder men who had memorized Spanish or Latin prayers and could repeat them verbatim without necessarily understanding their meaning. In the catechist meeting, prayer is democratized by translating a few orthodox Catholic prayers into the indige-nous language. Thus prayer becomes a collective, not an indi-vidual, activity. Under the ideology of the catechists, prayer changed from being an incantation to produce a desired effect to being a direct, personal communication with God.

A new sense of community has developed within the base group. The Bible is not only the medium between orthodox Q'eqchi's and their God, it is also used as a metaphor with which to talk about the Catholic base community: "The Bible is the center pole of our community." This sacred text is held to be the central focus of the group, its raison d'etre. It is given special powers to sanctify the congregation, deliver them from worldly troubles, and ensure their salvation.

The catechists' discourse on salvation has ramifications for ideas of community. Traditional Q'eqchi' religiosity paid little

attention to matters of life after death. Catechists now speak of
"changing one's own heart," of sweeping it clean of evil and
jealousy. This change at the level of the individual is fundamental. Ultimate responsibility for one's spiritual well-being and
salvation lies with the individual, not with the community.

The collective, however, is not wholly ignored; salvation can
be gained only through good works in the community. One
preacher stressed how "we will save ourselves by our works and
our words, as one community, older brothers and younger
brothers and sisters." Idioms of kinship (specifically, brotherhood) and community are invoked. Countless times the preacher will repeat, "We must help one another so that the community
raises itself up."

Mutual aid is not just an ideal but a practiced reality. The
most common form of help is a collection for a member at a
weekly meeting. Money is collected for those who have suffered
a tragedy—when someone has lost a maize crop, for example, or
when a relative has died and there is no money for burial, or
when someone is seriously ill and needs medical attention. The
base group organizes work parties, perhaps to repair a roof or
plant a maize crop for a widow or a woman whose husband has
abandoned her. Yet the base community is no substitute for
kinship bonds. Single women receive community aid only if
they have no sons to care for them. The work party does not
request payment in kind or cash, but does expect food and
refreshment during the day.

In one case, the house of an orphaned adolescent trio was
repeatedly robbed. During the Christmas period, when there
was no paid work, the community moved the children's whole
house a kilometer away, locating them closer to their neighbors.
This type of mutual aid was a feature of village life before the
catechist program began. It is a manifestation of traditional labor
reciprocity, which is now channeled through the base group.

In catechist discourse on salvation, then, we see the juggling of two orientations, one spiritual and another that accords more value to involvement in everyday problems.

Community projects are organized not only in the Catholic base group but also in the secular "betterment committee," which meets weekly to plan development initiatives and petition the government for materials and training. These existed in certain villages in the 1970s but were reorganized in all communities as part of the counterinsurgency strategy of the Ríos Montt government in 1982. The functioning of the betterment committees contributes toward ghettoizing the catechist group as a spiritual refuge. This specialization in the functions of community institutions contrasts with the lack of specialization in the prior civil-religious hierarchy, in which all responsibilities fell within the jurisdiction of a single institution.

Although they emphasize salvation, catechists do not shun worldly affairs. They get involved in development initiatives such as forming cooperatives and digging wells for clean drinking water. One or two of the catechists in a village are invariably involved in the betterment committee's work as well, often as president. They are the representatives of the community to the outside world, specifically to the army and the government. As one nun put it, "The catechists have the communities in their hands." Much of their activity, however, is undertaken outside of the weekly meeting, which only rarely serves as a basis for wider social action. Unlike the *cofradía,* the catechist meeting is not a forum for representation to outside political authorities. Like the elders before them, the catechists are the leaders of their communities because of their function as the principal ritual specialists. The weekly meeting legitimizes catechist hegemony in secular affairs but is not the sole platform on which political power is realized.

Did the catechist program lead to more institutional control

for the Church or to a decentralization of power? Both proposi-
tions are true to a degree. As Foucault has argued (1980:98),
power is not a unidirectional force; it eddies and flows in
different courses throughout the social network. Before the
catechist program, the communities and the Church were
disarticulated, allowing local idiosyncracy and independence.
Ultimately, the Church has extended its power greatly in the
communities and reduced their autonomy in religious practice.
The relationship between local ritual specialists and the parish
is closer, so catechist power within the institutional structure
derives in part from Church control itself. At the same time,
there is a new sphere of enhanced local independence within
orthodox Catholicism. Q'eqchi's now have direct access to the
Bible and a more autonomous relationship with the Christian
God, unmediated by foreign clergy.

CATECHISTS AND THE MOUNTAIN SPIRITS

In this section, I hope to complement the existing literature on
the catechist movement by focusing on the changes it wrought
in the traditional relationship with the landscape. Carlsen and
Prechtel (1991) have already begun this task by sensitively
exploring the effect of sixteenth-century Catholic evangelization on the Mayan concept of the "Flowering Mountain Earth."

Previous studies of the catechist program have had a more
sociological emphasis, concentrating on the collapse of the
civil-religious hierarchy and the conflict between young and old
men (Brintnall 1979; Colby and van den Berghe 1977; Falla
1978; Warren 1978). In what follows, I will investigate how the
catechists attacked many aspects of the earth cult but did not
wholly destroy traditional beliefs and practices. Carlos Cabarrús (1979:123), writing about Q'eqchi' catechists in the early
1970s, argued that they had rejected completely the tzuultaq'as
and all related rituals. This interpretation is simply incorrect,

and inevitably must be, because, in the words of Reinhard
Bendix (1960:92), "neither priests nor prophets can afford to
reject all compromise with the traditional beliefs of the masses."

CATECHIST COURSES AND THE TZUULTAQ'AS

> *A tzuultaq'a is not a god, there is only one God. All
> the priests taught me this, and I have been in two
> parishes. They say it is not good to request permis-
> sion to plant from tzuultaq'as. A mountain is just a
> mountain. They are wrong, those who say "our
> Father Tzuultaq'a," calling it "our Father" like that.
> Look at the old men who do the customs, they are the
> ones who get drunk and fight.* —Bex, a catechist

Through the catechist program, the priests sought to Christianize the Q'eqchi's, that is, to bring them closer in thought and
deed to the universal, modern Catholic church with its emphasis on lay participation, local groups, and Bible study. This
represented the most serious attempt since the sixteenth-century evangelization to replace existing community religion with
an orthodox Catholic strain.

The dissemination of information follows a dendritic pattern emanating from the Benedictine Centro San Benito in
Cobán. There, catechists from each parish come to receive two
to three courses per year, each lasting a few days. The courses
are written by members of the clergy but are taught by indigenous instructors, many of them urban Q'eqchi's who speak
Castilian and are often landless wage laborers. Those who have
been to Centro San Benito then teach the course in the parish, to
which catechists from the villages come every two to three
months. These catechists then take the message back to their
communities, where another course is held. By the time the
average villager hears the information, it is fourth hand. I
participated at each level of this process, and it is apparent that

the message becomes diluted, twisted, reformed, and rendered distinct from its original nature. The objective of this system is to ply the communities continually with Catholic doctrine. While it is generally effective, it also allows a great deal of catechist autonomy, which explains the degree of heterodoxy found "on the ground."

When the first catechists returned to their communities, most taught that the tzuultaq'as never existed and the old ways were misguided. Speaking about the first courses, Father Pacheco told me: "We started with a heavy emphasis on Christ to get rid of the [religious] syncretism. We taught the catechists to reject all that which doesn't coincide with the Gospel . . . and to hold on to and Christianize the rest."

The pamphlet for one course (*Xtenamitex li Dios,* "You Are the People of God") reads: "It is necessary that we [Q'eqchi's] reject fully the ways of our ancestors so that our lives bear fruit." The course portrayed the first evangelization in this way: "The priests taught the Maya that their gods had no power. There is only one Father, and that is the God our Father Jesus Christ." Christ was the standard-bearer of the catechists' religion, come to vanquish the previous gods. Whereas in the Andes, the mountains were Christianized early on through Christ apparitions on crags (Sallnow 1987:86), this did not occur in Alta Verapaz. The mountains are not associated with Christ in any way—only with the saints and the Virgin. Christ arrived in the 1970s as a substitute for the mountain spirits, to displace them rather than arrive at a syncretic compromise.

The courses targeted the mountain spirits and labeled them demonic. The priests especially discouraged sacrifices and rituals that involved alcohol consumption. The planting rituals were particularly offensive because they took place at Eastertime, competing with the Christian celebrations. Obviously, Jesus's death, burial, and regeneration fit well with agricultural symbolism. But the evangelizing Catholic church allowed no such concessions, as this catechist confirms: "We don't do any sacrifices any more as we're in the New Testament now. Jesus said that he's the only sacrifice, and the final one."

Regarding agricultural matters, the courses exposed cate-chists to cash-cropping and Western agricultural technology. The Church's orientation toward traditional religion was not forced on the catechists; they themselves helped to formulate it. One Q'eqchi' instructor defended the Church's position: "We taught them modern agricultural techniques. We failed some-what as we did not mention the ancient customs around the planting. But we couldn't have spoken of them, the catechists wouldn't have come to the courses." They yearned to learn more about the use of fertilizers and pesticides.

Agricultural "development" represented not only an attempt at economic betterment but also an attack on the tzuultaq'as at a more technical level. The cult of the tellurian divinity is based on subsistence agriculture, and the practice of cash-cropping excludes the tzuultaq'as. Thus, coffee and cardamom cultiva-tion and the ideology of development had an "elective affinity" with the religious discourse of orthodox Catholicism.

The degree to which catechists campaigned against the old ways depended on a number of sociological factors and individ-ual predispositions. I would estimate, very roughly, that during the 1970s and early 1980s, two-thirds of catechists followed an orthodox tendency and one third were more oriented toward traditionalism. The proportions were more balanced among noncatechist villagers.

Some parishes, such as those run by Salesians, were much more vociferous than others in their attack on "false gods." As a result, there was a certain degree of ecclesiastical pluralism, which catechists manipulated to legitimate a range of posi-tions. In one parish with an ultraorthodox priest, catechists who still practiced their planting rituals invoked the priest in an adjacent parish for validation. This latter priest had performed a mass and placed a cross in a cave shrine.

In the majority of villages, the catechists brought a radically new worldview and convinced the community to alter its behavior accordingly. In other areas, the catechists boycotted the customary practices and were left isolated with no following. Moreover, not all catechists accepted the orthodox campaign against the tzuultaq'as. Some attended the courses and listened attentively but paid no heed to the calls to Christianize religious practice. They attempted few changes in their communities and continued to perform the customs. One participant in the first courses told me, "Father Javier and the instructors didn't like Q'eqchi' customs. They pushed them to one side. They called them other gods, but their ideas weren't good. I still do my rituals."

CATECHISTS AND THE PLANTING

The discussion so far has been concerned with general changes at the level of discourse. To see how they have translated into alterations of concrete practice, let me reconsider the planting rituals. Planting is the maximum expression of the relationship between communities and the tzuultaq'as and offers the best insight into the cultural effects of the catechists.

I do not suggest that there is a clear, unilinear development from the traditionalists' customs to the catechists' doctrine. The processes run concomitantly and parallel, with a different balance of influences in each locality. There is an interplay of discourse and practice, with some elders taking on board the teachings of a more Roman Catholicism and some catechists adhering to their ancestors' ways. No neat fault line exists between traditional and Christianized planting methods.

At the level of overt discourse, traditional ideas hold little sway among the majority. Yet in practice, many elements of the planting rituals remain. Fasting and sexual abstinence are nearly universal. Catechists request license for cultivating the land, but from God, not the mountain spirit. Planters uphold many *awas* taboos, without actually calling them *awas*. Feasting continues in the same style—all eating at once, in a pervading atmosphere of silent shame.

Hot and cold distinctions operate in the catechists' planting. Planters offer *pom* and candles at various times. The heat level, however, is somewhat lower. The planters do not consume fiery fermented *b'oj*. There is no sacrifice of blood and flesh (both hot) to the earth. In the language of traditional symbolism, the catechists have had a cooling effect on agriculture. Yet they have introduced new types of hot elements, such as fertilizers and insecticides.

In sum, catechists continue much of the unspoken behavior of the elders without explicitly defining their reasons. This seems to be a pattern in catechist behavior—to continue using many elements of traditional rituals but to suppress the concomitant knowledge system. I am not sure whether some ritual acts are continued because of, or in spite of, the accompanying belief system. My intuition is that the catechists continue such customs as abstinence and fasting because they have not escaped the traditional motivations—that it is "dirty" and a sin to have sex because you are offending the corn and the mountain. It should be taken into account that the mountain cult has been developing in the context of universalist discourses for more than 450 years. Given that tzuultaq'as have been underground figures for so long, a disarticulation of explicit knowledge and practice is to be expected.

In explaining traditional ritual knowledge, catechists are much more likely to say "It's the custom" than an elder is. Mature catechists aged thirty to forty years understand the knowledge that underlies ritual, yet they suppress it, preferring not to give a detailed rationale. For younger catechists, the acquisition of local knowledge has been halted in its most critical stage by the catechist program. Young men, in gaining orthodox Biblical knowledge, relinquish the chance to learn the religious knowledge of their communities. The catechists practice remnants of rituals that survive as a legacy of the past, without understanding why. It is ironic that this is exactly what the catechists accused the elders of doing when they took part in the mass without having read the Bible.

The attitude of the clergy was a major factor affecting the survival of particular practices. Priests campaigned against only certain aspects of the tradition. This determined more than anything else what the catechists would extirpate and what they would tolerate. The clergy did not pull up belief in the tzuultaq'as by the roots; rather, they pruned its ramifications, such as the use of blood in rituals.

Cave sacrifice has been one of the customs hardest hit. Priests and nuns seized upon it as the most offensive of the "pagan" conventions, to be stamped out immediately. It was important that the priests actually prioritize an act for it to be campaigned against in the villages. This is perhaps one of the reasons why ideas like the food *awas* and sexual abstinence continued. The priests did not mention them directly as un-Christian; indeed, they probably did not even know about them. In general, the clergy's ignorance of traditional community practices is profound. I know of only one priest who has ever planted with Q'eqchi's. This nescience, like the incompetence of the state educational system, aids the survival of community traditions.

Local translations of catechist doctrine provide insights into the concrete processes of religious syncretism. In the planting vigil, catechists still refer to the seed as "being born," but they also perform rosaries during the night. Many continue the grab crop ritual but direct it to God, not the mountain spirit. A "civilized" God is offered cooked food, but not raw meat.

One planting taboo that has broken down almost completely is the prohibition on drinking coffee. Traditionally, coffee drinking would have led to the coffee *awas,* an expression of the opposition between subsistence cultivation and agroexport agriculture. Before the catechists and development initiatives of the 1970s, cash-cropping was not widespread. Coffee was produced only on the vast plantations, to which Q'eqchi' land and labor were easy prey. It is not surprising that this division has been bridged now that catechists have embraced coffee production for the market.

As I mentioned earlier, labor recruitment in the planting defines communal and ethnic boundaries, but religious conversions create new criteria for community labor pools. The ethnic boundary between Q'eqchi's and Ladinos remains, but a new intracommunal pluralism has developed through religious conversions. In some communities there are three separate pools of labor—the traditionalists, the catechists, and the evangelicals—where before there was only one. Religious affiliation, cutting across communities, has become as salient a basis of labor reciprocity as community.

CATECHISTS AND ILLNESS

The catechist program accepted traditional medicine much more readily than it did the cult of the mountain spirit. Healing methods weathered the catechist storm in part because the priests did not denounce them as backward or pagan. Q'eqchi' health care methods are even more obscure to the clergy than is the tzuultaq'a cult. Health care is not considered to be an aspect of religion by the priests, perhaps because they subscribe to a

Western dichotomy between the two. In the indigenous view, the two are undoubtedly interlinked.

In the early 1970s, the diocese started a health care program to parallel village structures. Owing to poor state health care provision in rural areas, the Catholic church set about creating an infrastructure to meet basic needs. This is the main channel for Western health care methods into the villages. Often the catechist is also his community's health promoter. Each parish coordinates courses in which the promoters learn about hygiene, first aid, giving injections, and taking blood samples to test for malaria. The Catholic health promoters are the basis for an international antimalaria program.

Catholic health intiatives did not supplant the traditional methods; rather, the two exist side by side. There is some competition, but cohabitation is the norm. Health promoters accept the *aj ilonel* (and may, indeed, be the *aj ilonel*) as legitimate, and vice versa. Catechists and promoters send their own families to see the curers to be diagnosed and cured through prayer, rituals, and herbs. Ultimately, the scarcity and high price of medicines weigh in favor of the village *aj ilonel*.

Patients accept both paradigms of classification and diagnosis of disease. For instance, people are willing to believe that an infection on the head is caused by bacteria and could also be avocado *awas*. All pharmaceutical pills, whether vitamins or antibiotics, are classed as hot or cold and must be taken in conjunction with the correct hot or cold foods. If a person is suffering from fever and is given an aspirin, it is assumed that it is a cold medicine. This is exactly the same principle on which traditional herbs and remedies are administered. Yet the *aj ilonel* is inclined to draw a sharper distinction between Western and traditional health care methods than does the promoter (especially when *the aj ilonel* is not a catechist or promoter). Spirit loss, says the *aj ilonel,* is uncurable by Western methods.

A Catholic health promoter teaches the scientific version of conception.

Traditional health care is facilitated by the fact that women play a larger role in curing than they do in subsistence crop production. This practice has insulated traditional beliefs because women are not as integrated as men into Church structures. Women are ultimately in charge of their children's well-being and are inclined to treat illnesses in the time-honored way. In a sense, pregnancy and infant health care constitute a semi-autonomous sphere of female control, partially isolated from men. Ideas of hot and cold in pregnancy firmly apply, and the expectant mother is treated with extreme care and reserve. Mothers continue to treat *awas* illnesses in children, and nearly all catechists I talked to still believed in this paradigm of disease.

Male catechists and health promoters have more success

with men than with women. There are many reasons why
women are less convinced by their ideas. There is a rigid
division of labor and segregation of the sexes, so non-kin men
have little chance to talk at length with women. Women's work
and social interaction are complementary but partly self-regu-
lated in relation to men. Historically, women have been less
exposed than men to urban and orthodox Catholic ideas and
education, and a higher percentage of women are monolingual.
They visit the towns and capital less frequently. It can be
concluded that the experiences of the two genders cause them
to assimilate orthodoxy at different rates. Gender boundaries
have meant that efforts to "modernize" traditional ways have
had an uneven, variegated impact. There are parallels here with
Andean history. In Irene Silverblatt's (1987) account, women
led Andean cultural resistance because men were the main
targets of the priests' efforts to stamp out "idolatry."

One area of health care that catechists find problematical is
spirit loss, especially the idea that a tzuultaq'a has captured the
spirit and expects an offering of *pom* in the shape of a human
being. In the past, the clergy has campaigned heavily against
witches. The use of fingernails, hair, and figurines in calling the
spirit back looks too much like witchcraft for the promoters.
Again, it is the elements that appear pagan in the eyes of the
orthodoxy that are crusaded against in the villages. Even
though many catechists may refuse to call a lost spirit, this has
had little effect because a large percentage of callers of the spirit
(*aj boqonel*) are women.

The perseverance of prior health care beliefs is a widespread
pattern in religious conversion. Redfield (1950:122) writes that
Protestant converts in Chan Kom rejected all manifestations of
Catholicism, yet continued to receive medical treatment from
the *h-men*, the Catholic ritual specialist and shaman. The
founding Protestant evangelist in Guatemala, Cameron Town-

send, found healing practices one of the most resilient areas of traditional belief. To his dismay, one of his leading Mayan evangelists set himself up as a folk healer with a Spanish edition of the Bible as his household altar (Stoll 1982:32).

The catechists are also trained to "cure" with the Bible, laying it over a patient as they incant Catholic prayers. The Bible is an effective curative symbol in a sense similar to that of the mountain spirit. Both are images of community that operate inside the personal boundaries of its sick members.

ETHNIC IDENTITY AND CATHOLIC ORTHODOXY

Overall, the catechist program has introduced elements from Ladino society into community cultures and launched a sea change in identity, just as the first evangelization changed traditional self-identification from "person" (*poyonam*) to "Christian" (*kristian*).

When questioned about the traditional customs, some catechists told me, "No, that's what our ancestors the Mayas believed." They consigned what was really the knowledge of their parents and grandparents to the status of ancient history. They would say of ritual knowledge, and especially of blood sacrifices, "That is stuff from the Old Testament, we don't do that anymore." If someone admits adhering to the mountain cult, they may call him, pejoratively, *Ch'ol wiinq,* meaning in this context "wild man," "Maya," or "jungle man." In using the term "Maya," they are distancing themselves from traditional religion and constructing a new, ultra-Christian, "civilized" identity. With their sights set upon a Ladino model of orthodoxy, the catechists reject an aspect of their Q'eqchi'-ness as savage and wild.

As I described in chapter three, a tzuultaq'a can appear as an ancient Maya, and its followers are seen to belong to the same category. The orthodox catechists distinguish themselves from other communities that still adhere to the old customs by calling them Mayas. Just as diversity in the earth cult was part of the construction of community identity, so communities now distinguish themselves according to the degree of their adherence to orthodox Catholicism.

Warren (1978:94) reports that the ideology of Kaqchikel catechists "proposes ladinoization as a means to achieving social and economic equivalence of Indians and Ladinos." Falla (1978:545) came to a similar conclusion about the program in Quiché, but there the impact on ethnicity was more accentuated. Catechist services were conducted only in Castilian, and the whole ideology of "development" was more widespread and well funded. In both Quiché and Alta Verapaz, however, catechists attacked traditional values and exalted in their place ones drawn from the dominant Ladino culture. To quote Carmack (1979:384), writing about catechists in Quiché: "Becoming a better Catholic meant the complete or partial abandonment of the whole world view, which also included the traditional agricultural methods."

Whether implicitly or explicitly, Catholic clergy and catechists used Ladino society as their model in reforming community culture. Catechists championed the national educational system, an institution that has, historically, imposed state ideology and Ladino-style socialization. State schools are a primary mechanism for extending the range of Castilian in the indigenous communities. The catechists also advocated economic motivations better suited to petty capitalists than to shifting cultivators. Previous mechanisms for marking ethnic boundaries have collapsed—for example, the export crop coffee is now drunk during many staple crop rituals. Catechists seek to further integrate community into the national and international market. They encourage the incorporation of Q'eqchi's into national society as voting citizens who participate in the legal system. The decimation of the *cofrades* was an essential stage in the assimilation of Q'eqchi's as national citizens. These pillars of community religious and political authority were created in the context of historical exclusion from Hispanic/Ladino national politics.

On the other hand, the catechist program has not always promoted a blind process of Ladinoization. It is possible for Mayas to take up Ladinolike activities without becoming identified as Ladinos; this is simply a matter of broadening the horizons of local identity (Watanabe 1992:219). Generally, the catechist program did not make Ladinos of the catechists but created a new, liminal ethnic identity. As van den Berghe and Colby put it (1977:115): "The position of the catechists is intermediate between the rest of the indigenous people and the Ladinos." Brintnall (1979:148) argues that the catechist program has been a source of "new Indian pride" and a forum for resisting Ladino domination. Among the Q'eqchi's as well, the assuming of Ladinolike attributes has been partial and focused only on certain aspects of local identity. Indigenous language, dress, and music continue to be highly valued. Some traditional touchstones of identity endure, as ethnic and community boundaries are maintained at certain critical points. Labor reciprocity during planting, for instance, continues to be practiced by members of the same community.

CONCLUSIONS

Catechists are willing agents of the institutional Church, expounding its orthodox discourse in their villages. One effect of their preaching has been to reduce heterodoxy, channeling local practice closer to that of universal Catholicism. As Weber (1952:336) argued, any religion must be universal to an extent for the hierarchy to maintain control. He argued that priests were the bearers of a cosmological systematization that "favored the primacy of universal gods" (1965:22). This means that peripheral cults, such as those centered on the saints or the local landscape, must be sloughed off—a ubiquitous process in Christianity and other world religions. Vatican II and the formation of base communities in Latin America provided the premises and instruments for this endeavor. Through the base communities, parishes achieved a revolution in the balance of power between generations, a shift in the basis of legitimacy of village ritual specialists, and the introduction of new religious and economic ethics. World religions, especially Christianity and Islam, have played a central role throughout history in undermining local bases of identification (such as community and ethnicity) in order to enhance their own universalist interests.[7]

Catechist activity affected the *cofrades* and the saint cults more than it affected rituals associated with the mountain spirit. At the level of village religious life, the catechists were more successful at extirpating elements of traditional Catholicism than at severing ties to the sacred landscape. There is a parallel here in Redfield's (1941:235) study of Protestantism in Yucatec villages, where evangelicals focused their antagonism against features of folk Catholicism (especially the saints) more than against "paganism." Yet I would urge caution in generalizing these findings too far, since Watanabe (1992:185) asserts that in Santiago Chimaltenango just the opposite occurred: the "cult of the soul" (including the mountain cult) has undergone more changes than the "cult of the community" (or civil-religious hierarchy).

By suppressing the earth cult, the catechist program had a sweeping impact on how villagers imagined their community. The ties linking all communities to one or two mountains became frayed (but not cut). The dreams of the elders that channeled the messages of the mountain spirits no longer provided the basis for a gerontocratic political system. The crushing of the gerontocracy and its replacement with externally legitimated authority meant that villagers looked more than ever to the outside world for the creation of community leadership.

The old ways of thinking about the community gave way to new ones, such as those based on the Bible as the "centerpole" of the community. The base group could not, however, claim to represent the whole community in all instances, as the *cofradía* did. Instead, it had to compete with secular state institutions such as the betterment committee and other religious groupings like the evangelicals and remnants of the *cofradía*.

New bases for association now preclude a single image of community. The traditional imagining of the community was based upon an unchallenged unity. Of course there were factions and dissent within the precatechist community, but these operated within a shared discourse and a single set of institutions. The catechists rent this unity asunder by changing the frame of the discourse and exalting another way of imagining community. Now there is a plurality of discourses and institutions, both religious and secular, that compete for hegemony. Religious pluralism has created communities within communities. The mountain spirit, previously a main focus for sociological tensions, became a totemic sign for just one of the competing groups. All told, this signifies the demise of traditional ways of apprehending the world.

It is hard to overemphasize the impact on identity of translating Catholic rituals and doctrines into Q'eqchi'. Anderson (1991:36) writes of how it is only possible to imagine the nation once particular conceptions lose their grip on people's minds, especially the idea that a particular script or language (e.g., Latin) offers a privileged access to truth because it is part of that ontological truth. Before the catechist program, the only languages suitable for interaction with God were Castilian and Latin. That their Mayan language could also be a language of truth meant it was now possible to begin thinking of Q'eqchi' as a unifying basis for an identity beyond that of the village.

Anderson (1991:115) discusses how pilgrimage is a vital element in the construction of an imagined identity, whether sacred or national. The catechists' meetings in Cobán set a precedent by being the first assemblies ever of village representatives from all over the Q'eqchi' linguistic area. The catechists became the pilgrims of a new type of sacred community.

As they discussed issues of common interest, the catechists constituted a parliament of deputies, the first modern Q'eqchi' intelligentsia. According to Gramsci (1971:103–104), for ideological hegemony to assert itself in a society, it must operate in a dual manner: as a "general conception of life" for the average person and as a "scholastic programme" or set of principles propounded by a sector of the intellectuals. As literate, self-reflexive cultural agents, the catechists are certainly the scholars of their communities and ethnic group.

Differing from Anderson's account of the demolition of the sacred imagined community that necessarily preceded secular nationalism, Q'eqchi' catechists replaced an insular sacred community (the *cofradía*) with a more universal one, the Catholic base group. Although one paradigm of organization replaced another, religion is still the sacred ground on which the community is imagined. Community identity thus ceased to be a closed shop and began to incorporate principles of universality and accept a wider basis of association than just the community. This created the necessary preconditions for the development of a class-based identity.

I would not like to overemphasize the degree to which the catechists rejected their traditional community religion and culture. In assessing the multiplicity of local effects of the catechist program, one should hold in mind the continuities that bridge the seemingly radical cultural discontinuities. Although drastic at certain junctures, religious change can also be seen as occurring along a continuum. No village is isolated from its neighbors, and in any one region there is a spectrum of competing discourses. Warren (1993:51, n. 7) has reassessed the impact of the catechist movement in a Kaqchikel community, writing, "Catholic Action's rhetoric was oppositional, whereas in practice its relationship with the civil-religious hierarchy was a complex pattern of negotiation, appropriation, resistance and reconciliation." If a complete cultural break had occurred, it would be impossible to explain the cultural content of the new ethnic resurgence among catechists.

In the context of certain continuities in practice and belief, the catechists introduced a fundamentally new way of apprehending the world that made it possible to imagine wider frames of reference such as class and the "pan-Q'eqchi' community." The next chapter deals with another process that has markedly affected the community—rural repression. These two events, the catechist program and the civil war, form the historical backdrop for a new indigenist movement, the subject of the penultimate chapter.

CHAPTER SEVEN

SURVIVING STATE TERROR

Any discussion of religious change and transformations of Q'eqchi' identities must include the political violence that the indigenous population has suffered at the hands of the Guatemalan army. The repression of the early 1980s was massive and wide-ranging, leading to physical displacement and cultural dislocation for those who survived. Q'eqchi's had previously known two historical events that had so profoundly affected them: the Spanish invasion and their dispossession of communal lands at the end of the nineteenth century. Judging from historical sources, the military massacres of the 1980s have been worse than those during the sixteenth century.[1]

Historically, anthropology has ignored the harsh realities of modern wars among the people being "anthropologized." The bulk of ethnographies that do consider warfare have tended to offer structural-functionalist analyses of intertribal feuding. The increased influence of Marxism on the discipline enhanced the study of armed conflict, but this time the emphasis was on colonialism and emerging nationalist republics. Anthropologists have been very slow to address armed confrontation between the modern nation-state and subnational social groups. Outside of Latin America, there have been some notable exceptions,[2] but the historical tendency is clear: most anthropologists have discreetly avoided serious investigation of modern warfare. They have gone the way of Evans-Pritchard, who, as he wrote about how much the Nuer loved their cows, neglected to mention that the government of Anglo-Egyptian Sudan bombed Nuer herds in the hope of subduing that recalcitrant colonial population. Evans-Pritchard made only a cursory reference to these issues in his introduction to *The Nuer* (1940:11), when an informant remarked, "You [the British] raid us, yet you say we cannot raid the Dinka."

Anthropologists working in Guatemala have responded to the country's crisis with remarkable degrees of both practical campaigning and insightful scholarly analysis.[3] I would like to see this chapter as a contribution to the growing literature on state terror against Guatemalan peoples. There have been no publications on Q'eqchi' experiences of scorched earth policies because most anthropologists have worked in the western highlands. Nor have previous studies focused in detail on the effects of violence on indigenous relations with the sacred landscape.

Researching themes of political violence and personal loss was a fraught and disturbing experience. It was here that my research methods were most adversely affected, for many refugee communities were severely controlled by the military and village civil patrols. I could not stay for any length of time in these villages but had to pass through them quickly, stopping for only a few days. My first tentative broaching of the subject aroused little response; as Kay Warren (1993:32) observes, the first legacy of the violence was silence. Once people did begin to speak, it was hard to know how to respond to emotional accounts of hardship and profound grief. People had few opportunities to publicly and verbally express their restrained feelings about the political violence, and my presence as a listener served as a channel for their catharsis. This line of research, which occupied my last months in the field, was cut short when my own brother died suddenly in a motorcycle accident in August 1988. After the funeral, I returned to Guatemala, but I could no longer tolerate refugees' wrenching accounts of loss and separation. Once I realized that I was no longer an effective ethnographer, I decided to return to England.

REVOLUTIONARY ORGANIZATIONS
IN ALTA VERAPAZ

After the overwhelming defeat of the guerrilla movement of the 1960s, the survivors began to organize among indigenous peoples of the western highlands. These revolutionaries were mostly Ladinos, either university students or disaffected army officers. The rebels did not at first consider the Q'eqchi's to be good "revolutionary material." The guerrilla leader Mario Payeras (1983:39–40) wrote: "We began hearing the Kekchi dialect and discovering the taciturnity of the people. . . . We were very suspicious of the silence that prevailed and the indifference of the inhabitants." Guerrilla organizing focused on the Mam, Ixil, K'iche', and other groups, with whom it had more success.

Revolutionary organizations in Alta Verapaz did not develop into a significant force until the early 1980s. The Guerrilla Army of the Poor (EGP), largest of the four rebel groups, had a presence in the south in Cobán and to the west in Chamá, Salaquím, and Chisec (see map 2). The Rebel Armed Forces (FAR) operated in the north of the department, in the Petén, and in Las Minas mountain range. The Guatemalan Communist Party (PGT) was also active in the eastern part of Q'eqchi' territory.

The rebels did not lay their foundation in Alta Verapaz but moved into the area once they had built up their forces in the western highlands. According to the Washington Office on Latin America (WOLA 1988:83), the EGP did not enter the area of San Cristóbal until late 1981, and "most spoke Ixil, but others were from the area; some were Indians and some were Ladinos." The guerrillas consolidated one of their strongest bases of operations in the area extending from San Cristóbal up to Chamá on the Chixoy river and across to Cobán.

One reason Q'eqchi's did not quickly join the ranks of the guerrillas was that there had historically been very little political or development activity in Alta Verapaz. Q'eqchi' villages were generally rather insular and inward looking, and their strong community identity obstructed wider bases of association. In other parts of the highlands, development initiatives, trade unions, and political parties had heightened indigenous people's awareness of their low economic and social status in the national society.[4] In Quiché, cooperatives flourished during the 1960s, creating links between communities and an infrastructure of indigenous economic self-organization. This process evolved alongside peasant leagues and trade unions that challenged landowner political hegemony. In addition, the "green revolution" enhanced smallholder self-sufficiency to the point where there was a labor shortage on Guatemala's exporting plantations during the late 1970s (C. Smith 1984:217–19).

By the late 1970s, the limits of development were reached as state and local elites began to assassinate community leaders. Jim Handy (1983:244) reports the death of 168 cooperative leaders between 1976 and 1978 in Quiché. Under such conditions it is not surprising that the ranks of the guerrillas grew. Development did not lead to an insurrection in Guatemala, but violent repression of development engendered support for an insurgency.

No such process of political radicalization through development organizations took place in Alta Verapaz. International

development agencies passed over the isolated Q'eqchi' territory in favor of groups with better access to major roads and
markets. The Catholic church was the only nongovernmental
organization in the region that coordinated widespread projects
concerned with education, health care, and agronomy. Yet the
diocese of the Verapaces did not support the creation of cooperatives on the same scale as those found in Quiché. Cooperatives
had already been formed by the government in many Q'eqchi'
areas but were mainly plantations expropriated from German
landowners. Being government run meant that they were often
managed by corrupt officials appointed as political favors.

Opposition political parties had only a weak presence in
Alta Verapaz. Those that did operate were parties of the landowners and urban Ladinos; they did not incorporate the indigenous majority. Trade unions had not organized among rural
workers. Since Q'eqchi's did not participate in mass seasonal
labor migrations to the coasts to the extent that other groups
did, they were not exposed to union activity there either. Trade
unions existed only in the two proletarian centers of the region—the Chixoy hydroelectric project and the copper mines
of the Polochic valley. Q'eqchi's worked in both, but many other
workers were Ladinos brought in from distant parts. The national peasant trade union, CUC (Comité de Unidad Campesina), had a foothold in the municipality of San Cristóbal,
where it began operations in 1980. The CUC had other bases,
but these were not consolidated. There was little established
organization before towns and villages were razed by the army.

After a time, the insurgent groups did successfully recruit
some members. It is difficult, especially many years later, to
assess the degree of their support. David Stoll (1993) argues
that support for the guerrillas in the Ixil triangle has been
overstated and asserts that most villagers' support for the rebels
resulted from their being caught between two armies. He

rightly questions the concept of resistance as a master trope for explaining how Guatemalans responded to insurgency and counterinsurgency. His view is echoed in Ignacio Bizarro's account of the war in the Tzutuhil area (Sexton 1992). In many communities in Alta Verapaz, there were those who either did not support the guerrillas or only threw their lot in with them as a temporary survival strategy. Yet it is undisputable that in large areas, the rebels operated within an infrastructure of solid support. Few of the sympathizers, however, actually became active combatants. As one source told me, "In terms of organization, they had a great deal, in terms of guns they hardly had any."

Initially, the main reasons for some campesinos' joining the ranks were related to the land. The vast majority of Q'eqchi's did not own their parcels, and the guerrillas promised that after the revolution there would be enough land for all. At the time, many communities lived as *mozos* on coffee, cardamom, and cattle plantations. Although organizing was difficult because of the landowner's authoritarian rule, many plantation workers came to sympathize with the revolutionaries. Living conditions on the haciendas were dire. The boss or his foreman controlled various aspects of Q'eqchi' life, making decisions over working practices, religious events, and education. A strong paternalistic element pervaded landowner-*mozo* relations. The owner was godfather to the indigenous children and the distributor of Western medicines in his capacity as local "doctor." He also had civilian obligations such as registering births and deaths in the municipality. The landowner granted permission for any local initiatives and could block, say, the construction of a school.

Economic exploitation was hidden behind a plethora of social relations, yet the reality of poverty ultimately left few mystified. One informant told me why he became a non-armed supporter of the EGP: "The problems started on the plantations because the landowners were looking for trouble. All the men and boys had to work for twelve days per month, come whatever. If you were ill, you had to work all the same. There was no pay, but we had permission to plant our own crops on *hacienda* land. Life was not sweet."

Other communities inhabited *baldío,* or untitled land. The territories had either been vacated when the German landowners were expelled in the 1940s, or they were primary forest, uninhabited since their prior occupants (Acalás, Ch'ols, or Lacandóns) had been brought to the Spanish towns in the sixteenth century. In either case, the villages paid INTA, the national government land ministry, for their land titles. The guerrillas urged nonpayment of these burdensome sums, and so won some support. One villager described the situation in Cahabón: "A brother came from outside and began talking to us and convinced some eight catechists. They said that the land should be held in common and that we should not pay INTA, because we paid for the land all those years that we worked for nothing for the plantation owner. Others wanted to pay for the land, and for each to have individual parcels."

In the 1970s, economic circumstances in Q'eqchi' communities were complex and changing quickly. Most smallholders and plantation workers were desperately poor. Yet Catholic development efforts and increased cash-cropping generated a new stratum of rural entrepreneurs. They rode the crest of increasing commodity prices for cardamom and coffee, and villages became more economically stratified. The majority of wealthier villagers came from the ranks of catechists, who were often among the first to identify with economic and social change. Informants repeatedly claimed that the catechists were the first to join the rebel forces.

Initially, at least, the guerrillas drew support not from the poorest sectors of the rural population but from Wolf's (1969: 291) "middle peasantry." Wolf comments (1969:xv) that tensions mount toward rebellion, and involvement in revolution grows, during the transformation from subsistence cultivator to maximizing capitalist farmer. This generalization fits the situation in Guatemala and the rest of Central America in the mid to late 1970s. The 1973 oil embargo led to a worldwide recession, an increase in the price of fertilizers, and a drop in commodity prices. Many middle peasants lost their capital, sank deep into debt, and, as Arturo Arias (1990:240) writes, experienced "sudden unexpected misery."

Catechist participation in the revolutionary organizations was prevalent across the whole of Guatemala. Lay activists were at the forefront of what Shelton Davis (1988:20) calls "a generalized social and political mobilization . . . in the Guatemalan highlands." Indigenous rebellion cannot be explained by purely economistic and "structural" factors. One exiled missionary offered a more idealistic explanation: "It wasn't just a matter of picking up guns for economic gain, for land. It was a religious and spiritual conversion that led to self-organization of the people . . . a complete change of life." Her view was that the catechist program and subsequent religious change in the communities had provided the necessary basis for political self-determination.

The two interpretations are compatible; most Q'eqchi's' material conditions were desperate, and the spiritual revitalization introduced by the catechists facilitated a radicalization of the villagers' political vision. In Marxist terminology, the catechists provided the subjective conditions in which a revolutionary situation could escalate. As old gods such as the mountain spirits were discarded, the tenets of the whole worldview were destabilized, especially those concerning political authority. If the mountain spirits were authority figures, some of whose characteristics were akin to those of the plantation owners, then the catechists' revolt against the authority of the tzuultaq'as likewise subverted their attitudes toward plantation owners and governmental authority.[5]

By combining a radical social message with the promise of a future religious golden age, the revolutionary war took on a millenarian mantle. James Scott (1977a:232) writes that "wars, plagues, revolutions, earthquakes . . . appear to destroy the normal categories in which reality is apprehended . . . and thereby provide the social soil for latent millennial beliefs to become manifest." The civil war certainly cultivated millenarian catechists, as did the 1976 earthquake that devastated the highlands, killing 25,000 people. The earthquake was deemed by many commentators to be a crucial factor in the development of a popular movement in Guatemala (Black 1984:101; Handy 1984:174).

Issues of social change were analyzed from a distinctly religious orientation, the villagers' actions being legitimated more in terms of the prophet Isaiah than of Marx. Catechists used the discourse of liberation theology, calling for the creation of the "Kingdom of God on Earth." Revolutionary organizations simply could not have recruited a significant number of Q'eqchi's had it not been for the catechists. Their role was critical not only because they were village leaders but also because they could translate the doctrine of political revolution into understandable local terms. The guerrillas' class analysis was retranslated into community ideology. Catechists spoke of the community versus particular landowners, or the community versus the local Ladinos and merchants, or the community versus the local Q'eqchi' representatives of the military. I never came across anyone who had ever thought he or she was fighting "the Guatemalan ruling class" or "the state." Perhaps this was a central weakness of the rebellion. Carol Smith (1990a:225) writes that the 1970s rebellion had little chance of becoming a successful liberation struggle because indigenous resistance developed in a primarily community-specific rather than a unified way. Just as in the localized rebellions of 1944, insurrection exploded at the community level; as Richard Adams (1990:157) writes, there was no "nationwide" identity that unified indigenous communities.

Many of the guerrillas from Quiché had been catechists and shared a common discourse with Q'eqchi' lay activists. In this way the catechist program in the highlands helped to bridge ethnic and linguistic divides among the twenty-two groups of Mayan descent. The catechists' role was analogous to that played by the Shona spirit mediums in David Lan's (1985) account of Zimbabwe's war of national liberation. Yet unlike the spirit mediums, the catechists embraced the values and religion of their nonindigenous opponents. Their creation of a new order involved rejecting, not exalting, the old ways.

In several parishes, the teachings of the clergy tended toward liberation theology, predisposing the catechists to the revolutionary groups. In a few places, the clergy actively endorsed their congregations' decision to support the insurgents. These were rare occurrences, however, and the majority of the missionaries took a neutral stand in the war. Others, such as the Salesian priests in Carchá, campaigned against the guerrillas, forbidding "their" catechists to join them.

The parish's position was not always a determining factor in guerrilla recruitment. In Cahabón, some catechists split with their spiritualist and conservative parish priest to form their own church. One informant related how they broke with the parish: "In 1981, the eight catechists who did not want to pay [INTA] for the land formed their own church. They had their own committee and ran their own courses. They were angry with the priest because they said that all he wanted to do was pray."

We should accord substantial weight to these subjective

factors in explaining rural rebellion in Guatemala. Class relations were important but were not a wholly determining factor,
since both landless hacienda workers and independent smallholders rebelled alike. Scott (1977b) has argued that isolated
smallholders are more likely to rebel, whereas Jeffrey Paige
(1975:42) sees landless rural laborers as being more disposed
toward revolutionary discontent. Peruvianists such as Henri
Favre (1984) have maintained that the core of Sendero Lumi-
noso activists are drawn from a "de-peasantized" class of people
who are alienated from their peasant economy and community.
Initially, this was the case for the Guatemalan revolutionary
movement, too, which drew its strength from western highland
communities that were fast becoming rural proletarians, on the
one hand, and petty capitalists, on the other. Yet once the
guerrillas gathered momentum, they gained support from
Q'eqchi's of a variety of economic strata. Perhaps we can
conclude from this, as Theda Skocpol (1979:115) has, that
political context is more important in determining rural rebellion than are particular economic conditions.

By 1982, the guerrillas were active in a large part of rural
Alta Verapaz. They harassed the army and killed local military
commissioners and auxiliary mayors. Oil production was severely disrupted as guerrillas sabotaged the pipeline that runs
along the Northern Transversal Strip. On September 15, 1981—
Independence Day—bombs exploded in three local military
reserve bases. The rebels used classic guerrilla tactics, and it
was nearly impossible for the army to catch them. Few large-
scale battles ever took place. To my knowledge, there were only
two lengthy engagements with heavy casualties around Salaquím and Chamá. When the army found it could not defeat the
insurgents in a conventional war, it turned its vehemence on the
rural civilian population. In the end, the villagers suffered far
higher losses of life than the armed combatants. This was the

most significant factor of all those that led Q'eqchi' communities to join the guerrillas.

ARMY REPRESSION

*They [Ladinos and Mayan peoples] are, thus,
locked in a fear-ridden embrace from which neither
can easily escape, and hence are captors of each
other.* —Richard N. Adams, "Ethnic Images and
Strategies in 1944"

The army reacted to its recurrent nightmare, loss of control in
the indigenous rural areas, with a level of violence unprecedented in the history of Guatemala. As many have noted
(Warren 1993:26), the war had powerful ethnic overtones; it
was an explosion of deep-seated national racism.

The ethnic hierarchy and structure of the army offers some
clues as to how a Ladino-dominated state can use a multiethnic
army to repress an indigenous majority. Crack troops are
mostly Ladinos and are depended upon for vital operations. The
infantry is headed by Ladino officers, but the rank-and-file
troops are mostly indigenous. Indigenous soldiers are generally
recruited by forced conscription and then stationed in an area
outside the domain of their ethnic group.

There is a great need for someone, perhaps through autobiographies, to document the process by which Guatemalan
Maya men are trained to become soldiers. The anthropology of
the army in Latin America is of the highest priority. In Guatemala and other strongly multiethnic countries, this would
entail documenting the army's discourse on terror and understanding the process of recruitment whereby young men are
turned into directed killers who then slaughter their own
communities. I talked to a few Q'eqchi' ex-soldiers who told me
fragments of stories about their role in massacres and how they
ate raw dog's hearts in training and so on. Yet I never established

a sufficiently long-term relationship with an ex-soldier to warrant writing in any depth about Q'eqchi' men's experiences in the army.

State terror began before the revolutionary organizations had established a presence in Alta Verapaz. In 1978, the Q'eqchi's suffered their first massacre of this latest cycle of violence when over a hundred villagers were killed in the central square in Panzós. Unarmed smallholders were coming to lobby the mayor about their petition for land when local landowners and soldiers opened fire on the crowd from the rooftops. The parish priest of Panzós at the time disclosed how the army had bulldozed mass graves three days earlier.

Such massacres became systematic government policy in the highlands from 1981 until late 1983, resulting in massive displacements of the population. AVANCSO (1990:11) reports that 80 percent of the inhabitants of the departments of Quiché, Huehuetenango, Chimaltenango, and Alta Verapaz abandoned their homes at least temporarily during 1981–82. Villagers did not have to be suspected of sympathizing with guerrillas to be attacked; the plan was to terrorize the entire indigenous population and separate it from guerrilla troops. Villages with developed local institutions such as cooperatives or schools were especially targeted in what one missionary described as "the army's 'preventative' measures." The army believed that such villages had the potential to become sympathetic to the revolutionaries, and this was enough to warrant their destruction. In its raids, the army set fire to houses, burned or cut down crops, and killed livestock. Survivors of massacres were then concentrated in towns where soldiers could control them more easily. The army created a no-man's-land, depopulated and devoid of crops and domestic animals, between militarized towns and the guerrillas' jungle.[6]

Massacres of Q'eqchi' communities began in 1981 in Chisec

and to the west of Cobán. WOLA reported (1988:73) that seven thousand refugees were held at the airstrip outside Cobán between September 1981 and March 1982. Operations then intensified to the west of Cobán. The majority of the villages between Cobán and Chamá were destroyed.[7] In some cases, their inhabitants were massacred; in others, the people had already fled to the jungle.

The government offensive then turned against the villages to the north of Chamá, which were mostly on *baldío* lands.[8] At the invitation of the landowners, the army used plantations such as Rosario and Esperanza as bases for their military operations. The landowners' complicity in the rural repression was more than passive support. They provided vital intelligence on guerrilla movements and sympathizers, giving lists of suspects' names to the army. Landowners settled old scores against recalcitrant workers. In the case of the plantation La Libertad, the *mozos* left the plantation to settle nearby forests. The incensed landowner denounced them as guerrillas to the military base. Soldiers arrived and tied fifteen men from the village to tree trunks and threw them into the river to drown.

In all, the Catholic diocese estimates that roughly ninety to one hundred Q'eqchi' villages were destroyed in Alta Verapaz.[9] Selective repression against individuals took place in hundreds of villages. This process had already begun in 1979–80, before the scorched earth methods became a generalized policy. Often only the lay activists were singled out. One catechist told me, "I was one of the first catechists in Chisec but all of them were killed in the years of violence. I only know of a couple who survived like me."

REPRESSION AND THE CHURCH

In the majority of rural villages of Cobán and Chisec, the weekly meeting of the Word of God was abandoned. To be involved in the Catholic base group was to be suspected of being a guerrilla. People feared to come together under any conditions. One villager remembered, "Our head catechist was killed and the rest fled. The meetings stopped for a year and then began again in 1983, with all new catechists. Some said that the army would come after us again. They said that we Catholics had started all the problems."

In areas that gave passive support to the armed struggle, catechists were among the first to supply food to the revolutionaries. The military were aware of this and extended their categorization of "revolutionary" to include all lay activists. The reality was that the majority of catechists were and are reformist in political orientation. Yet in such a polarized body politic as Guatemala, even a mildly reformist stance is interpreted as revolutionary by a ruthless and paranoid Ladino elite. One catechist remembered, "We spoke of the poor and how we have to share so people do not go without. The whole problem started over the Word of God, because we spoke the truth and how we will create the Kingdom of God here on earth. So we helped people, planted the crops of widows, and they called us guerrillas, but we weren't."

From the late 1970s on, members of the clergy continually received death threats. None were killed in Alta Verapaz, but the army kidnapped several and later released them. A few were officially expelled from the country, and others sought refuge in the capital or went into exile. In parishes that received the brunt of army violence, priests and nuns were under virtual house arrest. Missionaries did not perform any masses in Cobán villages for five years between 1980 and 1985. Clergy were afraid to travel in rural areas lest they be caught and executed by an army patrol. One missionary described the situation: "All we could do was to run a pastoral program from the office, to listen to villagers as they came into town and give them a bit of money and a bed for the night."

Not all missionaries were persecuted in this way. The split in the Church is still deep between those who espouse an active social role and those with a spiritualist, noninterventionist orientation. Some priests gave active legitimation to the army — for example, by traveling to villages in army helicopters. After the massacre in Pinares, Cahabón, the local priest performed a mass in the village with the military base commander. The Dominican called for reconciliation within the community, while standing next to the author of the recent slaughter.

INTO THE MOUNTAINS

The wind we set in motion should not be so strong as to strip the blossoms from the tree. —former EGP commander Mario Payeras, *Days of the Jungle*

The guerrillas could not defend the civilian population from the army onslaught and retreated to the jungle. They urged Q'eqchi's to accompany them and abandon their villages, a process that began in late 1981. A villager stated:

The army began to pass by every day and we heard that they were killing people in the communities, especially catechists. In Salaquím they decapitated people and cut off their ears and noses. There were planes and bombings. The brothers [the guerrillas] said, "Let's Go! Let's go!" before anything happened to us. We decided as a community to go into the mountains. Only a few did not and they went to Cobán.

The cohesion and unity of Q'eqchi' communities was striking. The majority of those that went into hiding in the forests did so en masse, with little dissent. Unity was based on the decision of a few male leaders. Ideological issues became secondary; people knew only that their lives were threatened and they must flee. So began the mass incorporation of the Q'eqchi's into the guerrilla ranks. Bishop Flores estimates that twenty thousand people in the diocese were forced to go into hiding in the mountains (America's Watch 1988:96). The rebel commander Mario Payeras (1983:71) wrote, "So many of our peasant bases managed to disappear when the army appeared. In less than a week we tripled our membership, augmented by the peasants who sought our protection." In Alta Verapaz, army repression achieved what political agitation alone could not: it brought the communities onto the side of the armed opposition.

Not everyone went with the guerrillas. Some sought refuge with the army itself, hoping that by openly siding with the troops they would be spared. The early eighties saw massive migration to urban areas as refugees hoped for safety in the towns. The squatter town called New Hope was created outside Cobán when hundreds of displaced people invaded vacant land. Others remained in their villages, fearing to escape, because this was a sure sign of guerrilla involvement in the eyes of the army. One man said, "We heard what the soldiers were doing in other places but we didn't run. We just prayed that they wouldn't come here."

Those who did not flee and showed strong allegiance to the army were organized into civil defense patrols, or PACs.[10] These were vigilante patrols, hewn out of the civilian population itself, armed and directed by the military. This counterinsurgency strategy has also been employed recently in Peru and the Philippines. In some cases, all able-bodied men and boys between about fourteen and sixty had to participate. In other instances, only a dozen or so men would form the core of the PAC. From the end of 1981 on, the patrols were employed successfully to control the populace both inside the villages and in neighboring communities. The army used the civilian patrols as the first line against the guerrillas, allowing the army to avoid the worst casualties. The PACs knew the terrain well and searched ruthlessly for slow-moving refugee groups. I repeatedly heard of atrocities committed by the Q'eqchi' patrollers of Chamá and Salaquím. The army's strategy was to divide the indigenous population internally and from the revolutionary forces via the PACs (Jay 1993).

The size, composition, and level of organization of refugee groups varied. Some had armed accompaniment for a year, many did not. Some were in contact with other refugee groups and coordinated their surveillance and patterns of movement, whereas others roamed in isolation. After 1983, those in hiding were consistently pursued by army patrols that scoured the jungle. The army also used psychological tactics against the refugees, flying over the forest canopy in helicopters, telling the groups to turn themselves in. They often used the voice of "Macario," the popular Q'eqchi' radio announcer who collaborated with the army for a time during the war.

Groups were cut off from markets, which soldiers monitored. The forest existence was communal; as one informant said, "In the bush we did everything together, no one had any more than the other." All resources were shared. The refugees built lean-tos from poles and thatched palms where everyone slept. Men, women, and children took turns keeping watch. People foraged for edible products of the forest, palms and roots. Communal work parties felled large trees in order to plant maize. This was a marked contrast to the usual method of clearing, where one man worked alone.

Most of the time was spent just surviving—finding enough to eat and avoiding the military. No informants reported the organization of any educational activities as was the case for established resistance populations in the Ixcán. The guerillas did little or no political work at the time; there were no attempts at "consciousness raising" or classes in Marxist doctrine. The

Civil patrollers and indigenous beauty queens marching with the army on Independence Day

absence of ideological training would later prove disastrous for the guerrillas. It is one of the reasons why the army, having captured refugees, could use its ideological finesse to incorporate them into the civil patrols and turn them against the guerrillas.

RELIGION IN THE MOUNTAINS

The catechists' religion survived the effects of civil war, but the war's ramifications on traditional community religion were devastating. Driving the indigenous population back up into the hills had an impact on their culture analogous to that of the sixteenth-century tactic of bringing them down into Spanish *reducciones*. Worship of tzuultaq'as could not be carried out in its full sense under nomadic war conditions. Q'eqchi's pointed out that the repositories of such knowledge, the elders, were among the first to die from malnutrition and exposure. Most married men knew how to petition tzuultaq'as on the day of the planting, but without *pom,* candles, and other offerings, permission would not be granted. Isolation from the markets meant that traditionalists could not feed their tzuultaq'as. Without sacrifice, the basic unit of reciprocity, the relationship with the mountain deity altered or decayed.

Because the mountain cult was highly localized, its practices were often abandoned when refugee groups moved to other areas. Traditionalists know the names of mountains and the characters of tzuultaq'as only in the immediate vicinity of their village. On occasion, they invoke the names of the Thirteen Great Tzuultaq'as in distant parts of Q'eqchi' territory, but their strongest relationship is with the hills within a few hours' walking distance of the community. Soldiers monitored nearby caves, denying the possibility of a spring offering.

The army and PAC patrols continually hunted refugees in the forest, so men thought better of traveling back to sacrifice in their local cave. People would not petition their old tzuultaq'as if they no longer lived within their ambit of influence. One man said, "How could I petition a mountain if I no longer live in front of it?" Because traditional ideas of sacredness are strongly locational, displacement from the original lands of the community created a chasm between the people and the mountain deities.

Followers of the mountain cult would not enter just any cave they encountered, according to one elder, "because we do not know its name." Lacking a prior relationship with a mountain and having noone to describe its name and character, it would

take many years of dreaming to initiate new relations with a
tzuultaq'a. The war stopped community sacrifices and large-
scale pilgrimages to cave shrines completely.[11]

Agricultural work in the forest was organized along lines
that differed from those of pre-war methods. Generalized labor
reciprocity replaced balanced reciprocity in the social group.
Collectivization of all productive labor is incompatible with
traditional religiosity. In communities with collective tenure,
the temporary right to cultivate a piece of land depends upon
who clears the bush. If private ownership of land exists in a
community, each man still clears his parcel individually. Clearing a piece of forest, then, states intended land use. Sacrifice to a
tzuultaq'a is the maximum expression of land tenure.

In pre-war communities, cooperation between unrelated
men during clearing occurred only in rare instances (e.g., to
provide for a widow). Traditionally, cooperation was institutionalized only during planting and harvesting. In the mountains, parties of refugees worked together at all points in the
productive process, so no one household had an exclusive claim
to the crop. As the planting rituals show clearly, only the
"owner" of the fields can petition for the mountain spirits'
license to plant and for the well-being of the maize. In the
absence of a definite "owner," noone petitioned before the
planting. In just a few cases, informants reported that the oldest
member of the refugee group would carry out the traditional
prayers and rituals.

Historically, farmers always performed a vigil the night before
planting. The refugees, on the other hand, planted when they
could—that is, when a patrol was not nearby. They often worked at
night or over the course of several days, planting at irregular
intervals. Again, pragmatic survival assumed primacy over customary practice. A nomadic existence and the inversion of activities from night to day wreaked havoc with prior customs.

So far as I could tell, the guerrillas did not actively discourage traditional beliefs and rituals. Several informants said that they actively encouraged them. In many instances, however, the guerrillas belonged to other indigenous ethnic groups with their own beliefs and rituals.

The experience of civil war did not totally destroy traditional beliefs. In response to their crisis, some refugees gave even more emphasis to symbols of community. A few communities that spent many years in the mountains accorded an accentuated guardian role to the tzuultaq'as. As they had done during sixteenth-century battles against the Spaniards, Q'eqchi's turned to their mountain spirits for guidance and protection. These refugees reported praying often to the tzuultaq'as and God to shield them from adversity. They petitioned mountain spirits for the right to pass through their domain with each new mountain they crossed. For these refugee groups, the tzuultaq'as took on the role of guardian angel, guiding the people through the forest and out of danger. One man told me, "The mountains collaborated with us. The mountains and the elders will never leave you. One tzuultaq'a told me in a dream, 'You go away from here because the dogs are coming.' So we left that place and five days later the army was there. The mountain looks like an old man with a beard. This is the mountain and God, too. We found wax from bees to make candles and gave thanks."

Another informant reported similar aid from the mountain spirits: "The tzuultaq'as helped us in the forests. He came to me in my sleep—a man all dressed in white. He told me of a place that would be safe and showed me how to get there. We all went to that spot and stayed for two years with no soldiers, no problems. Tranquil. Anyone, man or woman can see the tzuultaq'as, if you have the gift."

That collective symbols of the community should act as

protectors of villagers during war and social chaos is perhaps to be expected. I know of only one other instance, however, one documented by Watanabe (1992:214) in which the Mam-speaking residents of Santiago Chimaltenango were protected by their patron Catholic saint Santiago during military occupation. The "spirit" of the saint was said to have appeared at night on a white horse and attacked the military patrol, driving the detachment out of town.

Overall, the catechists' religion survived war conditions better than the earth cult did. As one lay activist related, "We celebrated the Word of God, too. We had guitars, a Bible, and song books, and we would sing when we were sure they weren't close by." Communities prayed on consecutive nights for God to deliver them. In the first years, they were accompanied by a few Catholic missionaries who lived in the forest for short periods. Their presence was vital in maintaining catechist religiosity. One exiled nun told me:

> We couldn't just abandon them up there fleeing in the mountains. I was forced out of the country but came back in to be with my people. We carried out baptisms and masses and helped in the organization of food. We preached about the reality of what was happening. We said that the Q'eqchi's were like the Israelites in the desert, fleeing the soldiers of Egypt.

The new religion of the catechists was more adaptable to refugee conditions than were the traditional rites. All it needed was a Bible; the songs and prayers were known by memory. The religion of the elders required monetary expense and religious paraphernalia that was unobtainable in the forest. A cosmology that had evolved in the context of isolated swidden cultivators was not flexible enough to adapt to the impositions of war. The change from sedentary settler to wandering nomad wreaked chaos on the customs. The catechists' religion was more appropriate and alluring under conditions of social upheaval. The mountain spirits were primarily concerned with agriculture and fertility, whereas God has a wider job description. Tzuultaq'as acted as protectors for some groups, but a majority reported an attenuation of their relationship with the sacred landscape. In this way, the Christian God gained a further edge over the mountain cult.

In a situation in which people from many different communities were jumbled together, usually far from their places of origin, it is not surprising that the traditional image of the community, the mountain spirit, began to fade. The catechists could then step into this vacuum of identity with a universal ideology that transcended the narrow confines of place, creating new sacred communities out of social chaos.

UNDER MILITARY CONTROL

Life in the forest lasted weeks or months for some communities, years for others. The refugee existence ended for many in the north of the department by the end of 1983, and for those nearer Cobán by 1986–87. One of the last groups delivered itself to the Catholic church in January 1988, but there are still Q'eqchi' communities in the Ixcán jungle.

Most refugees gave up their nomadic existence because of hunger and lack of protection. Hunger was the army's greatest weapon; the soldiers were mostly ineffective in physically capturing refugee groups. Informants told me countless times how they tired of seeing their children thin and malnourished and without medicines. The groups planted many crops, but army helicopters spotted and destroyed the fields. One man said, "All we ate for two years was bananas, wild spinach, and palms and whatever we could find. There were no domestic animals. We were always hungry and we just got sick of that."

Many refugees gave up because they felt defenseless against

the army onslaught. The main revolutionary force, the EGP, was defeated militarily and withdrew from Alta Verapaz by the end of 1983. Many commentators have judged the EGP's mass integration of indigenous communities into the guerrilla ranks to have been a disastrous strategy. Moving through the forest with whole villages denied the rebel forces the mobility necessary to fight a guerrilla war. There were too few guns to arm the population and too few revolutionaries to coordinate the civilians.

The military concentrated refugees in well-controlled areas—on army bases, near urban centers and on plantations. The primary role of these camps was to control movement and to separate the civilian population from the guerrilla groups in the mountains. The majority of refugees were held with strict limitations on their mobility for over a year, until the end of 1985. Those detained in the camps cultivated marginal subsistence crops on land in the immediate surroundings. With overcrowding, food supplies were meager. Toward the end of this period the refugees were allowed to work for short times on local plantations. This furnished landowners with cheap labor to rebuild the export sector of the war-torn rural economy.

A second role of the camps was to transmit the army's nationalist discourse. This brainwashing was perfected at the "reeducation" center at Acamal, near San Cristóbal, through which thousands passed (WOLA 1988). The sign at the entrance to the model village Saraxoch read "Antisubversive Village—Ideologically New," and this is exactly what the army wished to create: an ideologically new indigenous population. Specially trained officers of the army civil affairs section led ten "ideological talks" per day in the indigenous language. They showed films of life in the United States (showing "freedom" and prosperous people) versus life in Russia (ironically, showing soldiers). The director of the reeducation camp, Julio Corsantes, told America's Watch representative Jean-Marie Simon (1987:

179), "Now we don't turn them loose until we think they have totally changed their ideology. . . . Our desire is to have 100 percent success." The army was patently confident about its project; as the head of Cobán army-civilian affairs Major Figueroa said, "That is our obligation, to make them see the situation. . . . Indians are very susceptible, they are easy to ply, just like clay" (Simon 1987:178).

The army manipulated elements of local culture, playing heavily on indigenous notions of sin (*maak*) and culpability (Cabarrús 1979:35). As I described in chapter five, traditional ideas about the causes of sickness point to sin, either one's own or that of one's family, as the main source of illness. The army "counselors" extended this notion to include war-related difficulties in general. That is, everything the refugees had suffered was the result of their own sins. Those who had been in camps such as Acamal and Rosario related very similar stories. The phrase *nim li qa maak,* "our sin was great," was echoed in every interview.

Once Q'eqchi's had heard repeatedly how sinful they were, the army then told them that they could be redeemed if they repented their ways. The military represented itself as the savior of the people, utilizing explicitly fundamentalist religious imagery. Indeed, the whole process paralleled religious conversion as practiced by evangelical groups (see Stoll 1990). The army, understanding that a religious conversion had kindled rebellion, presumed that it would take another conversion to quell the uprising. In many camps, only the evangelical groups, whose ideology dovetailed with that of the army, were allowed to proselytize.

The army sought to turn refugees away from Catholicism by blaming Catholics and especially catechists for the violence. An ex-refugee in Acamal said, "There was no meeting of catechists in Acamal, even though we had celebrated the Word of God in

"Development Avenue" in model village Saraxoch, Alta Verapaz

the forest. The first thing they said to us was that we shouldn't
do the ritual. We wanted to, but were watched. It was not until
we got out that we started up again."

On the Esperanza plantation, no Catholic meetings were
permitted, but a branch of the Calvary evangelical church was
allowed to prosper. A pastor lived in the refugee camp and
celebrated frequent ceremonies. Not surprisingly, the majority
converted to the evangelical church as a pragmatic survival
strategy. The plantation and surrounding villages remain solidly evangelical. So while the Catholics were severely sup-
pressed, the evangelicals were clearly promoted by the army.
Whereas no mass was ever allowed in the camps, pastors visited
regularly. The Nazarene pastor in Cobán, Danilo Solís, told me,
"During those times of violence, we could go anywhere and

preach. Our movements were not restricted because we are non-political." This contrasts with the experience of many Catholic missionaries, who feared for their lives and remained in the towns.

Although the refugees were planting their maize crops again, they were bitterly poor and not allowed to go to market towns. They had no *pom,* candles, or animals to sacrifice to the tzuultaq'as. Nor were they allowed to come together to pray for the well-being of the crop. The time spent under army supervision, then, saw a suppression of both traditional religion and that of the catechists. All interactions were monitored and regulated by an army that denied refugees any autonomous social activity.

On military bases and in the Acamal reeducation camp, the army told refugees when they could leave and where they could resettle. In the western highlands, the army carried out limited "development" initiatives in the resettled communities to try to win the hearts of the local population. Such projects included providing sheet metal for roofs, food, and road building materials. They constituted the first phase of Ríos Montt's "beans and bullets" strategy, which used a twisted vision of development as a cover for counterinsurgency.

All Q'eqchi's got from the army, however, were the bullets. There were very few army "development" initiatives on the scale of those in the department of Quiché.[12] Perhaps the army felt that a deadly military blow to the civilian population was enough, and it was not important to win over hearts as well. The war caused the collapse of autonomous community developmentalism (Warren 1993:35–37), and the army did not begin to replace the material infrastructure created in the 1970s. Nor were there a significant number of foreign nongovernmental organizations providing economic assistance to villages in Alta Verapaz, as there were in departments such as Chimaltenango.

The talks in the concentration camps attempted to generate an ideological commitment to the state, but on the whole, they failed, except, perhaps, at the reeducation camp at Acamal. I was never in a position of full confidence with any ex-inmates of Acamal in order to judge the degree to which they were pro-army. They did, however, openly complain about the poverty, boredom, and restrictions on religion in the camp.

Overall, my opinion is that the brainwashing in the camps failed. All those I spoke to were clear as to who had burned their villages and chased them in the mountains. It would take more than a daily chat to dilute the experience of years in the forest avoiding the army. Coercion and an atmosphere of terror forced most men to participate in the civil patrols, not a deep ideological commitment to "fighting communism."

All the internal refugees in the country passed through the filter of the army camps, with the exception of about three hundred Q'eqchi's who were received and cared for by the diocese of the Verapaces in the disused convent in Cobán (AVANCSO 1990:49). This is the only case in the whole of Guatemala in which refugees and the Church outmaneuvered the military. It was possible in part because of the bishop's close relationship with the ruling Christian Democrats and his support from the departmental governor and the president. Bishop Flores met each of the six groups as they came in, malnourished, ill, and dressed in rags after up to seven years of nomadic existence in the mountains. The first group came out of the forest in February 1986 and delivered itself to the Church at a prearranged place. This occurred secretly, "because we were all frightened to death," as the bishop told me. The next group, in October 1986, received international press coverage as protection from military harassment. The last group sought refuge in the convent in January 1988.

The army was sorely chagrined because it had been deprived

of using the refugees to locate others in the mountains. Nor was it allowed to monitor the ideological disposition of the refugees. The military had wanted the refugees to accept amnesty, thereby admitting that they had been guerrillas. Several men were later kidnapped by the army. Two were "disappeared" from the first group during 1986 and never seen again. In a separate instance, nuns who were nursing the refugees physically obstructed an army squad trying to enter the convent. In another case, a refugee was kidnapped in an army jeep while walking in Cobán. He was questioned, tortured, and taken up into the mountains with an army patrol to locate other refugees. He led the patrol down a false trail and escaped one night during a torrential downpour. He made his way back to Cobán, still handcuffed, and into safe hiding. On occasions such as this, the diocese was in clear defiance of the military's "pacification" plans. At other times, the Church ingratiated itself by providing food and medicine to captured groups who were then relocated by the army.

"WE ARE LIKE SCRAMBLED EGGS NOW"

The varied changes in Q'eqchi' community organization during the war were such that I can only sketch out their most salient features here. Refugee groups have now resettled in roughly a hundred new communities, some on their original lands, others in new villages. There is a broad band that runs along the border with Quiché, from San Cristóbal to Playa Grande, in which none of the communities has its original composition. This situation prompted one villager to comment, "Laa'o chanchano chirmol anaqwan (we are like scrambled eggs now)."

The army had to give permission for each of the villages to be reconstituted, and it determined which sites would be chosen and who would live there. Previously, communities contained up to a hundred households, but the army model determined forty families to be the ideal size. For purposes of control, the villages were highly concentrated, all houses within several hundred square yards of one another. Every house should be visible from a single point. To facilitate this, the army bulldozed a hillock, on top of which sits the civil patrol hut, in the center of several communities. All this harks back to the Spanish *reducciones,* during which indigenous peoples were brought down out of the forests and settled in towns where they could be Christianized, controlled, and made to pay tribute. The concentrated town is a classic counterinsurgency strategy, also used by the British in Malaysia and the U.S. in Vietnam.

The "strategic hamlet" exists in strong contrast to previous patterns of indigenous villages, in which houses were surrounded by fields and often lay an hour's walk from one another. Social life was less intense in the old village than in the "urban center," as the army calls the new village. Evidence that Q'eqchi's dislike this arrangement is found wherever army control begins to relax. Concentrated communities are slowly disintegrating as families cautiously rebuild their houses progressively farther away from each other.

The majority of refugee villages are on *baldío,* or unowned, lands. People there are petitioning INTA for land titles, and some have spent all their resources on rogue surveyors and lawyers. Encroaching landlords continue to be a problem, and violence has broken out over boundary disputes. As elsewhere in the highlands, lack of access to land is the greatest economic problem for rural communities.

Although the rural insurgents were defeated, they seem to have won some benefits in relations between Mayan communities and landowners in certain instances. Many villagers expressed happiness at simply being off the plantations, whether or not they presently own the land they inhabit. A large number of landowners in violence-torn areas have not returned, or have sold their lands to INTA. Some informants pointed to an improvement in working conditions on the plantations since the war. One commented, with irony, "Before, on the Chamá plantation, no one was paid, but the *finqueros* [plantation owners] suffered too in the violence and they shot his wife. Now if people work there, they get paid."

These comments have wider relevance. The Tzutuhil elder Ignacio Bizarro Ujpán acknowledges that plantation owners would treat workers worse if there was no guerrilla insurgency (Sexton 1992:66). On the other side of Lake Atitlán, in the Kaqchikel community of San Andrés Semetabaj, the war seems to have had even deeper ramifications for ethnic and class relations. Kay Warren (1993:37) claims that the war there led to an exodus of Ladinos, which allowed a "localized agrarian reform" and greater Mayan control over municipal political and development organizations.

As Carol Smith (1990b:32) notes for the western highlands, the war, by creating more landlessness, has led to an increase in temporary wage labor. Almost all smallholders must now seek wage work in addition to cultivating their own lands. This decreases peasant self-sufficiency and provides a cheap labor pool for capitalist agricultural and a new *maquila* industrial sector.[13]

There has been a move away from paternalistic relations between landowner and tenant, and away from usufruct rather than wage payment. These former relations of production were not "precapitalist," as Salvadó (1978) argued, because plantations have been exporting for the world capitalist market since the nineteenth century. Yet relations of production are now more commoditized, and this is perceived as beneficial by many villagers. One fiery youth said, "Now many plantations are Q'eqchi' communities without the landowner. The plantations don't treat people as badly. It is like a naughty child—you hit it

hard on the head and it understands. We won something, there
are better conditions now even though we are poorer. If it gets
like before, we will rise up again."

Carol Smith (1990b) makes a dark assessment of the overall
economic reorganization undertaken in the western highlands
during the war, and many of her comments ring true for Alta
Verapaz. She argues that economic control replaced military
coercion as the main way of reducing the economic and political
independence of indigenous communities. Her research shows
that counterinsurgency methods have led to a drop in rural
incomes and regional trade, resulting in greater landlessness
and wage labor and a generalized expansion of more capitalist
forms of production. She sees the military as seeking to create a
corporatist state by making itself, rather than the private business community, the central institution in society. By devastating the rural economy and development gains of the 1970s and
replacing them with state and capitalist institutions, the military has ultimately undermined the bases for local autonomy.

POWER IN THE NEW COMMUNITIES

*I will defend my family, home and community
against any subversive attack or natural catastro-
phe.* —Item 1, Civil Patrol Code of Conduct

Community authority once stemmed from elders who were the
repositories of history, ritual specialists, and intermediaries
between their villages and the tzuultaq'as. They adjudicated
disputes within the community. Hierarchy was based on age
and prestige, but it was rather diffuse and was enforced by social
sanction, not violence. Traditional authority was transformed
with the introduction of the catechists, who were elected by the
community but legitimated by an external source, the Catholic
church. No sooner had they begun to usurp the power of the

elders than rural repression began with a vengeance and the civil patrols were instituted. There has been a general historical tendency, then, for village-based institutions to be replaced by those linked to external sources of power.

The army's reorganization of the village power structure was carried out in the name of "the community," as the Civil Patrol Code of Conduct makes clear. Its item 1 shows how the army sought to make the new surveillance functions as natural as those of combating a flood, an earthquake, or a forest fire.

The development of civil patrols has meant massive centralization of power in the hands of local men. This is backed by violence, that of the village PAC and the army. In reorganized communities, there is a often a core of men who dominate the patrol. They are trusted by the army for their loyalty during the years of repression. The head of a village PAC is chosen and supported by the military base. He reports to the military commissioner, a local man in the pay of the army. As America's Watch (1986) has documented, this system encourages despotism in which the patrol head dominates other villagers. His position is backed by the rifles of the patrol and by threats of denunciation as a guerrilla to the Cobán military base. Political violence is not enacted solely by outside institutions but is also "locally authored" (Warren 1993:38).

In other areas, all the villagers spent time in the forest and the army has no loyal supporters. In these cases, the patrols are not given guns. One patroller said, "The base told us that we'd get guns but they did not give them to us when we went to pick them up. They don't trust us who were in the mountains, just those who stayed in their villages and patrolled during those times. We still have to be watched."

In these communities, the army often selects catechists to head the patrol in order to defuse any antimilitary sentiments or activities. By co-opting the catechists, the army can occupy much of their time in the patrol instead of the church. Using the leaders of a previously hegemonic community institution, the Catholic base group, lends legitimacy and a semblance of continuity to the army's new local structures. The army also wishes to divide the catechists from their neighbors, since the PAC leader is meant to be monitoring his community relentlessly for "subversives." He is often the focus of suspicion, for his community may suspect that he is an army spy.

The polarizing effect of terror politicizes every act and has sown fear and suspicion throughout the highlands.[14] Suspicion is especially rife if only part of the community consists of refugees. The refugees are distrusted and watched by the rest. The patrol supervises mobility, and any exit from or entry into the village is noticed. Patrollers question unknown visitors as to their purpose and check their identification papers. This control is remarkably thorough. The patrol governs all intra-community relations, while the army is the controller of supra-community interactions. The "betterment committees," which meet with the PAC, take all petitions for development initiatives straight to the military. Whether they want to build a road or a bridge or install electricity or drinking-water facilities, villagers will at least notify the army before they take any steps. Although there are governmental departments that deal with these issues, communities petition the army first.

The army is the ultimate judicial authority in Alta Verapaz and the rest of the indigenous highlands (see Jay 1993:51). Disputes over land, adultery, animals eating others' crops, and even witchcraft accusations are continually carried to the army bases. Villagers perceive that the military exercises the real power, and they often approach them before going to the civilian authorities. As Beatriz Manz (1988:100) writes of the Ixcán region, "the totality of military authority has undermined all other power structures." This judicial involvement in local social relations facilitates military surveillance but also drains resources that might be used in actively combating the guerrillas. Ignacio Bizarro Ujpán, from Lake Atitlán, writes about how the military can become frustrated over being continually drawn into local disputes and vendettas that are not part of the counterinsurgency war (Sexton 1992:149).

Because religious symbolism is so important in constructing Q'eqchi' identities, we would expect the army to harness it to legitimate its position of power. This is exactly what has happened throughout the history of highland Guatemala. Robert Carmack (1990:121), writing about the nineteenth century, tells us, "The Indians' traditional religion was 'rationalized' in such a way that it provided ritual support for all things military (e.g., native priest-shamans were assigned to Indian militia divisions and even to bases in Guatemala City)." In modern-day Chajul, in Quiché, two of the religious icons on the church altar are dressed in the uniform of the Kaibiles, the elite army counterinsurgency troops (Simon 1987:91). The Kaibiles are named after Kaibil Balam, the last chief of the highland Mam kingdom at the time of the Spanish invasion.

A militarization of indigenous symbolism is also happening among the Q'eqchi's. The military-imposed system of social control could not have worked so effectively if it had not found some resonance in the indigenous culture itself. This linking of local tradition and military interests is apparent in item 10 of the Civil Patrol Code of Conduct, which reads, "I will respect community customs and traditions as well as the Civil and Military authorities" (America's Watch 1986:100).

Specifically, the army has attempted to appropriate the authoritarian symbolism of the tzuultaq'as for its own ends. The sign at the entrance to Cobán army headquarters reads "Cobán Military Base—Home of the Soldier Tzuultaq'a." The training program for new recruits is called the Tzuultaq'a Training

Program. Colonel Homero García, head of the army's department of information in 1991, told me, "We liken ourselves to the
mountain spirits because like them, we dominate the land, we
command over all who are in our territory." As this Ladino
officer spoke of Q'eqchi' symbolism so comfortably, I thought
to myself that the army has become the Guatemalan state
institution with the most profound understanding of indigenous culture, an understanding born out of centuries of sub-
jugating it.

How can the army so blatantly drape the mountain spirit in
battle camouflage? However Machiavellian its actions may
seem, the army has hit a cultural nerve, for the mountain spirit
has the potential to be the most authoritarian of deities. Both
tzuultaq'as and the army demand that permission be asked for
activities. Any building or agricultural labor requires the assent
of a tzuultaq'a, whereas most social activities require the
license of the army. The wrath of each is greatly feared, and their
penalties for autarkic activity can be disastrous. A tzuultaq'a
destroys crops; the army destroys not only crops but people and
whole villages. Both mandate their agents to execute their will:
the tzuultaq'as send jungle animals, and the army, civil patrols.
Both wield power violently and therefore are "hot." There are, of
course, vast differences between the two: for example, the
mountain spirits are benevolent in that they provide the fertility
of the earth. Yet the military seeks to appropriate symbolically
the autocratic facets of the mountain spirits.

This is simply a recent example of the way in which
historical processes have reshaped the nature of the mountain
spirits. As I have argued, the tzuultaq'a is a fluid and continually redefined symbol, not a relic of the Mayan past. The
character of the mountain spirits, whether in Guatemala or the
Andes, is the product of particular circumstances of the present
coupled with the symbolic legacy of the past. The tzuultaq'as

are often likened to the Germans, evidence that landowners of the nineteenth and early twentieth centuries had a profound influence on religious symbolism. The catechist program also altered the tzuultaq'as, rendering them less bloodthirsty for sacrifice. The upheavals caused by rural repression have had no less an impact, remodeling the nature of the earth gods. Tzuultaq'as have two customary functions in rituals—to give license and to participate in the renewal of fertility. Generalized violence has led to an accentuation of the authoritarian license-giving role, which suits army representations of power. The regeneration of crop fertility, a collective and more egalitarian process, has been diminished.

Tzuultaq'as do not yet appear in elders' dreams (as the Germanic figures do), as commandos in olive drab. Yet the historic competition continues over the tzuultaq'a icon, each pressure group seeking to mold it in its own image.

IMAGES OF NEW COMMUNITIES

Even with the war over, it remains difficult for communities to reinitiate certain rituals, especially ones that involved the whole community, such as the collective sacrifice (*mayejak*) during the planting. When I asked why this ritual had not yet been performed in reconstituted villages, the answer was often, "We must have unity and happiness of heart," or, "The elders are dead and no one knows how to do it properly."

Unity (*junajil*) is critical, for without it the basis for collective ritual is gone. Unlike before, the new communities are highly heterogeneous. They include people formerly from different communities, with different customs, perhaps different religions, and different experiences of the violence. "Unity" means originating in a specific locale and sharing its collective representations. Traditionalists owe allegiance to a particular mountain or group of mountains by virtue of being born and raised in their domain. As we saw earlier, community identity is based largely on a localized representation of the landscape.

Followers of the mountain cult owe little allegiance to tzuultaq'as they have not grown up with. The presence of new people prevents original members of the community from performing their rituals. If people are not certain that others in their community practice the same rituals in the same way, they will not advocate their performance. Ritual minutiae must be observed precisely or it is better not to perform them at all. Dissent during a ritual would be the worst possible scenario.

It is said that for rituals to take place, people must trust and have confidence in one another—an elusive element given the suspicion generated by the civil patrols. They must be "happy," another difficult criterion to meet under conditions of poverty and military domination. To carry out rituals when the necessary criteria are not met is worse than not enacting them at all. If a divided community offers a candle to a tzuultaq'a, it could split in half, symbolizing the mountain god's rejection of the gift.

The case of one village throws these issues into relief and shows how the creation of a new sense of community is a difficult, painstaking process. During 1982, the army merged two villages at a place some mid-distance between the two. For six years there were no community sacrifices to tzuultaq'as. In 1988, one of the villages moved back to its old site and immediately organized a collective offering at a spring, a manifestation of the local mountain god. The elders had been dreaming of a tzuultaq'a—the sign that a ritual was necessary. During the offering, the elders requested permission to return to their present place after many years of being away. One elder said, "We did not offer to the mountains in the last village because we did not know the mountains. We were just visitors there, we were two communities, not one. Now we are on our land."

Individual rituals survived better than collective offerings because they did not depend on an uncontested image of community. Elders provided the expertise for collective offerings, but most married men understood the basics of individually performed rites. Still, individual planting rites are now practiced with less frequency than before the war. Conversely, petitions for license to inhabit an area have spiraled in frequency because of mass displacements. In any major construction such as a church or house, a tzuultaq'a and the wood of the building must be fed in the *wa'tesiink* ("to feed") ritual.[15]

In the *wa'tesiink,* the offering creates a contract, securing license to use the raw materials and the land. The earth and wood are fed with blood and raw animal flesh, which act as substitutes for the human inhabitants of the edifice. If this substitute is not provided, the children and domestic animals may be "eaten" by a tzuultaq'a through a fatal illness. When communities resettled in a locality and built their houses, it was considered mandatory in most cases to perform the appropriate *wa'tesiink* rituals. Usually the most senior man was responsible for all of the houses. Even football pitches (often the first place to be cleared in a village!) were fed with flesh placed in the four corners of the field to forestall injuries among the players.

Like the planting rituals, the *wa'tesiink* expresses both the community and its contract with a tzuultaq'a, yet it seems to have weathered the violence much better. Perhaps this is because the *wa'tesiink* has been always an occasional ritual performed infrequently, whereas the planting rituals were regular annual occurrences. The extended nonperformance of a frequent ritual is more damaging than that of a rare event. Displacement from original lands may even have increased the frequency of the *wa'tesiink* ritual.

The repression did not affect traditional Q'eqchi' healing methods to the same extent as the earth cult. The resilient nature of shamanism and healing practices in the context of colonialism and violence has led Michael Taussig (1986), Norman Whitten (1976) and Barbara Tedlock (1992) to concentrate on them as markers of cultural survival. Infant sicknesses continue to be diagnosed and treated as before. Spirit loss has maintained its position as a major category of disease.

The persistence of traditional health care throughout the war also needs explanation. The refugees had easy access to medicinal plants, the majority of which come from the jungle. There were no Western drugs or medical attention to compete with traditional methods. Even more importantly, women are responsible for treating many types of illnesses, including spirit loss and children's sicknesses. Women are generally more resistant than men to outside influences because of a gender barrier that separates male and female activities and obstructs women from extracommunity relations. This means that women were less affected by catechist discourse and the nationalist onslaught of the military. These discourses were directed more at men.[16]

Like house feeding, curing rituals are performed infrequently. They are necessitated by irregular conditions, in contrast to renewal rites in the production process. Therefore, to put it crudely, their shelf life is longer. Catechists did not suppress traditional health care to the same extent as agricultural sacrifices. The catechists campaigned heavily against the *wa'tesiink,* with its blood sacrifice, yet its practice flourished under conditions of mass displacement. Given the violent circumstances of the early 1980s, it is not surprising that spirit-loss illnesses thrived. Causes of spirit loss include taking fright and falling, especially in the domain of tzuultaq'as, in the forest or by a stream. Since refugees lived in the wild territory of the mountain spirit, fleeing murderous military patrols, spirit loss was a frequent occurrence.

The war has meant the virtual disappearance of *cofrades* from community life. They still exist in some villages but only as shadows of the institutions they were ten years before. Their position was already seriously weakened before the guerrilla war began. In those few communities that have continued the *cofrades,* it is only because the financial burden has been redistributed. Money is now collected from all members of the village, and the festival is coordinated by a committee, usually with catechists at the head.

The decline of the *cofrades* means that one more element of collaboration between neighboring villages has been lost. In the past, villages would participate in one another's saint festivals, processions, and feasts. Each would carry its own saint's image on a litter to pay respects and bow to the image of the feted patron saint. Communities had their own complexes of relations based on the images, all now lost due to the repression. With them has also gone one level of intercommunity cohesion and cooperation—a loss that can only benefit the army in its drive to isolate and divide indigenous villages from one another.

NEW VILLAGES, NEW CATECHISTS

Because lay activists were the prime targets of army repression, few original catechists from the 1970s continue to be active in hard-hit areas. The refugee communities have a whole new generation of catechists. Repression continues, but in a less overtly violent form. Those loyal to the army, such as the despotic civil patrol leaders, assert that all Catholics are guerrillas whose activities should be curtailed. Catechists face continual harassment in many areas. Some do not attend parish courses because they are intimidated by the civil patrol.

Attendance is very low in many weekly meetings of the Word of God. The whole village will turn out, however, if a priest performs a mass. One missionary said, "People are frightened of coming together on their own as they will be accused. The patrol will say, 'There are those catechists causing trouble again.' They feel much safer when the priest comes because there can be nothing subversive about just having a mass and some baptisms. The faith and will to continue is there, people are just frightened of being marked."

The suppression of religious practice is clearly a counterinsurgency tactic designed to stifle all community organization that is not integrated into the military framework. Indeed, the sacred community is the only village institution that lies outside the military's structure. The other organizations — the civil patrol and betterment committees — compliantly implement and collaborate with military policy. The catechist program, especially now that the *cofrades* are decimated, is the only supracommunity social organization. Catechist courses are the only platforms on which Q'eqchi's from different villages can formally gather to discuss pertinent issues. For exactly these reasons, Thomas Bruneau (1980:225), writing about Brazil, says that Christian base communities are "the seed bed for popular initiatives under authoritarian regimes." Local Christian institutions, Protestant or Catholic, are one of the few bases for a resurgent civil society in indigenous areas.

In the present repressive environment, the new lay activists have abandoned many elements of liberation theology. The tendency in sermons is toward an escapist and spiritualistic doctrine that avoids calls for change at the level of society. Catechists instead exhort individual conversion and personal salvation. One long-time catechist said of present lay activists: "All they have on their minds is songs, and prayers and rosaries and doing them perfectly. Action is better than prayers. They are too spiritual and that is like the Protestants. They go around like there are no problems when there are so many and we need to be attacking them at the roots."

His point about Protestants is valid. The growth of evangelical groups has been dramatic since 1980, and this has influenced Catholics. Military control also makes salvation a safer
theme to espouse than radical social change. One urban catechist, preaching on the necessity of agrarian reform said, "I can
talk like this in town, but if one of our brothers said this in the
villages, he would disappear tomorrow."

Since it rolled back the revolutionary movement, the military has been vigilant for the slightest flicker of protest. Most
Q'eqchi's, and indeed Guatemalans, pragmatically avoid any
public discourse associated with the rebels. Some catechists'
support for the failed revolution gave a millenarian tinge to the
war, offering divine legitimation to human efforts to change the
mundane world. At present, catechists place more hope in
supernatural intervention to resolve problems of poverty and
political oppression. Bryan Wilson's (1975:272) comments
about millenarian movements seem to be vindicated here:
"When warfare has failed, revolutionist orientations become
more totally religious: reliance is now placed entirely on supernatural action."

Not all catechists uphold a spiritualist doctrine, however,
and a minority still advocate concrete actions to improve life
here on earth. This occurs especially in communities that are
homogeneous, made up solely of refugees who survived the
repression together. In these villages, there is a high degree of
social cohesion, trust, and mutual aid. Base groups coordinate
building houses, planting crops for widows, and pooling cash
resources during, for example, medical emergencies. This is not
to say that such mutual aid does not occur in communities led
by "spiritual" catechists, just that it is less likely. In any village,
no matter what the orientation of the catechists, the weekly
meeting of the Word of God increases the sense of integration
and community. The fact that it is the only regular rite that

reaffirms a sense of community means that the catechist meeting is of great significance.

In a small number of communities, the weekly catechist meeting is the only vessel for maintaining the collectivist culture of the years of refuge in the mountains. In one community, the catechists organized communal maize fields that belong to everyone, as they did during the years in the forest. The Bible continues to provide the platform for denouncing the army. This is done tangentially—for example, when catechists preach about the atrocities committed by Biblical Roman soldiers, the modern parallels are not lost on the congregation.

FROM PUNISHMENT TO SURVEILLANCE

The Mind of the people is the principle objective.— *National Plan for Security and Development* (Guatemalan military document, 1982)

A number of sociologists, such as Michael Mann (1986) and Anthony Giddens (1985), have drawn our attention to a qualitative difference between "premodern" and "modern" states, namely, the degree to which the state can exert its hegemony over the everyday life of its citizens. It is argued that the development of governmental structures in European states during the sixteenth and seventeenth centuries led to an increasing capacity of the state to intervene in social life and participate in the construction of social existence itself. With modernity, state relations with civil society become more intense and interwoven. During the Guatemalan civil war, the military modernized the state by sinking its institutional and discursive elements deeper into civil society than ever before. One reason the Guatemalan army's strategies have been effective is that it has made local people part of a national system of violence. The end result comes close to Gilles Deleuze and Félix

Guattari's (1988) notion of a "rhizome state," which sends its roots down into the soil of civil society and, by militarizing civilian life, affects its very constitution.

Anthropologists are just beginning to assess the new forms of state power in local communities that evolved during the most intensive phase of the counterinsurgency period. Anthropologists have generally underestimated the extent of military involvement in Guatemalan civil society via the civil patrols, the *cofradias* and other local institutions.[17] Yet it is equally important to stress that the state's strategies and effectiveness have not been homogeneous throughout all indigenous regions. I have previously disagreed (Wilson 1993a) with John Watanabe (1990:195) over his writing that state authority is "intrinsically foreign" to a Mam indigenous town. On reflection, this difference in views is more likely to be related to the differing degree of involvement of the military in Santiago Chimaltenango (where Watanabe worked) and villages in Alta Verapaz.

In Alta Verapaz, military structures are present inside the indigenous community, superimposing their own images over traditional collective images. The military is part of village culture, having long since insinuated itself into levels of local social meaning. This is also the case in the Andes, where mountain spirits (*wamanis*) function directly as allies (Earls 1969) or opponents (J. Nash 1979) of the state. In Guatemala, model villages and civil patrols are a logical historical progression of the army's agenda, in that once the army had physically imposed its control over a territory and exacted its brutal punishment, it moved to a new mode of exercising repression: surveillance. Foucault (1980:38) has drawn our attention to this same succession from punishment to surveillance of society by eighteenth-century European states. The state's increasingly sophisticated understanding of the mechanisms of repression means that it had to invent what Foucault (1980:39) calls "a synaptic regime of power, a regime of its exercise within the social body, rather than from above it."

Foucault's narrative of the historical development of ever more internalized forms of control is useful for analyzing the relationship between the Guatemalan state and indigenous communities. Foucault (1977) argues that modernity evolved new methods of social discipline, one of which was "hierarchical observation." He considers the panopticon, a concept of penal incarceration formulated by the seventeenth-century English philosopher Jeremy Bentham. The panopticon was an architectural design that entailed an observation tower in the middle of a prison, from which all cells would be visible. At any time, the inmates could not know whether someone in the tower was watching them or not. Yet the awareness of their own visibility meant that each would become his own policeman. Foucault (1977:202–203) writes, "He who is subjected to a field of visibility, and who knows it, assumes responsibility for the constraints of power. . . . He inscribes in himself the power relation in which he simultaneously plays both roles: he becomes the principle of his own subjection."

In indigenous communities, civil patrols serve the same surveillance function as the panopticon, creating a new field of visibility in which all can be seen. This is especially the case where the patrol hut is situated on hillock and each individual household is visible to the gaze of the army's local representatives. Villagers' consciousness of being in a visible space means that power functions automatically, lessening the need for active enforcement.

Foucault's writings on the body also have salience. In *Discipline and Punish* (1977), he argues that in modernity the body becomes an object of the exercise of new technologies of power. In Guatemala, the war led to changing notions of the body as the military increasingly reorganized the meaning of the body around the state's own notion of terror. Disappearances and torture meant a new language of control over the body—in Foucault's terminology, a new form of "biopower." Young male bodies in particular have become physical expressions of the state's dominance, for young men are the most likely perpetrators and subjects of torture and murder. These acts of political violence use almost exactly the same conventions in each case, as all languages must in order to communicate. Typically, bodies are left by the roadside with their hands tied behind their backs and a coup de grace delivered to the head. The roadside cadaver is the most potent sign of terror, proclaiming to each passerby the message of unassailable military authority. As Kay Warren (1993:31) writes, "For the public, violence was inscribed on the bodies of strangers, foretelling what might happen to one's own people."

The idea of a redefinition of the body applies particularly to the military's system of recruitment of young males. Carol Smith (1990b:10) writes that the army takes in (often coercively) seven thousand to eight thousand men between the ages of eighteen and twenty-four each year, mostly from rural, indigenous regions. This means that at any one time, 20 percent of the rural male population is serving a two-year stint.

By conscripting such huge numbers of indigenous youths, the army carries out a strategy of mass incarceration, ensuring that the guerrillas have less access to a significant potential resource base. It is a strategy also designed to inculcate in young men the state's regulatory norms and values, including nationalism, anticommunism, and deference to authority.

As in a prison, the army exerts its control over conscripts' bodily functions. Each day there is a timetable for activities— rising and sleeping, eating meals, even eliminating bodily wastes. The streets of Guatemala are full of distinctive signs of living bodies reshaped by the military's technology of power.

Army recruits are shorn of their hair, and they develop a new wide-legged gait and ramrod-stiff posture. The military's discourse on personal hygiene means that recruits are resocialized to see their bodies in a new way. Like young children, they are taught how to brush their teeth and comb their hair. The army suppresses the speaking of indigenous languages; Spanish is the only idiom permitted. This, too, is a material change in the conscript's physical being. Finally, sexuality is reformulated in the army, as young men visit local prostitutes en masse. In Cobán and most garrison towns, army personnel are the main presence at brothels.

Yet I would not push Foucault's discourse too far. There may be a general development from punishment to surveillance in the technologies of the Guatemalan state, but this is no neat transition: the two exist together. That is why Guatemala has historically had no political prisoners. The public spectacle of political murder is still a forceful expression of the absolutist power of the military.

Foucault perhaps erred by stressing too much the totalizing nature of surveillance. Writers such as Stanley Diamond (1974) have rightly pointed out that no state, no matter how perfect its totalitarian devices, can eliminate all contested domains and remove all bases for local resistance. We can see this in Q'eqchi' communities, where local religious institutions are recreating the basis for a resurgent civil society. Although the overall drift is toward greater state involvement in the social body, the state's discourse still has to compete with local formulations of traditional culture, such as those practiced daily by seers and midwives. In other parts of the indigenous highlands, community and national organizations such as the anti-patrol organization CERJ have undermined the unblinking gaze of the civil patrols.[18] In the Tzutuhil area, Ignacio Bizarro records the outspoken grumblings of local men when the army comes to their village to force them to do military drills and lecture them in anticommunist propaganda: "They said: son-of-a-bitch, motherfucker, go to hell. But they said these words in Tzutuhil. So when the *jefes* [Ladino officers] asked what they were saying, the others answered 'they are very happy (Sexton 1992:150).'"

CONCLUSIONS

Anthropological analyses of modern wars have tended to emphasize the "objective" economic and political conditions that give rise to rebellion. The effects of war have generally been judged in terms of changes in societal institutions and national-community power relations. The primary considerations of this largely structural style of analysis have been state structures, international forces, and class relations. This approach was initiated by the pioneering anthropological works of Eric Wolf (1969) and Samuel Popkin (1979) and influenced by the writings of political scientists (Scott 1976) and sociologists (Skocpol 1979). There are limitations, however, to relying solely on this social science tradition. Steve Stern (1987a:9) argues eloquently that it is unacceptable to deduce the "characteristic forms of consciousness" from the social structural category of a group. Such an economistic approach implies a mechanistic view of human agency and consciousness. Furthermore, it is ahistorical, ignores the cultural context, and tends toward an essentialist view of social groups (see Laclau 1985:30).

Since Wolf's study, an inordinate amount of attention has been focused on the structural and economic variables that determine armed conflicts (e.g., the level of capitalist "penetration"). This explanatory model, characterized by orthodox materialist analyses, seeks to objectify the meaning of revolutionary war but neglects the subjective perceptions of actors. David Stoll's (1993) book offers a thorough empirical critique of how a neglect of Ixil's own perceptions of the civil war led scholars to apply to their behavior the inappropriate trope of "resistance."

Anthropology's analysis of recent wars has differed little from that of political scientists or sociologists. Yet one of anthropology's historical strengths has been its ability to detail the subjectivities of actors engaged in a social process. Ethnographers are particularly well placed to relate the local, cultural meaning of contemporary war and its effects upon a people's worldview. Culturalist and reflexive analyses are needed to complement materialist and structural accounts, and these are beginning to emerge (e.g., Warren 1993). Yet apart from rare exceptions, anthropologists have generally commented from a safe distance, using the language of structural analysis. Taussig (1990:3) captures well this attitude toward terror, writing that it is "a matter of finding the right distance, holding it at arm's length so it doesn't turn on you . . . and yet not putting it so far away in a clinical reality that we end up substituting one form of terror for another."

In the anthropology of modern wars, I would encourage several avenues of research. Cultural representations of authority are vital for understanding why communities rebel. Each community has its touchstone symbols, such as the tzuultaq'as. Much can be learned by examining how these symbols become transformed during war. It is vital to consider competition over religious icons on the part of conflicting groups. Governments are likely to engage religious symbols as icons of orthodoxy, whereas rebels tend to redefine them as icons of subversion. In Q'eqchi' communities, the figure of the mountain spirit became a focus for competing interest groups. As Victoria Bricker (1981) found in highland Chiapas, the Mayas assert one vision of a god, the Ladino state another. Through the emergence of an indigenous Christ, Bricker writes (1981:161), "Christ became the personal protector of the Indians instead of the symbol of the oppressors." Similarly, the army used tzuultaq'as as authoritarian symbols, but for some refugee communities, the mountain spirits remained their protectors.

In the context of religious syncretism, how does war tip the balance in favor of one or another religion? In Guatemala, the war and its aftermath have produced changes in traditional religion and reinforced the rise of orthodox Catholicism. The traditional, community-based cult was particularly inflexible to the exigencies of war because it was unique to historical and relatively homogeneous communities and to highly specific localities. The orthodoxy of the catechists has fared better because its doctrine is that of the universal Catholic church, and it could adapt to conditions of displacement and material deprivation. Although in ascendancy when the violence began, the catechist program has now gained undisputed prominence over the traditional cosmology. The war speeded up what was perhaps an inevitable outcome.

War, whatever its other results, often accelerates the incorporation of indigenous communities into the national society. It does so economically by displacing huge numbers of people to the cities and by further commoditizing rural labor relations. On a cultural level, war fosters universal and orthodox religious beliefs. The very fact that indigenous communities were subjected to the unleashed brutality of the state made them aware of it as never before. Through terror, the Guatemalan state defined Q'eqchi's as national citizens and exerted its "right" to kill them. It exercised its monopoly over the means of violence, which meant that indigenous communities no longer had to contend with individual plantation owners and their local thugs but instead faced a national army representing a single state. The hope that a remote mountain village could just avoid and ignore the state and be left alone was shattered forever.

Although indigenous peoples were, on the whole, unconverted to the guerrillas' class analysis, they were exposed to wider bases of identity than just the community. Carol Smith (1990a:20) points out that the political consequence of the indigenous conception of community is to block the possibility of a pan-Indian struggle against the state. The indigenous imaginings of community through the mountain spirits and the *cofrades* had to be transcended for any real development of a widespread insurrection to take place. This is exactly what happened when the catechists accepted a supracommunal worldview that stressed class association and universal ideas of Catholic brotherhood. Guerrilla phrases such as "we the poor" united the communities in common cause against the state. Those on the side of the army went through a similar process. One adamant patroller told me how "we Guatemalans must fight the communist foreigners," showing how defensive paranoia is vital to the construction of a nationalist identity.

The chaos and social upheaval of the 1980s were utterly devastating for Q'eqchi' communities. People had just jettisoned old values for those of the catechists when these in turn were ravaged. Throughout the war, the military exerted its own imagining of Q'eqchi' communities: that they were ruled by soldier tzuultaq'as, each a local representative of the national Guatemalan army. In the wake of mass repression, the army imposed new forms of community organization, the civil patrols. These patrols translate army messages down to the local level and bind their representatives to the military base in Cobán, making all Q'eqchi' men "inner pilgrims" of the state, a crucial process in nation building (Anderson 1991:115). By speaking Mayan languages and manipulating traditional symbolism, the army represents the chief vehicle of Guatemalan national identity.

As Smith (1990a:273, 1990b) has recognized, the military is now trying to create a broad cultural consensus in order to incorporate indigenous peoples into the nation. The military interacts with communities effectively because it knows them well. It plans to extend its imagining of the nation, which means obliterating traditional divisions in society. This involves destroying community and non-Ladino ethnicity, the primary bases of non-national identity. Smith (1990a:282) speculates on the indigenous response to the military state and suggests either the development of a pan-Maya identity (which she sees as unlikely) or the "fragmentation" of communities, making it harder for the state to control them. Both, no doubt, are already occurring, and Maya revivalism is the subject of the following chapter.

The Guatemalan military's strategy toward Mayan peoples during the late 1970s and early 1980s was expressly ethnocidal (C. Smith 1988:206). Yet such attempts at ethnic obliteration usually fail on their own terms. The *matanza* in El Salvador in the 1930s (Anderson 1992) serves as an exception rather than as the rule. More often, culture is fragmented and its elements are redefined. Which elements survive, and why? How do gender barriers bolster resistance to culture loss?

War is not merely a one-way process of cultural attrition. A central part of the analysis of war must be cultural processes that take place after the devastation, that is, cultural reconstruction or "ethnogenesis" (Murra 1984; Whitten 1976). War affects society long after the last bullet is fired, and the creation of new cultural forms should be considered part of the anthropology of war.[19] One of the main consequences of the civil war for Q'eqchi's has been the formation of an indigenist revival movement committed to renovating the traditional rituals of the earth cult. Ethnocidal state policies imply ethnogenesis, and the two must be studied together if we are to grasp the full meaning of war.

CHAPTER EIGHT

THE INVENTION OF A Q'EQCHI' ETHNIC IDENTITY

The recent "indigenist" movement among Q'eqchi' catechists espouses a radical view of ethnicity. It promotes a politics of emergence that refashions identity around Q'eqchi' language, it encourages the renovation of aspects of traditional religion and culture, and it asserts the superiority of indigenous peoples over nonindigenous. Mayan revivalist movements, now prevalent throughout Guatemala, are one of the main focuses of present anthropological research (C. Smith 1991; Warren 1992; Watanabe 1995). Identity, more than any other issue, has generated dialogue between foreign and indigenous social commentators. The literature on ethnic resurgence, however, is much less extensive than that on state violence, partly owing to the recent and still indeterminate consequences of this new Mayan social movement. What material there is tends to focus on national rather than local expressions of revivalism.

There are both parallels and contrasts between Q'eqchi' indigenists's ideas and the ideology of *indigenismo* as it is commonly portrayed in Latin American history.[1] Like the *indigenismo* of early nineteenth-century Latin America and Mariátegui (1969), the indigenist movement in the Verapaces was initiated by educated, nonindigenous sectors of society. Although sparked by foreign Catholic missionaries, indigenist ideas were rapidly taken up by Q'eqchi's, especially by urban catechists. Pitt-Rivers (1973:19), quoting Bourricaud, writes, "Indigenismo is an ideology for mestizos," which, to an extent, excludes Q'eqchi' indigenist thought from the conventional category of *indigenismo*.

This present movement makes sense only in terms of recent historical processes, especially the catechist program and rural repression. The Q'eqchi' revivalist movement has been cast from the mold of two historical realities: the onslaught against the traditional image of the community by the bearers of a universal religious orthodoxy, and a military domination that precludes class identity. These processes are still at work today, and it must be remembered that everything described in this chapter takes place in the context of a militarized society (see Wilson 1993c).

Indigenist catechists, like the original catechists before them, constitute a revitalization movement that enacts a conscious plan of cultural reform. Yet the two movements have worked with dissimilar images of what it is to be Q'eqchi'. Whereas the first catechists valued the modern and deprecated the autochthonous, the indigenists exalt the traditional and erect defenses to exclude the Ladino "other." Anthony Wallace (1961:155) writes that "in chronically extreme situations, [revitalization] movements may develop every ten or fifteen years." He expects this only in "small, tribal societies," but Q'eqchi's (a large, nontribal linguistic group) have experienced two such movements within the space of fifteen years. The extreme situations that have fostered revitalization movements include subsistence crisis, war, falling commodity prices, sweeping religious change, and rapid cultural transformations.

The foremost expression of traditional Q'eqchi' religion and community, the cult of the tzuultaq'as, has been a central concern of both revitalization movements. The earth deities were largely attacked by the first wave of catechists, who combined an antitraditional stance with a class-based political philosophy. Catechist discourse attempted to sweep away all previous religious, political,and economic forms. In some areas catechists supported armed insurrection against the dominant order and called for the creation of the "Kingdom of God on Earth." As Yonina Talmon (1962:130) observes, millenarianism can have a strong antitraditional element, rupturing with established religious norms "in a desecration of their most valued religious symbols."

The state repression killed hundreds of lay activists and caused the collapse of the catechist program in many areas. Scorched earth policies of the early eighties had devastating consequences for local social organization and culture, leaving a lasting stamp on the catechist effort and other Church work. Now the previous catechist discourse is inverted, embracing a severe suppression of class politics and a reworking of religious traditionalism. The original catechists disparaged the mountain spirits, but now tzuultaq'as are accorded a primary role in the indigenists' sense of "becoming" Q'eqchi'.

In the wake of these successive waves of change, the relationship between religion and social change has altered little. Bricker (1977:257) writes that all Mayan revitalization initiatives are "an attempt to throw off the yoke . . . of 'foreign' domination." The catechists, whatever their discourse, constitute the main channel for social protest. The clergy were the prime instigators of both currents in the catechist program. Faced with crises at its indigenous base, the Catholic church has reacted repeatedly with the same strategy—the creation of a revitalization movement.

ETHNIC REVIVALISM AND
THE CATHOLIC CHURCH

There is a dual nature to Q'eqchi' belief at the moment, the Word of God and the traditional ideas. They are separate and the catechists do not know how to bridge the two. We want them to be able to speak of both together. — a Catholic missionary

Indigenist ideas have been common currency in Guatemala and Latin America since the colonial period, but their preeminence in the Church at this particular time demands explanation.

The military defeat of the National Guatemalan Revolutionary Unity (URNG) and the destruction of trade unions and peasant organizations has foiled class politics in contemporary Guatemala. When the revolutionary movement had looked poised for victory, reformist sectors of the Church were sympathetic to social change. The utterly crushing defeat of the insurgents in Alta Verapaz meant that liberation theology was persecuted and driven underground by secular and religious authorities alike. This contrasts with the situation in other areas such as Quiché, San Marcos, and Sololá, where the war between the army and URNG continued into the 1990s.

Statements about indigenous ethnicity, on the other hand, do not draw as much attention from the security forces. The Cerezo administration (1986–91) itself used indigenist rhetoric in a populist bid for public approval. In 1987, the government paid large handouts (U.S. $400) to highland *cofrades* to parade in front of foreign dignitaries in the capital. Such cynical manipulation of indigenous culture was accompanied by a profusion of utterances about the value of the indigenous heritage of the nation. In this environment, there is more scope for public social comment in the idiom of ethnicity than in that of class. The indigenist missionaries of today are not the Marxists of ten years ago. They are highly critical of the insurgents and those with a purely Marxist orientation. Many people with the latter tendency have either been exiled to Mexico or killed, or they now confine their activities to the capital.

Initially, the main interests of indigenist missionaries were not overtly political but ecclesiastical. Their intent was to effect changes in the liturgy by incorporating selected symbols of tradition. They explicitly drew upon the pronouncements of Vatican II and Latin American Episcopal conferences and on experiences of missionaries in Africa to "Africanize Christianity." They called this process an "enculturation of the faith" and a "Q'eqchi'-izing of the Church." Political considerations, however, remained subdued until Q'eqchi' catechists put them center stage.

The initial aim of the indigenist clergy was selectively to introduce elements of what they saw as Mayan culture into the celebrations of the mass. They burned *pom* incense and candles, placed palm leaves on the altar and walls, and sprinkled pine needles on the floor. This was the custom in a *cofradía* celebration, or whenever traditionalists invoked the sacred. The Catholic service might be held in the round, as opposed to having everyone face the front altar, thus expressing a perceived "Q'eqchi' egalitarianism."

In some masses, large quantities of maize ears surrounded the altar and were raised by the catechists along with the sacraments before communion. This practice recognized the sacred status of the subsistence crop and allowed the participation of lay activists. The priest might introduce corn tortillas to replace the imported wafers that symbolize the body of Christ. I never saw alcoholic *b'oj* used as a substitute for wine, however, owing to its continued rejection by the catechists. In the indigenists' mass, blood sacrifice remains taboo and is still seen as belonging to an archaic, pre-Christian past.

In the indigenist mass, elders now play a larger role in leading the congregation's prayers, assuming the duties of the *aj k'atok,* "she/he-who-burns" the *pom* and candles. This was traditionally a principal role in the community offering to a saint or a tzuultaq'a, but it was appropriated by catechists when the weekly meeting of the Word of God began. In these instances, initiatives by the clergy are having an effect in the villages. Elders are generally pleased at these developments because they are reintegrated, albeit in a lesser role, into new expressions of older rituals. The elders seem to be regaining some influence over how the community is imagined through ritual.

Often the priests are more experimental with indigenist ideas than are the catechists. One priest organized elders to dance in the traditional style to marimba music during a mass. Dancing is held to be taboo by all catechists because of its associations with *cofradía* celebrations, drunkenness, and licentious behavior. In another case, a priest performed a mass requested by the elders for the well-being of domestic and wild animals, a request that might have been refused only a few years ago. An elders commission at the level of the diocese was formed to further elders' interests. The elders' role in the liturgy, however, is still decorative and less important than the catechists'. The elders do not have access to the central locus of ritual power—the Bible and its interpretation.

Although this process has only recently begun, many of the changes I encountered in the mass were superficial and tokenistic, motivated by priests' own preconceptions of a monolithic Q'eqchi' culture. An indigenous missionary candidly referred to the process as "still at a folkloric level."[2] One priest acknowledged the limitations of his approach, saying in an ironic tone: "We foreign priests can change some rites, use more candles, and burn more *pom,* but this is only the primary level. The profound incarnation of belief has to wait until the ordination of indigenous priests."

Yet producing Q'eqchi' priests might not solve the problem so easily. The Q'eqchi's presently in seminary are products of a process designed to Ladinoize its Mayan subjects. One seminarist from Sololá told me, "The seminary swept away my identity as an indigenous person. I returned to my village and I wasn't like before because I had learned to depreciate my culture. Those who are conscious of their culture don't find a space; many are expelled or refused ordination if they identify with the people."

The overt discourse of "Q'eqchi'-ized" masses does not incorporate traditional deities of the autochthonous religion. The tzuultaq'a icon remains just as marginalized as before. So far, all that has been incorporated is some of the ritual paraphernalia used in the earth cult.

For many missionaries, the indigenizing of the liturgy is an extension of the historic plan of the catechist program—the evangelization of the Q'eqchi's. The Catholic hierarchy recognizes that previous efforts failed to rout the remnants of traditional religiosity. So the indigenist current represents in part a new strategy in the long-running extirpation of indigenous idolatry. A U.S. missionary commented: "The culture has to be taken into account if the message is to reach the people's heart. Right now I don't know how deep the faith of the people goes."

The attitude of most clergy suggests that the indigenizing of the liturgy is undertaken with the intention of making Q'eqchi's more Catholic rather than making Catholicism more Q'eqchi'. In the eyes of many priests, if Q'eqchi's are to be more Christian, Catholicism must contain more traditional religious elements for Q'eqchi's to relate to. This perspective does not apply to all clergy; there are a few who genuinely respect the religious autonomy of villagers. Ironically, the motivations of some missionaries in introducing indigenist ideology—the extirpation of idolatry—are wholly different from the Q'eqchi's' reasons for accepting this discourse—reconstruction of culture and identity. This situation echoes Weber's comments on the unintended consequences of religious doctrines.

The balance between center and periphery in the Catholic church is delicate and dangerous, and so must be highly controlled by the hierarchy. They are careful to keep close rein on any movement among the laity, be it charismatic, indigenist, or radical materialist. Studies among Catholic base communities in Brazil (Bruneau 1982) and other Latin American countries (Cleary 1985; Gismondi 1986) have described similar relations between base community and institutional Church.

Some missionaries virulently oppose the indigenists' plans for the Church, however orthodox they may seem to be. They fear that indigenizing the Church means rendering it open to "pagan" influences, never a point on which the Catholic church has historically been comfortable. One Salesian priest said during a pastoral conference in the diocese, "There must be an equilibrium so that we do not reject the universal values of the Church. We must follow the Church line, but perhaps with only a Q'eqchi' flavor."

Those clergy closely allied to orthodox liturgy and doctrine are also more likely to be conservative politically. During a pastoral conference of the diocese, they vented their anger against the indigenists: "These types are the ones who whip up the people and then the army kills everyone and they run away to leave us to pick up the pieces. . . . These courses will breed hate and violence between races. . . . To give these courses is like putting a match to dry brush. We in the Church must confine ourselves to spiritual issues only."

The same old division between conservatives and liberals has surfaced over the issue of ethnicity, just as it crystallized over class in the late 1970s. At present, the indigenists have the support of the bishop and hold key positions in the institutional structure. We must view the Catholic church, then, as a heterogeneous institution with different theological and ideological currents and tensions both between clergy and laity and within the two groups themselves. Because no one group commands complete control, there can be only a partial consensus. Opposing sides may attempt to become independent from one another but are always bound within the same institutional structure.

REHABILITATING THE ANCIENT MAYAS

The relationship between clergy and catechists is hierarchical, although the latter are semiautonomous of the missionaries' mandates. One of the central methods of transferring doctrine is through the courses for catechists. The "formation committee," which is composed of clergy, creates a set of courses, the first two being called "The Path of the Israelites" and "The Path of the Maya People." Though written by missionaries, the courses are translated into the indigenous language and taught by Q'eqchi's, allowing them to influence the content. Course teachers are usually urban catechists, those most exposed to indigenist clergy and Ladino national culture and with the strongest desire to reconstruct Q'eqchi' identity.

The courses were the first serious effort by the diocese to inculcate catechists with the indigenist current of thought. I participated in several courses given in different places and was able to form an opinion about their aims and degree of local acceptance.

In the courses, Q'eqchi' identity was not so much recreated as created. As I argued earlier, a strongly defined pan-Q'eqchi' identity did not exist traditionally. People would refer to themselves as being from a certain locality, community, or municipality. Q'eqchi' was simply the language spoken, and the word

Q'eqchi' denoted linguistic proficiency more than ethnicity. In the courses, the Catholic church used the concept of "Q'eqchi'-ness" to mean shared cultural values and attributes, which in reality might vary. A language-based ethnic identity that was historically weak was thus greatly strengthened. Catechists were quick to begin using this terminology and now refer to themselves as "we the Q'eqchi'."

Eric Hobsbawm and Terence Ranger (1983) have drawn attention to how an "invented tradition" is central to the project of any collective identity. The catechist courses taught that "the Q'eqchi'" were descendants of the ancient Mayas of the Classic period. In the past, most Q'eqchi's held a low opinion of their ancestors and sought to distance themselves from them. Usually Q'eqchi's referred to Mayas as "savages" or "wild men." The most common term was "Ch'ol men," because the Ch'ol tribe was still living in the jungle when the Q'eqchi's were living in Spanish *reducciones*. As I mentioned earlier, this label is still used as a disparaging epithet by catechists against those who continue to practice customary agricultural rituals.

The courses contradicted prevailing opinions about the ancient Mayas, exalting traditional culture above that of the present. They detailed the achievements of Mayan science and astronomy. They idealized Mayan social structure, teaching that the land was owned by all in a blissful state of primitive collectivism where everyone shared resources equally. Marxism and ethnic revivalism both painted a collectivist picture of the Mayan past. It was said that there was no alcoholism. Any unfortunate aspects of Mayan culture (such as human sacrifice) were said to have been brought by foreigners such as the Toltecs—explicitly drawing a parallel between the Toltecs and modern-day Ladinos. The courses contradicted themselves when referring to Mayan religion. Often they depicted Mayas as monotheistic believers in the Judeo-Christian God. At other times they recognized that the Spaniards had introduced the "Word of God," but "it did not come to sweep away the ideas and soul of the Mayas." They stated that remnants of Mayan culture still exist and must be recovered to bring back the peace of the Mayan golden age. In sum, the courses invented a Mayan tradition, encouraged its recovery, and implicitly promoted a political program of pan-Mayanism.

The reactions of the catechists were generally positive, for the message connected with their shared experiences of cultural loss. Often the courses would turn into effervescent discussions of particular customs, with catechists excitedly volunteering memories of their forebears' practices. The youth of the ethnic revivalists is of significance: these men are the sons of the first catechists of the 1970s. They identify primarily with the symbols of their grandparents. New icons of community are not just about changing collective representations but are also part of an intergenerational psychological drama.

In the courses on the Mayas, the atmosphere would become electric and animated, with many catechists declaiming at once, finally able to relieve repressed beliefs and doubts. Catechists would repeat verbatim the sayings of elders, especially their claims that corn harvests were pitifully low these days because people had ceased to perform their rituals to the tzuultaq'as. They recounted stories that repeated the theme of the sacrificial contract whereby farmers would be repaid with bountiful crops in return for sacrifices of fowl to the tzuultaq'as. In one instance, they asked the Q'eqchi' course instructor if this were true, and the latter replied yes. Catechists asked in disbelief, "Should we really go to the mountain to ask permission?" and the instructor replied, "Go!" For the first time, the Church was giving credence to some aspect of the tellurian image of the community.

Catechists accepted some of the ideas contained in the

indigenist courses, but they reworked the elders' knowledge according to their own criteria. The treatment of tzuultaq'as is a good example of syncretism in action. Catechists' adherence to monotheism is airtight, and they reject the ambiguity of their fathers on this issue. The elders said that the mountains had *xtioxilal,* or godliness. Some elders were not too sure how many gods there were in all; many said only one, but others said more. Catechists held fast to the idea of only one God. So where do tzuultaq'as belong? They clearly are sacred, but what is their place in the Catholic hierarchy of sacred beings? Catechists and clergy agree that the mountain spirits are like guardian angels in that they are not gods but carry out a protective role. In one course, a catechist said, "God created the mountains and left them down here to watch over everything while He is in the sky."

The catechists selectively emphasize the good aspects of tzuultaq'as. The wrathful and destructive nature of the mountain spirits is glossed over as they are incorporated into local official Catholicism. Perhaps this is because of the emphasis given in the catechist program to the New Testament and to Jesus as a wholly benevolent God, most unlike the God of the Old Testament and the traditional tzuultaq'as.

The orientation of the courses toward Maya and Q'eqchi' identity has spilled over into the conception of the mountain spirit. In the past, tzuultaq'as encompassed both nonindigenous and Mayan ethnicities. They appeared as white landowners but always spoke Q'eqchi'. Today's indigenist catechists, with their disdain of whites, reject their elders' view and assert that tzuultaq'as are their ancestors, the ancient Mayas. We cannot know whether tzuultaq'as were white-skinned gods before the Spanish invasion, but indigenist theology plans to indigenize them thoroughly. This position contradicts that of the army, which seeks to appropriate the paternalistic and authoritarian aspects of tzuultaq'as.

Urban catechists celebrating the "Word of God" in a corn field

The indigenizing of religious icons extends to the Virgin Mary, who has become an *aj k'aleb'aal*, "a-girl-from-the-corn-fields." From the lily-white Ladina on the church altars, she has become, in the words of one lay preacher, "a campesina like any one of our girls. She was not from the towns, and she couldn't speak Spanish either." For tzuultaq'as and the Virgin, language proficiency (being monolingual Q'eqchi'), skin color (being dark skinned), and place of origin (being from the mountains) are the criteria most important in their conversion into "Q'eqchi'-ized" divinities.

Not all catechists accept indigenist ideas. Opposition to the courses depends on a variety of factors, including rigid adherence to Catholic orthodoxy, landlessness, urbanization, and the influence of evangelical groups. The Catholic church is a heterodox institution, and some parishes, such as those of the Salesians, have produced extremely orthodox and antitraditionalist catechists who are antagonistic to the ideas of the courses. Salesian priests protested to the bishop over the courses' contents and instructed their catechists to boycott them.

In urban areas and on plantations, some catechists balked at renewing the rituals because they owned no land, and discussions took a radical turn: "The Mayas had their land, and lots of it, but now it is owned by the bosses so how can it be sacred?" Also: "How can we do the ancient customs around the land if it isn't ours anymore?" And: "We have no land. People work in town and don't want anything to do with the traditions."

The catechists were drawing a direct link between the land-tenure system and the survival of their customs. For them, the agroexport economy was incompatible with the persistence of cults of tzuultaq'as. The capitalist plantations caused landlessness, proletarianization, and changes in the nature of the community, thus rendering futile any attempts to replicate exactly the old religion.[3]

In areas with a high incidence of evangelicals, the catechists were reluctant to return to the old customs. One Q'eqchi' nun made it plain when she said, "Some catechists run their church like the evangelicals, with no saint images or incense. They are frightened because there are so many chapels around." Many of those most adamantly opposed to the new trends are from the towns. These lay activists tend to be involved in the new salvationist and charismatic current within Q'eqchi' Catholicism, a result not only of Protestant conversions but also of military repression.

The generational conflict still simmers unresolved, obstructing a revival of customs. Younger catechists are more accustomed to Catholic orthodoxy and are less exposed to the

methods of their fathers. Their most common objection to the
ways of the ancestors concerns alcohol. Many catechists are
radical teetotalers, often in reaction to their own previous
alcoholism: "But all the elders want to do is drink." And: "The
elders keep their secrets, they won't share their knowledge with
us, only if they've had a bit to drink."

To many catechists, tzuultaq'as represent tarnished images
of lost communities. The catechists see no way to return to
previous modes of apprehending the world, modes their religious institution helped destroy.

It is too soon to tell what lasting effect the courses will have
on the everyday ethos of villagers. To quote one catechist:
"Some things are difficult to explain in our communities, like
the idea that everything is alive, so I'll choose the bits I can say."
Ultimately, it is up to each catechist what to tell his congregation back in his village. The response in the communities has
generally been positive toward the religious facet of indigenist
thought. The villagers' support, however, has been even more
united and favorable for indigenist economic policies, as I will
detail later.

THE PREDICAMENT OF
ETHNICITY

Urban catechists hold the most radical views on Q'eqchi' ethnic
identity. At the same time, the most vehement opponents of
ethnic radicalism also live in urban areas. I believe both subject
positions have the same explanation. In the towns, catechists
feel most acutely the challenges to traditional identity that
come from Ladinos, the state, evangelicals, and national urban
culture in general.

Urban catechists have seized upon language as a marker of
identity. They consciously speak Q'eqchi' in their homes and
communities, scolding those who talk in Castilian. Seeking to

"purify" Q'eqchi', they purge it of its many Iberian borrowings. One man joked, "We talk with one foot on the ground and one in the saddle," meaning that they speak neither pure Q'eqchi' nor pure Spanish. Rural Q'eqchi's speak their native language with more fluency and with less contamination from Castilian. Yet those who have any contact with urban centers and markets (that is, the majority) speak a Q'eqchi' littered with Castilian words. This is the case even among monolingual Q'eqchi' speakers. To remedy this, catechists have renovated dozens of archaic words (not used commonly for centuries) to replace the Spanish or "Q'eqchi'-ized" Spanish. For example, they now use *poyonam* instead of *kristian* to mean "person." This practice is in part a return to their secular pre-Colombian identity, which changed when Q'eqchi's became "Christians."

Urban catechists have also urged the formal use of archaic greetings and partings by juniors toward male and female elders. These phrases had hitherto persisted only in the most isolated areas. Urban Q'eqchi's are inventing new words for foreign concepts that had always been communicated in Spanish. The catechists demonstrate great imagination in this process, exploring the full expressiveness of their language:

English	New Q'eqchi'	Literal Translation
airplane	so'sol ch'iich'	vulture metal
radio	raabinob'al soon	music listening-place
telephone	raabinob'al aatin	word listening-place
electric light	kaxlan xam	chicken/foreign fire
eyeglasses	kaxlan lem	chicken/foreign glass
television	mu sa' kaxon	shadow in a box

Catechists are teaching the members of their communities to use the Mayan counting system, which had been largely forgotten. Most Q'eqchi's could count to twenty, but after that they would use the Western system. I met only one ancient elder, a curer and suspected witch, who could count up to four hundred in Q'eqchi'. Youths especially enjoy learning the vigesimal Mayan system.

The catechists' emphasis on language is supported by the work of IGER, a radio education program backed by the Catholic church.[4] The Catholic radio station, broadcasting in the vernacular, is the infrastructure for the program. IGER functions in over four hundred villages and is managed solely by Q'eqchi's, who provide the materials and teacher training for catechists. The catechists then return to their villages to give literacy classes in Q'eqchi'. IGER operates out of the parishes, so its area coordinators are urban catechists. They are the ones most influenced by its philosophy, which accords high value to Q'eqchi' language and customs. IGER held indigenist convictions before they became part of the catechist movement. IGER's role was crucial during the recent change in the orthography of Guatemalan Mayan languages. It provided the network and information to make the changes understandable for villagers whose ability to read in their own language was tenuous at best.

Benedict Anderson (1991:44) draws attention to the rise of "print capitalism" (e.g., newspapers, mass book publishing) in the formation of new types of imagined communities. Until very recently, the Bible and religious publications were the only written documents in Q'eqchi'. They forged new textual links between members of a disparate linguistic community. The constitution of the Guatemalan republic was printed in Q'eqchi' in 1987 as part of the government's nationalist project—one more episode in the perennial competition between the sacred community and the nation-state over villagers' imaginations. In this context, however, the radio is more important than print; the Catholic station blares in every home, beginning at four in the morning to suit the schedule of its agricultural audience.

Along with renovating their language, urban catechists are pressuring the Church to use Q'eqchi' more at all levels. They harass priests to learn their language. The cathedral has yet to hold regular masses in the vernacular, and this is a sore point for some, representing what they feel to be the exclusion of Q'eqchi' by the Church hierarchy. The *hermandad* of Calvary, a brotherhood that coordinates the events and processions around Easter week, has in the past conducted its prayers, songs, and liturgy in Castilian, even though all its members and participants are Q'eqchi's. In the last few years, after a prolonged tussle between catechists and conservative elders, all Holy week events have taken place in Q'eqchi'.

The perceived ethnic identity of saints' images has become a point of contention, as I realized during the planning of a procession of the Virgin of Guadalupe. The "Indian Virgin" is a symbol of the evangelization for indigenous peoples throughout Latin America (Friedlander 1975). She is also a symbol of peasant and indigenous resistance; Zapata's troops fought under her banner in the Mexican Revolution. Before the day of the Virgin's procession, urban female catechists argued over whether to dress the image in Ladina or Q'eqchi' clothes. In the end, Mary went on parade in indigenous dress—a woven blouse and a *corte*, the dark-colored skirt worn only by Q'eqchi' women. During the 1850s, the dressing of crosses and Catholic icons in indigenous clothing was a principal feature of the War of the Castes in Yucatán (Villa-Rojas 1978:100).

In another incident, the best-known local saint image, the Christ in Cobán's Calvary church, was to be taken down and cleaned. The image was originally carved in the form of a blue-eyed European. After hundreds of years of incense and candle smoke, the Christ was completely black, like the main religious shrine in Guatemala, the Black Christ of Esquipulas. A wealthy plantation owner, descended from German coffee entrepreneurs, offered to pay the cost of specialist cleaning. Yet she arranged the matter solely through the bishop, bypassing the

Women catechists in a procession of the Virgin of Guadalupe

hermandad made up of indigenous catechist caretakers. She encountered great resistance from the *hermandad,* who did not like the idea of a white Christ or her manner of ignoring the Q'eqchi's in charge of "their own" church. Similarly, Sallnow (1987:77) records how the cleaning and whitening of the Señor de Temblores led to riots in Cusco in 1834. In the end, the Calvary image was cleaned, demonstrating the power of the hierarchy and its financial patrons over the indigenous congregation.

Urban indigenists' attitudes toward Ladinos are generally more combative and aggressive, expressing a resentment motivated by centuries of subordinate status. The catechists, taking great pride in their Mayan past, boast of how their ancestors militarily defeated the Spaniards. Racial equality based on a notion of Christian brotherhood has always been part of the catechist program. The indigenists take the egalitarian ideology a step farther by actively questioning how it can be achieved in practice. Their contempt for Ladinos and those Q'eqchi's who aspire to Ladino status is explicit. In their sermons, the catechists extol the virtues of being a Q'eqchi' and denigrate Ladino culture, language, and perceived lack of religious convictions. They appropriate God for their own, since it is written that God is with the poor, and all Ladinos are viewed as being rich. Ladino economic and political hegemony is resented and seen as ultimately based upon deceit and skulduggery. Ladinos are referred to as "thieves" and "foreigners."

The catechists are not entirely original in their insulting of Ladinos; the practice seems characteristic of ethnic relations throughout Mesoamerica (Bricker 1973). Among the Tzotzil, it is said that "a woman sinned with a white dog and so gave birth to Ladinos" (Guiteras Holmes 1961:157). Although this attitude has featured in ethnic relations for many years, it has not entered into the public discourse of Catholicism until now.

Catechists bring pressure to bear upon the young people of the communities to prevent them from becoming Ladinos. They instruct the youths to be proud of their indigenous attributes. Girls are coerced most heavily of all and are discouraged from wearing makeup, Western jewelry, or trousers. Only women still wear traditional Q'eqchi' dress, and the pressure on them to maintain it is great. Warren (1993:46) observes that for ethnic nationalists, women are "powerful metonymic representations of community" who stand for "the essentialist construction of Kaqchikel identity." Perhaps this explains why the ethnic identity of Virgin icons is contested so hotly.

Q'eqchi's traditionally used Spanish Christian names and Mayan surnames. Some indigenist catechists are now giving

Q'eqchi' first names to their children, some of which have to be completely invented, especially girls' names. All of the foregoing practices amount to a radical process of boundary maintenance in relation to the minority Ladino population that lives in the towns and monopolizes military, political, and economic power throughout the province.

INDIGENISTS AND URBAN IDENTITY

An emerging ethnic identity is most noticeably present in the major towns. Urban Q'eqchi's encounter discrimination daily, and this judgment of inferiority is both internalized and reacted against. Indigenists are reacting against a structure and ideology of inequality with deep roots in history and national society. Such discrimination is most exposed and acute in the towns, where national institutions and the Ladino elites who run them are based.

Q'eqchi's are often called *inditos,* or "little Indians," by Ladinos. Every year on the day of the Virgin of Guadalupe (December 12), Ladinos dress their children up as *inditos,* putting them in stereotypical Mayan dress and covering their faces in greasepaint. This is the equivalent of a Sambo costume and is perceived as a parody of indigenous dress. While Q'eqchi's are proudly parading their Indian Virgin, Ladinos undermine the occasion by making a mockery of indigenous dress and identity.

Each year Ladinos celebrate the day of Tecún Umán, the last K'iche' king, who, legend has it, was killed by the lance of the conquering Pedro de Alvarado. Indigenous children are taught in school, and in Castilian, about the "glorious" defeat of their culture hero (i.e. glorious, but defeated).

Communities close to urban areas are less dependent on traditional knowledge than are people in isolated villages, due to exposure to local Ladinos and heightened contact with other regions and the capital. Ladino ideas, especially political ones, are hegemonic in urban areas. Castilian is more widely used, and with it come national and international cultural influences. There is also a higher degree of religious pluralism in the towns because evangelical groups maintain their head offices in Cobán. The only institutions of the weak civilian state structure are in the towns as well, and their power is largely confined to these areas. Q'eqchi' men living near the towns stand more chance of being seized and forced into military service. Education and health care services are largely restricted to urban areas. The only hospital in Alta Verapaz is in Cobán, enabling urban Q'eqchi's to visit it often, whereas distant areas rely more on traditional healing methods. There are no pharmacies in rural areas. Urban Q'eqchi's are more likely to speak Castilian and to receive at least some schooling or literacy training. One Q'eqchi' teacher told me: "Thank God the government education programs are so inefficient. It has saved our culture in the rural areas. Education is one of the main methods of bringing in Ladino values."

Q'eqchi' communities are constructed very differently in the towns compared to the rural areas, where villagers live in monolingual, relatively homogeneous communities. Urban neighborhoods are not bounded communities with the same sense of shared history, because there is a great deal of movement into and out of their blurred borders. Catechist groups have become the main structures for the imagining of urban Q'eqchi' communities. Originally, the Catholic clergy actively opposed the setting up of base groups among Q'eqchi's in the towns. Only a few years after the catechist meetings started up in rural communities, they sprang up spontaneously among urban Q'eqchi's, but not among Ladinos.

Urban base groups draw people from both the towns and their hinterlands and are only loosely based on geographical proximity. Their recruitment is based much more on occupational category and kinship than is the composition of the rural village group, which is based on locale. In the urban base groups I knew, more than 60 percent of the members were related by kinship, and conversion to the group generally followed kin lines. Often, the reunions take place in the house of each member in rotation, which means that many participants travel up to two hours to be with their brethren. There is an almost desperate quality to this desire to reinvent a sense of community in the towns.

Many urban Q'eqchi's are alienated from the land and work as wage laborers, which means that the earth cult cannot be the central representation of urban notions of community. Whether their work is agricultural or in crafts, their landlessness is ultimately incompatible with the traditional religion, which is specifically centered on a sacred geography and ensures human and maize fertility. Without a piece of land, however small, the link with the tzuultaq'as is considerably weakened. When asked why they ceased to practice their customs, urban Q'eqchi's repeatedly responded, "Well, we haven't any crops, have we?" Ownership of the land, even if not legally recognized, is essential to geographic images of community.

Urban Q'eqchi's are most affected by government efforts to "integrate" (read "Ladinoize") indigenous peoples. At the same time, their involvement in traditional Q'eqchi' culture is lessened by landlessness and involvement in capitalized industries. The absence of the village structure gives a different meaning to collective rituals such as *cofradía* celebrations. The community sacrifice to the tzuultaq'as before planting is not practiced at all. Traditional health care methods are supplanted by clinics and hospitals.

On the other hand, the exposure of urban Q'eqchi's to priests means that they are also more influenced by new indige-

nist currents within the hierarchy. When the indigenist movement got underway, urban catechists were the first to understand its ramifications. It is exactly these urban catechists who
are the course instructors. Inculcated with the discourse of the
indigenist priests, urban Q'eqchi's took the ideas to their logical
conclusions in a more explosive fashion than did the villagers,
whose community identity was not as problematical.

When questioned why he thought a radical ethnic consciousness developed more rapidly in the towns, a missionary
replied, "These catechists tried to be Ladinos and failed. They
weren't accepted, so they became the most adamant Q'eqchi's."
This analysis does not apply in all cases, but without a doubt
the identity of urban Q'eqchi's is the one most threatened by the
Ladinos. Indigenous identity is continually under attack, yet
becoming accepted as a Ladino in Cobán is difficult. Urban
Q'eqchi's are constantly pressured to Ladinoize but seldom are
fully accepted as Ladinos.

Local memory plays a central role here; the categorization of
one's family forever influences the ethnicity of the individual.
This is partly because Ladinos constitute a very small percentage (less than 10 percent) of the population of Alta Verapaz.
Neither fluency in Spanish nor the adoption of Ladino dress and
customs can easily erase local memories and collective histories. Ladinoization is possible, especially through extended
residence in Guatemala City, but it is difficult. Even when
becoming a Ladino is feasible, the whole process carries with it
psychological traumas that are often underestimated by anthropologists.[5] These contradictory tensions have led to a
revitalizing of age-old symbols in order to relocate and
recreate an identity. In doing so, urban catechists have
focused upon the same symbols (e.g., tzuultaq'as) that the
catechist program denounced in its early years. We see, then,
a cultural reorientation by urban indigenous people, facing

not inward toward the town center but outward toward the surrounding mountains.

Drawing from Fredrik Barth's perspective, a general point can be made here: that a renovation of traditions and a radical stance on ethnicity is most likely to come from those caught in between two ethnicities, on the boundary where categories blur. Wolf (1969:291) expressed this idea in class terms, writing that neither the most downtrodden nor the well-off but the middle peasantry is most likely to rebel.

These general comments have historical precedents in Mesoamerica. In Bricker's reading (1981) of Mayan history, colonial and postcolonial religious revitalization movements were often led by Ladinos or Ladinoized indigenous people. In 1708, a Ladino instigated the first miraculous cult of the Indian Virgin in highland Chiapas. The Quisteil rebellion of 1761 was headed by Jacinto Canek, a Maya who was literate and spoke Spanish, having been educated by priests (Bricker 1981:70). A defecting Ladino led the 1867 Chamula uprising for a short time. In recounting the Caste War of Yucatán, Bricker (1981:92) refers to a mestizo group located between the Indians and the Ladinos. Originally, Ladinos were the "Spanish whites," and mestizos were an ambiguous intermediary group with no fixed community allegiance. True to their liminal status, mestizos fought for both sides. The leader of the Mayas was Jacinto Pat, an educated mestizo plantation owner (Bricker 1981:98). The inventor of the cult of the Talking Cross was José María Barrera, a mestizo.

To sum up, we can see that a problematical community identity combined with daily discrimination by Ladinos stokes up the fires of radical ethnic revivalism in the towns.

OUR FOOD, OUR WATER

The first wave of catechists became caught up in an insurrection against the state. The new indigenist catechists' program is expressed in an organization called Qawa Quk'a (literally, "our food, our water"), which is directed not only inward at Q'eqchi' communities but also outward at the market and Ladino material culture.

This catechist association developed within the structures of the Catholic church during a meeting between laity and missionaries. Catechists demanded that the Church help them defend their livelihood and community cultures in the face of spiraling inflation and expanding global markets. These issues—inflation and cultural transformation—were inextricably linked in the eyes of both rural and urban Q'eqchi's. The clergy were taken aback by the demands, for their prevailing discourse was highly spiritual and concerned largely with sacred and intraecclesiastical issues. Pastoral programs were limited in scope and size. Catechist courses offered little instruction on pragmatic secular issues such as cooperatives or agricultural techniques. Nor was any information available on constitutional, legal, or human rights. Generally, Catholic gatherings avoided the wider economic and political situation in the country. Since the terror of the early 1980s, catechists had shown little initiative and independence, generally echoing the views of a cautious clergy.

In this context, the clergy were surprised when catechists spontaneously began making demands after one man complained of material conditions in his village. Catechists called for immediate action—not so much for the Church to save them but for communities to organize themselves. One catechist mocked the spiritual orientation of the Church, saying: "We can't wait for everything to fall from heaven. We can help one another too." Lay Q'eqchi's delivered an ultimatum to the clergy, several of whom agreed to participate in future meetings: "We hope that the Church helps us. Jesus died to save his people; which of you clergy are with us? If none, we will continue on our own." The catechists, faced with deteriorating living conditions in their villages, were looking for an umbrella discourse other than class to unite their communities in action.

Catechists formed Qawa Quk'a primarily to channel their reaction against local and global markets. They exalted all that was "traditional," linking their dependence on markets to the drastic changes in their traditional communities and culture. In its first public flyer, the group stated its position in a characteristic opening paragraph: "We are a group of Q'eqchi's who have realized that we are losing the ancient ideas which our ancestors left us and we realize that each day life is more expensive and we see our children living in misery and do not know what tomorrow will bring for them since everything we buy is more expensive and whatever we sell brings a lower price."

In one five-month period during my fieldwork, prices on basic foodstuffs increased by 22 percent. The price of cardamom, the main cash crop, had fallen to 25 percent (U.S. $20 per 100 lb.) of its 1980 value. Catechists bemoaned their dependence on cash crops for money and merchandise, which traders managed to bring even to the most remote villages. They subjected Ladino middlemen to heavy criticism for paying low prices for cash crops and then selling them in town at 100 percent profit. Truck drivers, another group comprising mostly Ladinos, also were attacked for charging high prices to drive goods to market or back to the villages, thus inflating the price of consumer goods and depressing commodity values.

Catechists remembered days when there were much less cash-cropping and consumer participation by indigenous communities. The present state of affairs, they said, was the product of the last fifteen years. Many criticized the way in which villagers were seduced by advertising into wanting every new item on the market: "New things come amongst us and they tell us we want them and we are just accepting them and it is killing us. We've become used to them and it is hard to give them up."

Catechists agreed upon a course of action that included a consumer boycott and other efforts to defend their position as producers. The boycott covered Western market goods, which would be replaced by autochthonous items of traditional material culture. For example plastic containers would be replaced with earthenware pots, Mexican mass-produced hats with straw types, Western medicines with plants and herbs, and soap with pig's fat and plant resins.

This boycott would be implemented slowly, giving villagers time to get used to the changes. There were also good security reasons for doing so: the military is vigilant for any hint of collective organizing. At one meeting a catechist said, "We must do this quietly. If we say, 'Don't buy these things,' misfortune will befall us. The merchants will become angry." Nevertheless, the Catholic radio station that broadcasts in Q'eqchi' has been the main method of transmitting the messages of Qawa Quk'a.

On the whole, the boycott list includes more women's goods than men's. Men's clothes and agricultural tools (especially machetes) are two types of goods that involve participation in the market, yet they are excluded from the boycott. Some women's clothes are also purchased, but other articles are woven and embroidered by women themselves. The boycotting of foodstuffs, manufactured soap, and plastic vases is likely to affect women's labor more than men's, so the boycott entails added work for women in particular.

A withdrawal from the market necessitates villagers' learning old skills and arts. Catechists called for the teaching of pottery, weaving, crocheting, curing of animal diseases, soap making, and traditional medicine. These abilities have not been completely lost and with effort could be revived. In the hinterlands, most women can weave cloth and men know how to make hats and tough rope bags from corn husks. Closer to the cities, such traditional knowledge has faded away completely due to the availability and acceptance of market goods.

Qawa Quk'a called for a complete reassessment of agricultural practices by Q'eqchi's. Formerly, villagers mixed cash and subsistence crops. I never met a Q'eqchi' villager who grew only coffee or cardamom, owing to the religious and economic significance of corn. All those with sufficient land potentially to reproduce the family unit had at least enough corn planted or stored for twelve months' subsistence. Only after subsistence needs were met was cash-cropping attempted. Still, the catechists urged people to reduce cash-cropping and diversify so as to minimize their dependence on any one crop (especially cardamom). This was phrased in the elders' language of reverence for maize and other crops: "We must give importance to the holy crops—maize, beans, chile, tomatoes, and cacao."

Qawa Quk'a discouraged the use of fertilizers, insecticides, and herbicides. Catechists came to accept elders' earlier pronouncements that they "burn the soil." This was a radical departure from previous developmentalist postures, which recommended chemicals to swell cash crop harvests. "Scientific agriculture," however, never definitively implanted itself due to a lack of capital. Now such agricultural techniques are perceived as a debt trap that produces an unhealthy dependence on cash crops. Once fertilizers are used, they must be continued in following years. Their cost is high for the average villager, and one bad harvest means hardship and debt. Qawa Quk'a also encourages the planting of xayau (a plant that yields a red dye) and groves of copal trees. Every community once cultivated these crops, but they have now become commercialized and available only through the market. Thus, self-sufficiency is advocated as the most desirable agricultural policy.

Qawa Quk'a is organizing to defend the price of commodities produced for sale by the villages. It attempts to create an administrative structure to mediate between representatives in each parish. This network would bypass the market completely and arrange barter between different crop-producing regions so that all can fulfill their needs cheaply. For goods that must be sold at market (e.g., cardamom, for which villagers have no use), they are looking for credit and loans to buy trucks in order to transport produce themselves. Villagers are organizing warehouses so that they can sell to middlemen in bulk, as a collective, instead of as individuals with no bargaining power.

The tone of the Qawa Quk'a meetings is fearful but determined. Catechists tell stories of benevolent middlemen or plantation owners who paid decent prices or wages and were driven away or killed by ruthless businessmen. They realistically fear the wrath of both the military and mercantile capitalists whose profit margins will be adversely affected. The scope for Qawa Quk'a to organize on the plantations is small because of the watchful eye and repressive tactics of the landowners and their foremen. In their own communities, indigenist catechists have to be wary of the civil patrols, the local eyes and ears of the army. For this reason, the group asserted in early public announcements that it was made up only of Q'eqchi's, so as not to appear associated with any politicized (read, revolutionary) Ladinos. Official policy accepts Ladinos in meetings only if they do not dominate affairs. Catechists openly discuss the possibility of one of their organizers being killed or disappeared and how the organization would react. The general attitude is fatalistic and somewhat martyrlike: "Well, they may kill us but if it is for helping our people, that's okay."

After the first few meetings, delegates returned to their communities to gauge opinions. They reported a positive response. To many villagers, it all seemed like common sense. Though they were fearful, the general consensus was to carry on with the plans. Communities did petition for much more information and instruction from the Church on the national constitution, legal rights, and the political situation in the country. The constitution of the republic was only recently translated into Q'eqchi'—the first time ever into an indigenous language. Only a tiny percentage of Q'eqchi's read newspapers; most glean news from the radio, which they generally distrust. The reaction against the economic situation has been forceful but restricted, in that it has not yet branched out into criticism of the government or the army.

INTERPRETING STRATEGIES OF AUTARKY

One explanation for the revival of traditionalism is the ecological crisis in Alta Verapaz. Elders assert (with credibility) that the fields do not produce bountiful crops as they did before. This, the traditionalists say, is because the Q'eqchi's have forgotten the tzuultaq'as, who really provide their sustenance. One elder said, "The mountains are ignored now and they feel sad. Look how small the ears of corn are." Declining productivity is also the result of decreasing land resources in Alta Verapaz. There is simply less land for more smallholders. With the boom in the cardamom industry in the 1970s, previously less-useful land became cultivated by large landowners. Meanwhile, the indigenous population increased sharply, and migration was not enough to relieve the pressure on the land. Slash-and-burn agriculture requires vast tracts of jungle, which are no longer available. Its continued practice has led to the decimation of primary forests, radically decreased rainfall, erosion, and, in short, tragic ecological consequences.

One Western analysis would say that environmental degradation is caused by relations between people: unequal access to the land and extension of the agroexport economy. For the elders, however, ecological crisis results from the breakdown in relations between people and the conscious environment, specifically the mountain spirits that inhabit and constitute the landscape. Science is not seen as a valid source of explanation for ecological problems; instead, it is part of those problems.

Q'eqchi' strategies of autarky can also be understood with reference to a changing relationship with regional and global markets. In the last twenty years, the majority of Q'eqchi' communities have placed a stronger emphasis on cash-cropping while maintaining their central focus on staple crops.[6] Wolf (1969:xiv) was correct to remark that a smallholder usually "favours production for sale only within the context of an assured production for subsistence." A market-oriented strategy was advantageous for a time, but has now become catastrophic as commodity prices plummet. Production oriented toward the market is inelastic because cash crops represent an investment of time (coffee takes five years to bear fruit) and money. At present, many Q'eqchi' communities perceive the market as highly unfavorable to their interests. Their response is not to the market itself but to their increasingly deteriorating relation to markets.

Before cash crops became so prominent, there were still markets, and community social organization has not been "precapitalist" since the mid-1800s. Taussig's (1980) work has been criticized for characterizing Andean subsistence-based economies as precapitalist and for basing the whole of his thesis on a supposed economic dualism (Sallnow 1989). Campesinos need not have "one foot in the pre-capitalist economy" to perceive the evils of capitalism.[7] Whether in the Andes or Mesoamerica, a rigid distinction between village and capitalist economies is flawed because it underestimates the historic integration of the two.[8] Furthermore, Q'eqchi' smallholders did not reject the market until it began to work to their disadvantage. Putting aside their own "alienation" and any inherent contradictions of capitalism, they were avid participants in the market while it benefited them. Modern Mayan lifestyles necessitate access to cash and markets. As for the Q'eqchi's, they began to criticize elements of modernity in the idiom of traditional culture only after their economy was ravaged by war and commodity prices fell.

The present reaction to the market is probably temporary, and if or when the prices of commodities (either traditional crops or new ones) increase, Q'eqchi' cultivators may once again turn to the market for supplementary income. The prevailing state of affairs is part of the cycle of vacillation between openness to, and insulation from, the market, depending on prices of export commodities and cycles in the world economy.[9]

Economic cycles resulting in peasantization coupled with economic conservatism are hardly unique phenomena; they have been documented in subsistence economies the world over (Scott 1976, 1977a; Wolf 1966:43–47). Scott (1977a:233) proposes that Asian peasant movements are based upon the same factors we see in Guatemala, namely, "an intrusive state and the development of a commercialized agrarian economy." In the Guatemalan case, the military state's campaign of mass repression decimated a growing commercialized peasant sector. The war halted production and ruptured links to markets. In its aftermath, catechists can promote self-sufficiency as a viable strategy with greater ease. Many refugee communities are only just meeting subsistence requirements anyway.

What needs explanation, however, is the discourse that runs concurrent with a reaction against the market and Western goods. The retreat to economic conservatism has been coupled with an idealistic valuing of indigenous culture by religious lay activists. Specifically, why are the mountain spirits and their surrounding rituals the focus of this renovation movement? Why does this ideology appeal to and unite Q'eqchi's with radically different means of production—some cash crop producers, others working class consumers?

If rural Q'eqchi's identify the market as the fount of their economic oppression, then it is not surprising that they hark back to a golden age of subsistence agriculture when they depended less on the international market. Here is a case in which resistance to the market serves as one explanation for the reinvention of tradition and the signs of the ancestral community. When the market threatens the source of livelihood, there is a resurgence of the traditional cult of the earth deities that comes hand-in-hand with a revaluation of traditional agricultural practices and an idyllic isolationism.

A UNIFICATION OF URBAN AND RURAL ETHNIC IDENTITIES?

We have seen how tzuultaq'as are chosen as symbols of a radical Q'eqchi' ethnic identity, but why have both urban and rural Q'eqchi's come together around these figures? Why would rural villagers assume the same stance as urbanites with different lifestyles and occupational statuses? Recent history has united the cultural and religious interests of urban and rural Q'eqchi's as never before. Both have experienced similar transformations of their worldview stemming from an evangelization spearheaded by young, male lay activists. Another important factor explaining the attitude of the villagers is their dislocating experience of civil war.

Indigenist discourse unites rural and urban Q'eqchi's but has a different resonance in each area. The ethnicity of urban Q'eqchi's is especially compromised, and they compensate by radically affirming their indigenous identity. This stance has a

less militant tone in rural areas, and some time ago may have
had no relevance at all. Yet the catechist program brought many
of the ambiguities of identity from town to village. It not only
shifted Q'eqchi' religious belief closer to that of Catholic orthodoxy, it also brought with it a new economic ideology, that of
development. A religious ethic and economic relations reinforced one another in a truly Weberian fashion. That rural
Q'eqchi's have been drawn into capitalist relations of production and distribution in recent years means that once the market
works to their disadvantage, they are more likely to revolt
against its concomitant cultural (Ladino) attributes.

The military repression unleashed against Q'eqchi' villages
had disastrous implications for traditional culture. Army attacks led to displacement from original lands, mass urban
migration for safety, and the abandoning of traditional religious
practices. Not since the 1870s, when foreign landowners dispossessed Q'eqchi's en masse, had an event so fundamentally
affected the isolated mountain villages. In these areas, customs
and lifestyles have undergone profound dislocations. We see,
then, a conjunction of interests between urban and rural
Q'eqchi's caused by their different but parallel experiences of
dislocated community and ethnic identities.

The attenuation of traditional mechanisms of identification
has led to the creation of new formations. Norman Whitten
(1976) and John Murra (1984) have called this process "ethnogenesis." This term is perhaps more accurate than "renewing
traditions," "revival," or "revitalization" because the new religious formations and ethnic identity are something novel.
Ethnogenesis is the act of cultural creation in response to
ethnocide. The ethnocidal policies of the civil war and the
original catechist program carried within them the seeds of
ethnogenesis, presently being sown by the indigenist intelligentsia.

Although ethnogenesis purports to be the unearthing of previous customs, it is innovative on many levels. Indigenist catechists forge new forms out of a past cultural matrix, but they are partly distinct from the traditions. Cultural memory is selective; in the words of Warren (1992:199), it has the "explicit goal of affirming what has now become problematic: the continuity of Mayan ethnicity."

To this end, the indigenist catechists have set about renovating rituals belonging to the mountain cult, but according to their still rather orthodox tendencies. The rituals could not be exact replicas of ancient practices. Only some villagers still live under the conditions in which the mountain cult traditionally thrived. Those affected by landlessness, urban migration, orthodox Catholicism, and cash-cropping must invent a new image of the community. Even if their material circumstances are compatible with the earth cult, subjective conditions in the villages seldom are. The restructuring of the communities by the military and orthodox doctrines of Catholicism and Protestantism prohibit the exact replication of past collective representations.

Bricker's study (1981) convincingly demonstrates that the "Indian King" has been a key figure of religious revitalization and anti-Ladino movements in Mayan history. The figure of the tzuultaq'a fulfills an analogous role. It too is idealized in opposition to a Ladino view of the sacred and becomes a benevolent guardian and protector, also in the role of a Maya. Both types of religious renovation have been led by "deindigenized" groups. In highland Chiapas, mestizos have played a vital role. In the case of the Q'eqchi's, both urban and rural catechists (but especially the former) have been the catalysts. However, tzuultaq'as are different kinds of Mayas than are Q'eqchi' villagers. They are ancient Mayas and, like the Ch'ol men, savages from the forest. The mountain spirits express two poles of ethnicity: the ancient Maya and the foreigner. Q'eqchi's fall into neither camp but somewhere in the middle, and tzuultaq'as represent their unresolved cultural paradoxes.

Using Barth's terminology, we could say that those at the ethnic boundary between indigenous and nonindigenous are the critical group to consider at this point. It is they who live at the edges who feel least comfortable about their ethnicity. Those who inhabit the boundaries within a society are those with the most acute sensitivity to where the boundary is set and those who have the greatest interest in altering perimeter lines. The catechists are, in this sense, like the *kurakas* of colonial Peru—the middlemen between two worlds, the mediators between external, institutionalized power and the community. The mediating class sees the contradictions most clearly, or has aspirations to power only to see them shattered. Significantly, Wolf (1969:292) also points out that anthropologists have deemed this group to be both the main bearer of rural tradition and the "most vulnerable to economic changes wrought by commercialism." This explosive mixture of adherence to traditionalism and exposure to the vagaries of capital provides the best framework for understanding why catechists have revamped tradition and rejected a total reliance on export agriculture.

Frank Salomon (1981:164) vividly describes the dramatic embracing of indigenous identity by Quechua-speaking Quiteños, who occupy a "peculiar position as an unnamed, unrecognized, but nonetheless distinctive group in the space between two cultures." Urban Q'eqchi's have been inhabiting a similar space for some time, but recent events have also dragged rural Q'eqchi's into this liminal ethnic state in which the individual feels "an inner clash, a volcanic conflict of two worlds that both exist within him" (Salomon 1981:171). Whereas formerly only urban Q'eqchi's had to redefine themselves, now villagers, too, want to hear "the voice of the 'mountain mothers'" (Salomon 1981:168). Another parallel between the *yumbo* dancers of

Quito and urban Q'eqchi's is the bond they create with surrounding mountains. The *yumbo* dancers receive their stamina
and dancing skills from the mountain *apus,* and they take spirit
names from "the place names of mountain spirits" (Salomon
1981:174).

Although the catechist program is one of the instigators of
the "inner clash," uncompromising Catholic orthodoxy and
radical indigenous revivalism are the two sides of the coin of an
identity crisis. To quote Salomon (1981:172): "The conflicts . . .
which cannot be solved on cultural 'home ground' because that
home ground itself is precisely what is in question, are projected out onto the two screens of extreme Christianity and
extreme paganism."

The indigenist current is only the latest phase in the ongoing
innovations in Q'eqchi' identities. Its effects may be lasting or
transitory. It could be that as in Chan Kom (Redfield 1950),
some communities will soon reject the new identity of the
indigenist catechists and their isolation from agroexport production. Redfield's notion of "progress" is neither chosen nor
rejected by Q'eqchi's in the long run. Developments over time
flow and eddy, expressing the nonlinear nature of history and
traditions. Villages choose a variety of paths, some defined in
terms of "progress," others in opposition to it, and still others
utterly indifferent to it.

Ultimately, holding onto an essentialist dualism of progress
versus tradition helps us not at all. The same statement extends
to other commonly reified dualisms such as mestizo/indige-
nous, capitalist/precapitalist, Christian/pagan, and so on. All
these dualisms are without eternal foundations; they are historically and contextually transformed. Among the Q'eqchi's, they
are negotiated by various groups at different times in diverse
places and are represented in the recurring symbolism of the
tzuultaq'as.

ETHNIC REVITALIZATION AND
NEW SOCIAL MOVEMENTS

Movements based upon ethnic identity have been called "new social movements" because they develop outside the traditional paradigms of Marxist discourses. Yet, as historical analogies show, the processes involved in these movements are part of a long history of ethnic struggles that share many of the same features and evolve out of similar contradictions. Gonzalo Aguirre Beltrán (1956:42) writes that the ideologies of all Latin American "Indianist" movements combine ideals of economic autarky, autochthonous religion, and ethnic segregation. The Q'eqchi' indigenist movement has parallels in Peru, where a pan-indigenous identity did not form until the Taki Onqoy uprising of 1560–70. This identity was based on the separation of the indigenous and Spanish worlds (Sallnow 1987:58–60). The Taki Onqoy movement manifested a total rejection of Spanish food, clothes, and names (Wachtel 1973; Zuidema 1966). In present terms, Qawa Quk'a resembles the Kataristas of Bolivia (Albó 1987) in being a grassroots, indigenous group with little prospect of turning to violent methods to achieve its aims.

Another analogy with Andean movements lies in the failed Huamanga revolt of 1613, which Steve Stern (1987b:47) argues led to the creation of the insulating institutions of the "closed corporate community" in the area. Similarly, the defeated revolt of Guatemalan indigenous groups in the 1980s sparked moves for community insulation, but in the form of regional organizations such as Qawa Quk'a now that the *cofrades* are ineffective.

The "newness" of the movements derives mainly from the fact that many of those writing about new social movements are reformed Marxists who have realized that their analysis must move beyond Marxist objectivism and incorporate actors' own frameworks of understanding. Having said this, I also admit that many of the ideas from the new social movements school are very useful in this context. One such idea is that not only is power present in every aspect of social life, but also "to an even greater extent every power relation is penetrated by social life" (Evers 1985:48). As Ernesto Laclau (1985:29) writes, "The political ceases to be a level of the social and becomes a dimension which is present, to a greater or lesser extent, in all social practice. The political is but one of the possible forms of existence of the social."

This theoretical approach allows the possibility for the political to be influenced and even partially determined by all forms of expression of the social, without according a priori status to any one of them. Among the Q'eqchi's in particular, power is imbued with religious and agricultural symbolism, which is the main idiom in which political decision making takes place.

A lack of understanding of the role of religious ideas and identity in the politics of everyday life leads to statements like that of Manning Nash (1989:114), who asserts that Mayan ethnic groups in Guatemala demonstrate an absence of political strategy compared to other "subordinate" minorities such as the Chinese in Malaysia or Jews in the United States. The violent nature of the Guatemalan state as compared to the U.S. or Malaysia has rendered Mayas seemingly without a voice or direction. In my view Nash is overstating his position; Mayan communities do have a political strategy, but one that is subtle and understated. Tilman Evers (1985:51) draws our attention to the "microphysics of power" that underlie the macro phenomena of power and are often overlooked by analysts like Nash and many political scientists. Political structures, whether structures of domination or of relative independence, do not exist outside everyday social practices.

Q'eqchi' political strategies (and there are many) are Brechtian in their everydayness, in their lack of organizational structure. Religious ideas contain a fount of resistance and self-preservation that has served as a basis for a new social movement when the organizational aspect was provided for it by the indigenist catechists. To use a Gramscian phrase, the indigenist catechists represent a war of position, not a war of movement. Wars of movement have been repeatedly squashed by the military-state apparatus. When supracommunity organizations (such as political parties, trade unions, and armed revolutionary groups) that represent political aspirations are dashed, ideas return to a clandestine life in the community, where they can be nurtured. There they are transformed and gather momentum until they are given shape by another, often different set of premises, through which they can again challenge the status quo. When previous discourses such as class can no longer unite communities, other discourses such as those promoting ethnic identity become hegemonic.

Everyday positions of resistance should not be looked down upon as immature forms of politics; in fact they are highly sophisticated, with mass political potential. Indigenist Q'eqchi' strategies are intentionally unintelligible to Ladinos (and many western social scientists, no doubt including this writer) and incommensurable with Ladinos' formal political categories. As such, they are more resistant to being co-opted, controlled, or destroyed. I agree wholeheartedly with Evers when he writes (1985:59), "Weak and fragmented as they are, the new social movements thus hold a key position for any emancipatory project in Latin America. They are it."

Scott (1985:28) criticizes social science for romanticizing peasant wars of national liberation and ignoring the silent and anonymous forms of class or ethnic struggle that peasants employ. He is right when he says that we need to understand what the peasantry does "between revolts" as much as we understand the revolts themselves (Scott 1985:29). This is one of the main messages of this book: that although armed revolt is not on the present agenda for the majority of Mayas in Guatemala, they continue to wield ordinary "weapons of the weak" in their daily strategies for autonomy.

Qawa Quk'a is one of hundreds of indigenist movements all over the Americas, the majority of which do not receive attention from outside observers. It will probably be assimilated into community discourses and melt into everyday practice like the overwhelming proportion of such movements. Its potential to effect change is more social than formally political. Though its institutional structure may fail or be repressed out of existence, indigenist ideas are likely to affect ethnic relations for many years to come.[10] Its principles may no longer be channeled through an organization, but they will be absorbed into daily practice — diffused, but still present.

CONCLUSIONS

Strident revivalism among catechists has different motivations in rural and urban areas, the latter being more prone to radical expressions of ethnic identity. Indigenist discourse provides the ideology to unify people in a pan-Q'eqchi' alliance. In a sense, the same role was played by liberation theology in the late 1970s. In both cases, catechists unified disparate groups by espousing a religion-based ideology bent on overturning present relations of economic and cultural inequity. Stern (1987b) is right to comment that the message of Indianism is directed more at indigenous peoples themselves, in a bid for unity, than it is at Ladinos.

However radical they purport to be, ethnic movements can never completely sweep away the present in favor of the past. The revived mountain spirits and their associated rituals are as modern as they are ancestral. There has been selectivity on the part of clergy and catechists involved in the indigenist project. Barth (1969:35) writes well about this process, saying that

> much of the activity of political innovators is concerned with the codification of idioms: the selection of signals for identity and the assertion of value for these cultural diacritica, and the suppression or denial of relevance for other differentiae. The issue as to which new cultural forms are compatible with the native ethnic identity is often hotly contended, but is generally settled in favour of syncretism.

In ravaging the traditional images of community, the catechist program created the necessary preconditions for an ethnic revival. Ethnic revivalism does not merely follow changes in material conditions. After all, the crisis in the rural economy in the late 1970s did not lead to a stronger ethnic identity. The present ethnic revival has been made possible by the pan-Q'eqchi' dissemination of ideas and the unfolding of a capacity to imagine identity in terms of a community wider than that of a person's immediate circle of kith and kin. By embracing certain attributes of Ladino society, the catechists of the 1970s incorporated principles of universality that allowed them to transcend the narrow boundaries of the community. This laid the groundwork for the emergence of a new Q'eqchi' identity with enough general features to forge meaningful links between communities that were not possible before. To use Anderson's phrase, it established a new mode of apprehending the world.

After the scorched earth policies of 1981–82 and the military consolidation of control in 1983–86, there was not even a flicker of organized protest from catechists. Perhaps Taussig (1980: 153) is vindicated in this instance: "Political struggle starts with the determination to resist ideological encroachment," so that symbols of indigenousness are seized upon as markers of resistance. The Catholic church triggered this process in the beginning, but as also happened with liberation theology, the catechists have assumed independence from the institutional hierarchy and are deciding their own course of action.

The catechists broke the old template of imagining the community, but the revolutionary and developmentalist models failed. Catechists, however, remained the bridge between communities, the charismatic leaders who could construct collective images to combine communities in common endeavor. Now indigenist catechists seek to construct an ethnic identity and end up reconstructing old community images that preceded the catechist movement. In their search for elements of the past in the present, they come across strands of ancient practice in health care and agricultural production. The indigenist catechists create a new identity, basing it on a revamped and Mayanized mountain spirit. The Mayas in the mountains are their only link to a past that is itself contested.

Finally, it must be recognized that Mayan revitalization groups are forming all over highland Guatemala. A pan-Mayan identity is forming through bilingual education, Catholic and Protestant churches, radio stations, and national indigenous groups such as CONAVIGUA (National Coordinator of Guatemalan Widows) and COMG (Council of Maya Organizations). Mayan intellectuals are formulating nationalist programs for cultural and territorial autonomy (C. Smith 1991). Such groups have flourished all over Latin America in recent years, campaigning around the Columbus quincentenary in 1992 and the UN Year of Indigenous Peoples in 1993. The processes I am describing are not wholly new; they merely represent one twenty-five-year segment of a long history of transformations of indigenous identities.

CHAPTER NINE

IDENTITY RECONSIDERED: THE PAST IN THE PRESENT

Cultural change transpires not only in a linear, diachronic fashion but also in cycles, returning to refashion prior cultural signs. Ethnographers have written extensively about religious conversion, most of them stressing its finality. Few have emphasized the tenuous nature of apparent innovation. Perhaps this is because only a handful have returned to their place of fieldwork after several decades. Robert Redfield did just that, and in *A Village that Chose Progress* (1950:114) he wrote of how "change . . . was more apparent than real." Rendering the title of his book somewhat ironic, he describes how seventeen years after a whole village converted to Protestantism, it reconverted back to a blend of Catholicism and Mayan religion. Redfield was forced to relegate the Protestant episode from the status of an event of major "progress" to the status of an "unsuccessful mutiny" (1950:113).

Within "syncretized" religions, there is an ever-shifting flux, a sequence of oscillations. The pendulum swings between an indigenizing of Christianity and the Christianizing of indigenous beliefs, and writers such as Frank Tannenbaum (1943: 402) have questioned which has been the historically dominant tendency. Whatever the present balance in Guatemala, it is clear that since the Spanish invasion, traditional beliefs and Christianity have become intertwined and contradictions are still being played out. The relative influences of the orthodox and the vernacular move in cycles and remain unresolved. Further, the constitutional nature of global and local elements is not static but is itself transforming internally.

We should approach indigenous revitalization movements in Guatemala in the light of these comments. As Eva Hunt (1977: 249) writes of Chiapas: "These armed rebellions were viewed in religious terms as nativistic movements, and involved a clear attempt on the part of the Indians to reinterpret Christian symbolism to fit the needs of their ethnic group." Religious intermixture is but one of the cultural contradictions within community and ethnic identities. Indeed, identity should not be seen as a bounded Aristotelian concept but as an assortment of paradoxes that interact dynamically without ever being reconciled.

Why is religion so often the stage on which Mayan community politics are played out? Part of the explanation lies in the way in which local political languages the world over draw from a syntax that is not wholly constructed by the discourses of colonialism (Prakash 1992:183). Mayas have sought to elude the uniform and controlled identities conferred by a system of dominance and find new, untrammeled cultural domains which then serve as foundations for alternative visions of identity. They are engaged in a continual quest for alterity. Local religious expressions have never stood completely outside Ladino elite discourses of political authority, but they do represent autonomous local interests more than any other cultural idiom. This characteristic is prevalent throughout the Guatemalan highlands; Kay Warren (1978:60) writes that ethnic "separatism is most clearly achieved in the realm of religion."

Throughout Q'eqchi' history, key images of identity have been expressed in a religious medium. Preinvasion Mayan communities gave primacy to religion, and Mayan states in the Classic period have been described as theocratic (Thompson 1954:266). Since the Spanish invasion, the Catholic church has been the external institution with the most prolonged presence in indigenous communities. Catholicism was one of the main points of contact between colonialism and indigenous peoples, and community political representatives were legitimated by holding religious offices as well. The Catholic church has exerted the most important external influence on the identity of Mayan groups, partly because of the Mayas' exclusion from formal political structures (that is, the state). Indigenous peoples have sought representation in religious structures, and, as elsewhere in the world, an indigenous intelligentsia has developed primarily within the Catholic church. This local literate elite has, historically, encoded both the interests of Catholic universalist identity and those of a particularized ethnic identity.[1]

In terms of overt resistance, often a wider rebellion begins within the community structures of the Catholic church itself, whose ecclesiastical discourses provide the ideological mortar that cements communities together.[2] Revolt in the Mayan area erupts in defense of the community, and so has invariably drawn upon religious images and institutions. Religious organizations have served as key channels for discontent directed against Ladino authorities. Waldemar Smith (1977:13) writes that the K'iche' uprisings of the 1920s and the Tzeltal rebellion of 1712 were both "based on an expanded and ad hoc version of village institutions," notably the cofradía.

Mayan rebels have used Catholic symbolism in their movements against Spaniards and Ladinos over the centuries, and these Catholic symbols are the focus of competition between conflicting groups. Talking saints appeared in the Tzeltal rebellion, in which indigenous rebels referred to themselves as "soldiers of the Virgin" (Bricker 1981:62). In the latter half of the nineteenth century, the Yucatán peninsula was in the control of an incipient Mayan state. The main religious symbol during this War of the Castes was a talking cross, and the rebels were called "the people of the cross" (Bricker 1981:113). The holy crosses of the rebels were dressed in indigenous clothing (Villa-Rojas 1978:100), and so the Christian symbol was indigenized.

The widespread insurrection of Guatemalan indigenous peoples against the state in the 1970s and 1980s should be seen as part of this history. Although the guerrilla movement is formally Marxist, the rebellion developed inside the village religious structures (the Word of God catechist meetings) and rode the back of a spiritual conversion to the catechist program. Revolutionary catechists identified with the symbolism of Exodus, referring to themselves as Israelites and the soldiers/government as Egyptians. The guerrillas espoused the unification of Ladinos and Mayan communities in a combined class struggle. Their military defeat was a major factor in the development of radical indigenist movements, which advocate an alternative, separatist view. Religion still furnishes the organizational structure and discursive medium binding communities together in political action.

It is apparent that Mayan communities tend to focus upon a particular religious figure—Christ, the Virgin, or a saint—around which the orthodox and the vernacular feud. These struggles channel the surrounding reservoir of ethnic, economic, and political tensions. Victoria Bricker (1981) has shown how issues have coalesced historically around the figure of the Indian Christ and the Virgin. All documented Mayan revitalization movements have reinterpreted Catholic symbols to integrate them into indigenous experience. Such was the need for an

Indian Christ that the inhabitants of Cancuc crucified a Tzeltal boy on Good Friday in 1868.

Among the Q'eqchi's, tzuultaq'as have been the focus of collective tensions. The indigenist revival is unique in that it is focused on a Mayan image, not on a symbol of Catholicism. To my knowledge, there is no previous documentation in anthropological or historical literature of the renovation of an overtly Mayan deity. As David Gow (1979:74) has explained, Mayan movements have been Christian in their overt symbolism, whereas Andean movements such as Taki Onqoy have been more disposed toward using autochthonous icons. Gow qualifies this seeming oversimplification, recognizing the native symbolism present in Christian iconography. It is no accident, for example, that the Virgin appeared on the mountain Tepeyac, nor that the cross, successor to the Mayan tree of life, is the focus of many revitalization currents. Because Gow is writing about general tendencies within Andean and Mayan movements, I think his basic thesis is sound.

Referring to the Andes in the sixteenth century, Gow (1979:58) points out how "victims" were cured of the dancing sickness during a September festival associated with the Pleiades (Onqoy) constellation, which was linked with the fertility of maize. The participants in Taki Onqoy were possessed by the *wak'as,* local figures of the pre-Inka landscape. Community shrines were associated with these mountain spirits, so perhaps there is a greater parallel between Taki Onqoy and the renovation of tzuultaq'as than originally meets the eye.

The Q'eqchi' indigenist movement seems to lie somewhere in between traditional Mesoamerican movements and Taki Onqoy. It developed within a Catholic structure, yet it employs the indigenous symbolism of a native deity. Catechists approach tzuultaq'as not as indigenous people reinterpreting a Catholic symbol (as happened in the Chiapas movements) but as Catholics reinterpreting an indigenous symbol (unlike the Andean movements).

Why are tzuultaq'as repeatedly the focus of Q'eqchi' cultural revitalization? As I have stressed throughout this book, representations of the landscape are central to community and ethnic identities. Q'eqchi's call themselves "sons and daughters of the earth" (*ral ch'och'*), "people of the cornfield" (*aj k'aleb'aal*), or by the name of the important local mountain. The village's agricultural fertility and human well-being are dependent on this mountain, and major community rituals are directed at the local religious topography. These community identifications were traditionally more important than being ethnically "Q'eqchi'."

Q'eqchi' identities have not been fixed for all time but have been undergoing transformations since before the Spaniards arrived. After the invasion, the Q'eqchi' word for "person" changed from *poyonam* to *kristian*. More recently, this usage changed again with the commencement of the catechist program, when activists sought to reconstruct local identity during meetings of the Word of God. In the context of rapid economic and religious change, coupled with the upheaval of civil war, it is not surprising that some Q'eqchi' villagers champion a reconstruction of "traditional" identities. Indigenist catechists gain their popularity from this nostalgia, for they propose a revival of "ancient" rituals and an improvement in the relationship with the land, as much in the economic realm as in the sacred.

As in many instances elsewhere, religion serves as a space for resistance and cultural preservation. According to Michael Sallnow (1987:267), sacred landscapes are a means with which to legitimate domination (for the army or German landowners) and a means with which to resist it (for the indigenist catechists). Which persona of the tzuultaq'as is revealed depends on historical circumstance. Like the devil in the Bolivian tin mines, the mountain spirits can be evil landowners or champions of resistance (J. Nash 1979).

One reason for the revival of the tzuultaq'as is local economic difficulty. The present discontent is caused by spiraling inflation of prices of consumer goods and falling commodity prices. This situation would have had less impact on Q'eqchi' villages twenty years ago, but with increased participation in cash-cropping, encouraged by the catechists, smallholders are now dependent on the market as never before. When this dependency leads to deprivation, villagers repudiate not only the market but also the "modern" agriculture that precipitated the crisis. Further, they reject capitalist agriculture's associated religious ethic—orthodox Catholicism, catechist style. Tzuultaq'as represent the antimodernist religious component of the traditional subsistence economy and are the symbolic personification of an agricultural strategy of self-sufficiency. Their revival underlines the importance of including culturalist explanations in understanding economic behavior. There is nothing necessary about the link between economic difficulties and a rejection of modern agriculture. Specific perceptions of and responses to economic circumstances are mediated by local cultural discourses, in this case religious ones.

There are also more culturalist explanations of the importance of tzuultaq'as that accord weight to the internal characteristics of their symbolism. In traditional religion, tzuultaq'as represent many features of the sacred. Tzuultaq'as wear many masks and can accommodate many more. They encompass all boundaries, subsume all divisions and dualities. The mountain spirits not only envelop distinctions but also recognize them and mediate between them. Mountain spirits stand at the gateway to the supernatural, mediating between communities and other divinities.

The integrated diversity of tzuultaq'as is repeatedly manifested. Tzuultaq'as are both male and female, mother and father,
good and evil, god and demon, spirit and matter. They unify the
earth and the sky, controlling events on land along with rain and
the movements of the celestial deities. Their character is authoritarian and open to manipulation, being both goodwilled and
vengeful. Kind as well as vicious, they are always unpredictable
and capricious. The tzuultaq'a figure encloses different ethnicities — "wild" Maya, Q'eqchi', and European.

Because the mountain spirit contains a variety possibilities
of expression of ethnicity, gender, and the sacred, it is the focus
of the sociological and symbolic contradictions that surface in
Q'eqchi' communities. The multifaceted character of the
tzuultaq'a allows a range of interpretations to be made by
competing interest groups such as traditionalists, catechists,
the Catholic clergy, the army, indigenist catechists, and Protestants. Each of the different factions created among Q'eqchi's by
economic and political processes emphasizes one set of features
over another, thereby defining themselves. Every faction appropri-
ates an image of the mountain spirit, but there cannot be complete
hegemony of any single discourse. Each group can have only
partial influence in this inveterately pluralistic situation. Which-
ever current is preeminent cannot be divorced from the concomitant sociological factors outlined in this book, such as emerging
economic differentials, civil war, and the strength of institutional
churches. All these influenced the construction of new historical
Q'eqchi' identities. Though they form part of a chronological
transformational sequence, all the strands created by these processes coexist in Q'eqchi' communities.

MAYAN IDENTITIES AND TRADITION

The most widespread approach to Mayan collective identities is
materialist and relationalist, and it sees indigenous cultural

patterns as responses to state and Ladino hegemony. This approach has had a major impact on how Mayan histories are written: those influenced by Fredrik Barth have tended not to do history at all, and those inspired by Eric Wolf have seen history as beginning only after the Spaniards arrived.[3]

Among others, Carol Smith's (1990a:220–22) materialist reading of the indigenous past bears many hallmarks of this approach. She argues that indigenous identity is "not fixed in 'tradition'" but is renewed in each generation and is created dialectically in opposition to the Ladino world. Local belief emphasizes the continuity of a group's tradition, but according to Smith, "all tradition could disappear" tomorrow and indigenous identity would remain.

This approach is certainly not wrong and has led to many valuable insights, but it is, I think, one-sided. The point that indigenous communities are partially the product of external relations, particularly with Ladinos and the state, is wholly acceptable. Yet this functionalist and synchronic view overlooks the way in which indigenous identities remain powerful and distinctly "traditional" even when their specific meanings are altered through their articulation with successive historical moments. Religious tradition, in particular, historically frames identities, providing the idiom for and limitations to the way community is portrayed.

Q'eqchi' experiences have shown how, even under cataclysmic circumstances, tradition will never just "disappear." Instead, tradition is continually readjusted to the circumstances from within a monumental matrix carried forward from the past. The mountains still loom over Q'eqchi' communities, casting their shadows on all present reformulations of the community. There is an immense inertia in local representations of shifting ethnic boundaries, even though change is wrought by events of epic scale such as civil war and Catholic reevangelization. Identity, then, remains a process of constrained refashioning.

Relational and materialist views of identity tend to neglect indigenous agency and deny the autonomy of nativistic cultural constructions consciously developed by indigenous peoples. As Robert Carmack (1990:130) argues, indigenous cultural forms are not dialectical reflections of Ladino culture. Robert Carlsen and Martin Prechtel (1991) have illustrated convincingly how Atiteco symbolism "embodies its own history." The religious archetype of *Jaloj K'exoj,* in the sense of the "Flowering of the Dead," is a core sign of cultural memory, grounded in the past activities of the ancestors.

Kay Warren's (1992, 1993) social constructionist discussion of Kaqchikel identity displays perhaps one of the most nuanced and insightful approaches to indigenous history in Guatemala. She conceptualizes history as both fragmentary and continuous in her exploration of local discourses on religious conversion and war. These cultural processes imply both breaks and continuities, especially in the individual's sense of self. In her interpretation of the narrative about transforming selves, "Peel Off Flesh, Come Back On," Warren (1993) shows how evangelicals' conversion stories evoke traditionalist Kaqchikel constructions of the person.

Despite my emphasis on the past, I am not making a sentimental argument for undefiled traditional communities. A romanticized essentialist view has little framework from which to cope with the impact of modernity, other than bemoaning its savaging of the "pure" indigenous community. John Watanabe (1990:201) counsels against the naive reification of traditional indigenous communities that represents them as "fragile mosaics of 'shared poverty,' political insularity and cultural inscrutability that then shatter irrevocably under the impact of global modernity."

NONFOUNDATIONAL HISTORIES OF IDENTITY

Social thinkers have been too ready and willing to dismiss other peoples' pasts. In exalting form over content, they apply structural paradigms that are insensitive to their informants' sense of cultural memory. This has been the legacy of approaches to identity informed by structuralism, structural Marxism, and poststructuralism. The latest postmodernist trends in social theory have inherited from structuralism a relational approach to meaning and a presentist bias that mitigates against a subtle treatment of histories that invoke tradition and authenticity. In denying all prior and integral bases of identity, postmodernism has taken structuralism's relational view of meaning to its logical and sometimes extreme end.

Postmodernism generally expresses an even more synchronic perspective on culture than that of Barth. In anthropology, the synchronic has held sway because of a variety of influences, including Malinowski's functionalism, Lévi-Strauss's structuralism, and the usually short duration of fieldwork. Postmodernism has only exacerbated this disciplinary predisposition. J.D.Y. Peel (1989:213) is right to question the notion of the present as a viable, distinct object of study: "The present has often been treated by anthropologists as a sort of temporal plateau, coterminous with the duration of their fieldwork, inhabited by structures and categories; but it is much more evanescent than that, no sooner come than gone, really no more than a hinge between the past and future."

Some of the most influential postmodernist statements on identity come from James Clifford. At the beginning of *The Predicament of Culture* (1988:1–4) he invokes the dadaist poet William Carlos Williams, whose work expresses the "predicament of ethnographic modernity," in a world where all peoples suffer from "lost authenticity" due to the "cultural incest" of "scattered traditions." According to this view, when marginal peoples enter the modern world, they quickly lose their distinct history and are no longer able to invent their own future. The demise of genuine traditions means that "there is no going back, no essence to redeem. . . . Such authenticities would be at best artificial aesthetic purifications" (Clifford 1988:4).

Clifford's own vision (1988:9) is of an interconnected world made up of an "unprecedented overlay of traditions," where everyone is "'inauthentic': caught between cultures." This predicament leads to a continual process of "personal and collective self-fashioning." For Clifford (1988:10), identities are "mixed, relational and inventive"; he conceives of "collective identity as a hybrid, often discontinuous inventive process." Clifford (1988:12) is suspicious of any attempts at returning to "'original' sources, or gathering up of a true tradition." He writes that "if authenticity is relational, there can be no essence except as a political, cultural invention, a local tactic." Because of the global nature of local identities, ethnographic histories are condemned to oscillate between two metanarratives: homogenization and loss, and emergence and invention. Both narratives are relevant, and each undermines the other's ability to tell the whole story.

This last point accurately captures what writing this book actually felt like. I realized that neither loss nor invention described "the whole story" for all Q'eqchi's, and each point that confirmed one reading demanded a contrary qualification. In trying to include every counterpoint in the narrative, I engaged in a constant process of self-vetting to make sure that processes of homogenization and emergence received equal regard. Q'eqchi' identities certainly are hybrid, as Clifford puts it, and a number of social actors from within Q'eqchi' communities are engaging in a competitive process of collective self-fashioning. Revivalists' discourses on tradition do not lead to an exact return to an original authentic state (whatever that may have been) but partially reinvent icons of tradition according to the present cultural and political context. The past is not fully recoverable, and the activities of the revivalists can be at best fragmentary and selective.

Yet there are other areas where Clifford's claims impose too many limitations—specifically, the idea that any concept of tradition is never more than just an ideology of the present, a discourse that legitimates today's political position. Clifford's preference for deconstructing any concept of tradition to show how it is a capricious tactic reinvented in the present context does not enable us to explore cultural continuities and fissures that might tell us why certain traditions are possible and others are not.

Clifford himself (1988:15) anticipates criticism of his book's approach, admitting that "its Western assumption that assertions of 'tradition' are always a response to the new . . . may exclude local narratives of cultural continuity and recovery." Clifford asks who has the right to speak for a group's identity, yet what right has he to deny all those in the twentieth century their sense of authenticity and generally to deride their own understandings of tradition?

Clifford can only criticize modern versions of tradition in this way in relation to his own unstated conception of what "real authenticity" might be. By emphasizing the uniqueness of the twentieth century, Clifford suggests that authenticity is a possibility only of the nineteenth century and earlier. His predicament of culture is exclusively modern, which implies that a "genuine" authenticity and tradition can only be (romantically) premodern. Yet identity was problematical and hybrid long before the advent of modernity. Clifford's conception of "real authenticity" (and he must have one to show how all existing ones are illusory) is far too immaculate and idealized to be a useful working concept for the rest of us. Clifford's "hidden" definition of authenticity is also too universalist; any workable definition of authenticity must be local and contextual, and historical as well as relational.

All renditions of tradition (including the premodern) transform through time, but simply because they are shaped by present political strategies and global cultural influences does not mean a particular tradition can no longer be judged more or less authentic. If we employ less pristine and chaste concepts of "authenticity," "origin," and "tradition" that allow for ruptures and outside influences as well as continuities, then they become more useful as categories in thinking about identities. Watanabe (1992:x) takes a valuable step in this direction with a pragmatic approach to authenticity, arguing that authenticity inheres in what people make of themselves, not in primordial properties of their culture. He asserts that people experience change but can still retain an abiding sense of who they are. He allows for contingencies and fragmentation by indicating that "no people ever self-consciously encompass the totality of what they are about." I would add that notions of authenticity are embedded in the premises for the conventional sociality of a place and in the shared memory contained in collective representations.

Authenticity is certainly problematical, but not only because there is disarticulation with the past. Discontinuities are linked to the past because they always have to be discontinuous in terms of something, that is, prior cultural patterns. Social processes are not orderly and rule bound but can be paradoxical and indeterminate. Yet even contradiction can be comprehensible through reference to the past. As J.D.Y. Peel (1989:199) writes, "Even the sharpest kind of identity change, such as religious conversion, becomes intelligible only in the light of continuities and criteria of value, which run from past to present."

Breaks with the past (e.g., through evangelization) often occur as oppositions to the past, and those oppositions are constructed in relation to previous cultural icons. We can never know, as Redfield confessed in his writings on Protestant conversion, whether an interruption is eternally final. The ethnic revivalists' politics of emergence, despite its often invented nature, sends impulses of cultural memory leaping across the synapses of discontinuity and rupture. My final point on historical discontinuities concerns agency. Cultural ruptures, even if they are externally triggered, do not transpire outside of the consciousness of local agents. If one conceptualizes cultural change in terms of radical breaks, one presumes passivity and an unconscious status on the part of the actors involved.

Clifford maintains a disdain for any notions of historical causality and a predilection for cultural flux and unpredictability, both of which are touchstones of postmodernism (see Lash and Friedman 1992:1–30). This free-floating view of culture reflects well one fashionable North American image of its *own* identity and history, in which unhampered consumers choose from a cafeteria menu of personal identities. Yet this image is overly presentist because social actors are not wholly free to reinvent themselves and that which preceded them.

Rosalind O'Hanlon and David Washbrook (1992:164), among others, argue convincingly that individuals are not free to reinvent either global relationships or their culture at will. Social relations are not as voluntaristic or individualistic as many postmodernists would have them, but are framed by past and present social discourses and structures. In terms of local substantive knowledges of social life, the social is never "in the last instance groundless," as Ernesto Laclau (1985:37) argues, for its possibilities of expression are limited by its own past.

And as with Friedrich Engel's view of determination by the material base, one never arrives at the postulated postmodern "last instance" anyway.

Although the various currents within postmodernism do not generally highlight historical explanations, their philosophical or metatheoretical influence on social history has been beneficial in that it has dealt a seemingly fatal blow to essentialist conceptions of identity and foundationalist approaches to narrative.[4] It is surely right to argue that the impact of political economy on cultures and identities is not predetermined but must be contingent in each instance.

Benedict Anderson's (1991) approach is particularly useful for tracing the historical trajectory of an identity without lapsing into essentialism. Anderson argues that changes in a people's model for apprehending the world are necessary in order to rethink identities. In Alta Verapaz these changes were effected through processes of reevangelization and civil war. For most Q'eqchi's, the community is still imagined in the idiom of religion, but a more defined ethnic identity has also developed within this discourse.

In the traditional communities described in chapters three through five, the communal images are the local saint and the mountain spirit(s). These are not static images; they have incorporated elements of events such as the assimilation of the Ch'ol tribe in the sixteenth century and the growth of agroexport plantations in the nineteenth century. The earth gods express collective land rights and are actively involved in the community's agricultural production and human reproduction. The local landscape operates inside the boundaries of the individual psyche, appearing in human form in dreams and occasionally interfering with a person's soul. The imagining of the ethnic group is not as elaborated as is that of the geographical community. These Q'eqchi's imagine their ethnic identity by references and pilgrimages to the Thirteen Great Tzuultaq'as that delimit their territory.

The catechists and evangelicals swept away previous models for imagining community and broke the connection between identity and the landscape. A new set of images such as the Bible — a universal text — and an orthodox global brotherhood were put in place. During this period, external entities such as the state and Catholic and Protestant churches exerted greater control over local imaginings of identity. The concept of "community" expanded to include more than just the geographical village. The limited number of coherent icons of traditional identity became subordinate representations in the context of a competing plurality of images. With the decline in importance of local identity came an increased awareness of ethnicity, as catechist pilgrims met regularly from disparate regions. More important than this, however, was the growing sense of class identification, as people perceived "we the poor" to be more relevant to events than "we the Q'eqchi'."

During the war, traditional forms of community identity were dealt a heavy blow. Refugee status deepened the chasm between people and their landscape. After the war, the army reorganized communities physically. By reshaping the mountain spirit into a "soldier tzuultaq'a," it sought to insinuate itself into traditional forms of imagining community. The military altered local institutional organization to fit the army's structure of control and emphasized surveillance over punishment as the main mechanism of repression. Because of their link to the state, civil patrols became the most powerful internal community institutions. The patrol leaders, in their monthly reports to the military base, became what Anderson calls "inner pilgrims" of the state (1991:115). In these ways, the military cultivated national identity at an unprecedented level in Q'eqchi' communities. The breakdown of previous forms of community association had unintended consequences for ethnic identity because it created possibilities for new forms of imagining "the Q'eqchi'."

Anderson (1991:11) argues that the secular rationalism of eighteenth-century Europe gained ascendancy because of the demise of the traditional community and because religious modes of thought did not address philosophical questions of existence for the masses. Nationalism could fill these existential gaps and so increase its ambit of influence. Yet the Guatemalan military has so far failed to entrench nationalism among Mayan peoples. In the context of persistent social inequality, Mayan counterhegemonic discourses have merely shifted from community to class to ethnicity. Collective religious images continue to subvert national identity.

The renovation of past images of the community such as the mountain spirits by indigenist catechists is carried out not so much to recreate the traditional community as to enhance ethnic identity. Catechists are developing new ways of imagining "the Q'eqchi'" so as to move beyond the community to higher levels of association. This strategy has also strengthened pan-Mayan links across Guatemala and even pan-Indian ties across the continent.

In this book I have sought to show how the symbolism of the landscape and icons of the community provide continuity to the past under the impact of modernity. What could be a more modern experience than surviving the full onslaught of twentieth-century means of mass destruction, wielded by the one ethnic minority that controls the nation-state? Cultural reconstruction is going on, and Q'eqchi' identities and communities are patently not what they were. Yet indigenous peoples are the active agents in this reconstruction, and their responses are shaped by their cultural history. What I am proposing is a synthetic approach: that we see both the legacy of past content without distilling any essence from it, and that we recognize the influence of Q'eqchi' interactions with Ladinos and their state without losing sight of how history mediates these interactions.

Q'EQCHI' PRAYER IN THE CAVE SACRIFICE

1. Ay Tiox Ay Tzuultaq'a ex inna' inyuwa', arin wankin rub'el aawoq, rub'el aawuq' at wa'. Chaakuy ta xaq inmaak. B'antiox aawe xinru xinchal jarub' chi tzuul, jarub' chi taq'a, jarub' chi leeg, chi kutan. Anaqwan wankin arin sa' Qaawa' Siyab', b'antiox xaq aawe xaak'e we xinru xink'ulun toj arin at inyuwa'. Sa' xk'ab'a' xnimal xloq'al aawankilal, laa wiinqilal, laa tioxilal, laa wuxtaan, laarahom, laa santil kawom.

2. Wanko sa'in, sa' li santil na'ajej a'in, naqanaw naq wanko chaawu at inTiox, naqanaw li ani wan chink'atq, li ani ink'a' naoso'. B'antiox aawe xinb'eek xochal atwa'. Kutan saqeu toj arin sa' xnimal aaloq'al. Laa'in ka'chinin chaawu Qaawa' Tzuultaq'a. Laa'at tz'aqal nim ut tiix.

3. B'antiox xaq aawe xoaak'ulun chi aatinak aawik'in, chi seraq'ik aawik'in, chi tzamankil qatenq'al qakawilal qasahilal, chi yechi'inkil qamayej chaawu. Waaye' li qasantil pom, waaye' li qasantil kandeel, waaye li qasaqi utz'uj, aaay Tiox, raxi pom saqi pom q'ani pom, saqi ceer raxi ceer q'ani ceer.

4. Arin wanko sa' laa santil ilob'aal, laa santil muheb'aal. Ka'ch'in aawa aawuk'a' tink'e aawe anaqwan. Waaye li loq'laj pom, li loq'laj usilal. Anaqwan arin wankin chiru li Qana' Po, li

Qaawa' Saq'e, li Kak Chaim, chiru li Oxlaju Tzuul, li oxlaju Taq'a sa' xk'ab'a' xnimal li qawa quk'a'. Wa'eat inyuwa', chaak'e chaawoq chaawuq' chaawu. Wa'eko.

5. Arin wan ink'as, li jo'chial jo'k'ial jo'nimal xink'atok chiru li tzuul li taq'a rik'in li waqlaju pesos. Naru nintoj nink'at chiru li Qaawa' Qana' Tzuultaq'a re naq toaak'ut ut toaab'eresi. Arin wankin chixtojb'al li loq'laj k'iche', li loq'laj che'k'am. At nimajwal Tiox, at Qaawa' Tzuultaq'a, chinaatenq'a ta xaq. Taak'e laa b'endicion sa'xb'en ink'al. Ok qe chi aawk. Ninpatz' laa liceens chi k'anjelak chiru li loq'laj Tzuultaq'a b'ar naqataw li qawa quk'a'. At Qaawa' Siyab', chaak'e weesil rik'in li Qaawa' Tiox. Maataqla li xuleb' chixwa'b'al ink'al. Chaak'e aawuxtaan sa' inb'een ut sa' xb'een walal k'ajol. Laa'in aj ——————— . . .

6. Naqab'aanu jo' ke'xb'aan li qaxe'qatoon aj Maay, jo'ka'in xe'ra xaq li qaTzuultaq'a. Laa'ex neke'xk'e li qatzakaank, li qawa quk'a', li qasahilal, li qakaxlan, qawiimq, qatoomq. B'antiox xaq aawe Qana' Itzam, Q.Tulux, Q.Chiaax, Q.Chimam, Q.Xukaneb', Q.Raxche', Q.Raxuntz'unun.

7. Xik xaq qe at Qaawa'. Xoaak'ul sa' laa santil muheb'aal. Chaakuy qamaak, laa'o yal wiinqo. Taak'am qab'e re naq maak'a' li raylal, li rasa. Taqak'ul ut b'ar toruuq tohilaanq, aran tohilaanq jo' nakawaj laa'at. B'antiox xaq aawe.

Q'EQCHI' PRAYER IN THE GRAB CROP RITUAL

At inTiox at inyuwa', chaakuy inmaak, b'antiox xaq aawe naq xaasi ke jun chik kutan rub'el aawoq rub'el aawuq'. Laa'at tzaqal nim chiwu ut q'axal numtajenaq aawuxtaan, atQaawa'. At Qaawa' Saq'e, Qana' Po, Qaawa' Kak Chaim, cheek'ul ta xaq li mayej a'in. Wankin arin chi xpatz'b'al inliceens. Ok we chi aawk sa' li loq'laj kutan a'in. Xik we chi muquk. Ok qe chi k'anjelak chiru li loq'laj Tzuultaq'a b'ar taqataw li qawa quk'a'. Chaak'e laa bendicion sa' xben ink'al. Chaak'e chi k'iik ink'al. Chaak'e li hab'. Chaawil re naq maak'a tixk'ul. Tintz'aamaaq aawe re naq li k'a'ru ninaawk, a'an we, moko re li yak ta, moko re li k'iche' aaq ta. Maataqla eb' li xul chi xketb'al ink'al, chaaxoc re naq ink'a' te'k'ulun. Nintz'aamaak eere Qaawa' Xukaneb', Q. Kojaj, Qana' Ak'tela', Q. Chitu, Q. Woloq', Q. Mucano, Q. Sa'pok, Q. K'ixmes. Cheerab'i ut cheek'ul intzamahom.

THE SUN'S ELOPEMENT WITH THE MOON

God gave light to the stars and moon and sun. He told the sun, "You will watch over all that is on the land." The sun came down to see the land and its animals. He came way down. He saw a young girl, the moon, weaving outside her house. The hummingbird fed on the flowers, he fed on the yellow flower (*q'antzum*). His feathers were so very blue-green (*raxrax*), like glass/mirror (*lem*). The girl called her father, the tzuultaq'a, and asked him to hit the hummingbird. He took his *puub'* (gun, previously blowgun), and hit it.

The girl put the dead bird next to her and stroked it as she wove. When it became late, she took it to bed to sleep with it next to her. Her father, the king, the tzuultaq'a, was sleeping. The hummingbird heated up again. He said to her, "You screwed me over, now I am going to screw you." He spoke with her (*raatinankil*, a euphemism for "have sex with"). He said, "Now we must flee," and they flew across the water.

The king, the tzuultaq'a, looked for them, he could barely see them. They were far, far away. He looked through a tiny piece of glass/mirror (*lem*) with smoke on it. Just a little bit of them showed and he saw them fleeing. He threw a lightning bolt to kill the sun, but he hit the moon. He killed her with lightning and she fell bloody into the sea. Her blood covered the sea. The sun gathered her blood into thirteen coffins and put them in the corner of the house. In twelve of them were different animals, the snake, the deer, the *tolokat*, the *pakmaleb'*, the cricket, the butterfly, until in the thirteenth box was the moon.

NOTES

CHAPTER ONE

1. I characterize Wolf as a historicist for portraying indigenous culture as a product of the colonial period, but Watanabe refers to him as an essentialist for seeing culture as fixed and immutable. The positions can blur into one another at times, and perhaps both should be seen as historically reductionist, the difference lying only in the epoch that is emphasized. Whereas essentialists reduce culture to that of the pre-Columbian period, historicists give preeminence to the centuries of Spanish rule.

2. This tendency is not necessarily essential to Barth's method, and some have used his ideas to study social change and the history of identity in a more sensitive fashion, e.g., Cohen (1975, 1985). My criticisms are therefore directed more at the application of the relational approach to identity in Mesoamerica than at Barth's own work.

3. Barth himself, to give him his due, seems to be trying to make amends, writing that ethnicity is a matter not only of structure but of life experience as well (1984:83).

4. Hunt's (1977) otherwise insightful work on Mesoamerican symbolism is perhaps not the best example of this trend because she also argues the case for continuity with the past without demonstrating concretely how culture and religion became transformed over time. For not exploring thoroughly enough the historical processes that interacted with community culture, she could perhaps be faulted, to paraphrase Wolf, for short-circuiting four centuries of history.

5. I am by no means the first to see this useful application; for example, see M. Nash (1989:127). Is a theory of nationalism applicable to ethnicity? Worsley (1984:247) is correct to place these two forms of identity on the same level of analysis: "Nationalism is also a form of ethnicity, but it is a special form. It is the institutionalization of one particular ethnic identity by attaching it to the state. . . . When those interests are to obtain a State of its own the group becomes a nationality."

CHAPTER TWO

1. See Cancian (1965), Favre (1973), Reina (1966), W. Smith (1977), Vogt (1969), Wagley (1949), Watanabe (1992), and Wolf (1967).

2. For a short overview of the historical roots of the term *Ladino* in Guatemala, see Watanabe (1992:55–56).

3. Across Mesoamerica, the chicken is a totem of the Spanish. Bricker (1981:5) writing about Mayan groups in highland Chiapas, asserts that *kaxlan* is an indigenized pronunciation of *Castellano,* or Castilian, but I am unconvinced. In Q'eqchi', *kaxlan* means only chicken, and Castilian is pronounced *Kastiyaan.*

4. See Whetten (1961) and the early work of Adams (1959).

5. These figures are based on documentation from the government land ministry, INTA (Instituto Nacional de Transformación Agraria), 1984.

6. Figures are based on information from INTA (1984).

7. In using these estimates I am concurring with Carter (1969:137).

8. Of course the whole category of "subsistence" is culturally relative, because few, if any, agricultural societies regularly plant only enough to stay alive.

9. Carter's average was 3.5 hectares for the community of Chichipate (1969:137).

10. Carter (1969:76) records that twenty-five pounds of seed are needed for each *manzana* (roughly 2.8 acres) of *milpa,* or corn field. However, the quantity depends on the corn type employed—*ninqehal* is planted sparsely (1.5 meters apart) because the plants and ears are large.

Some common Q'eqchi' maize types are *k'amb'ob',* with a seven-month growing season; *ninqehal* ("big ear"), the most common type in the highlands, requiring five months' growing time; *kok'hal* ("small ear"), five months, used mostly in the lowlands; *xhal tz'i'* ("dog ear"), five months, with short stalks; and *chaklich',* which needs six months' growing time. Beans are often mixed and planted with the corn. Three types are used: *lol* (large, black, and kidney shaped), *nun* (small, colored, and round), and *ch'ux* (multi-colored and round).

11. The Quetzal (Q) is the monetary unit of Guatemala. It was valued at Q2.7:U.S. $1 at the time of my fieldwork.

12. Traditionally, marriage was a process, not a single ritual, since few were married by a priest or in a registry office. The parents of the groom visited the bride's parents three times, pleading with them for their daughter and offering presents. If the presents were accepted and all drank to seal the contract, the groom moved in with his parents-in-law. The bride was usually consulted throughout, and could, in fact, call the marriage off at any time during the period of bride service. Nowadays, marriage is arranged with fewer intermediaries and is occasionally solemnized in the municipal building or by a priest.

CHAPTER THREE

1. Hunt (1977) has argued that in Mesoamerican cosmologies, each god comprises dualisms that split into further dualisms, yet the divisions are integrated into a single image.

2. Among the K'iche', mountains are male and valleys are female (Carmack 1979:382). This is also the tendency in the Andes, where male *wamani* (mountain spirits) dwell in the peaks, whereas plateaus are more the domain of the mother earth matrix, *Pacha Mama* (Isbell 1978:59; J. Nash 1979:122). Exceptions to this tendency are the Mam mountain gods, or *witz*, which can be male or female (Watanabe 1992:67).

3. See Thompson (1939) on the moon in Mesoamerican symbolism.

4. *Batz'uunk*, from the noun *b'atz'*, or monkey.

5. *Liceens*, from the Spanish *licencia*.

6. God is called Tiox.

7. Historical accounts (Bossú 1986) give Pre-Columbian Q'eqchi' words for "God" as *ahau* (king) and *mam* (grandfather).

8. Studies of indigenous peoples of Latin America have tended to distinguish between the highlands and lowlands, but the Q'eqchi's should not be placed in either camp. They have historically lived in both areas, being on the edge of the sierra of Chamá. Present-day Q'eqchi's are a mixture of various assimilated ethnic groups, many of them lowlanders such as the Ch'ol and Lacandón, who were brought together in the Spanish *reducciones,* or concentrated ("reduced") towns (Sapper 1985). These towns were built on a grid pattern, and in them, indigenous peoples could be concentrated under the control of Spanish ecclesiastical and military authorities.

CHAPTER FOUR

1. During fieldwork, I participated in eight plantings, mostly in the environs of Cobán. Apart from this, I interviewed over one hundred informants from many different regions about their planting rituals. Some of my information, then, is based not upon observation but on what people told me they did. Even in the plantings where I participated, I could document only acts and speech such as those of the vigil, meals, planting work, and some of the *awas* taboos. Individualized actions and beliefs are an unknown quantity. Ultimately, one can never know which God/gods a person is praying to when alone in his field. In the realm of individual action, there is always room for clandestine practices and beliefs.

2. See Bloch (1986:176) and Sperber (1975:113) for influential formulations of this approach.

3. A variant of this story was also recorded by Burkitt (1918).

4. Menchú writes (1984:71) that prohibitions on bread also serve as a rallying point for indigenous ethnicity among the K'iche'. According to Wilk (1991:139), Q'eqchi's in Belize are careful to divide the sacred realm of corn production from the profane sphere of the main cash crop, rice.

CHAPTER FIVE

1. Watanabe (1992:190) refers to a similar Mam sexual division of labor in curing between female herbalists and midwives (*xhb'ool*) and male diviners (*chmaan*).

2. I will not address the debate over whether the hot/cold distinction is autochthonous (Redfield and Villa-Rojas 1934:372) or imported (Foster 1953:202–204) to Mesoamerica.

3. Silverblatt (1987:24) reports how in Andean communities, in contrast, it is said that a woman would be swallowed up by the mountain if she were to approach the shrine of a mountain-ancestor.

4. Vogt (1976:79) reports that in Zinacantán, the spirit is recovered by the Earth Lord, and Watanabe (1992:191) describes how captured Mam souls must work for the *witz* in his subterranean plantation.

5. The future transitive of the verb *toch'ok* is used, but the object is unspecified, so it could be either "you" or "it."

6. Guiteras (1961:297) describes a similar ritual in highland Chiapas, where the seer (in Tzotzil, *ilol*) calls the soul and sends his or her own out to search for that of the patient. J. Nash (1970:150) details "soul-calling" by the Tzeltal.

7. It would be interesting to delve into the European associations between infants and staple grains, which led to their both being kept in a Greek *krippe* or Old English *crib*.

CHAPTER SIX

1. See Saint-Lú (1968:426). The verses of the evangelizing songs are reproduced in Estrada Monroy (1979) and Bossú (1986).

2. Burnett (1989) gives a thorough summary of the historical relationship between the Guatemalan state and evangelical groups.

3. Anthropological studies of evangelical groups among indigenous peoples in Guatemala include those by Emery (1970) and Annis (1987). Schackt (1986) has written about Q'eqchi' evangelicals in Belize. For Mexico, Redfield's account (1950) of Protestantism in a Yucatec village still stands as a landmark.

4. Stoll's (1982) study of the activities of the Summer Institute of Linguistics in Guatemala reviews the history of this organization.

5. W. Smith (1977) documented a similar collectivization of the *cofradía* fiesta in San Miguel Ixtahuacán when capitalized agriculture commenced there. His analysis is overreductionist, however, since he explains this phenomenon wholly in terms of "rational" economic motivations.

6. See Berryman (1984a), Boff (1985), Bruneau (1980, 1982), Cleary (1985), Dussel (1976), Gutierrez (1974, 1983), Lancaster (1988), and Levine (1980, 1986).

7. See Peel (1989) for a richly detailed example of both Christianity and Islam at work among the Yoruba.

CHAPTER SEVEN

1. See Casas (1909), Estrada Monroy (1979), Juarros (1981), Remesal (1932), and Ximénez (1929).

2. For example, see Bourque and Warren (1989), Lan (1985), Popkin (1979), Riches (1986), Warren (1993), and Wolf (1969), and more recent material on the conflict in former Yugoslavia (Bringa 1993). In 1993, the organization Anthropologists against Ethnic Violence was set up in the United Kingdom.

3. See AVANCSO (1990, 1991, 1992), Carmack (1988), Falla (1992), Krueger and Enge (1985), Manz (1988), Richards (1985), Sexton (1992), C. Smith (1990a, 1990b), Stoll (1990, 1993), Warren (1993), WOLA (1988), and others.

4. See Berryman (1984b), Black (1984), Brintnall (1979), Falla (1978), and Warren (1978).

5. The religion of the catechists corresponds to Leach's model of an icon of subversion, yet their belief in a unitary God refutes Leach's thesis (1972:12) that "visible hierarchy among deities goes with egalitarian politics among men; isolated monotheism goes with hierarchical politics among men." For Q'eqchi' converts, the move towards monotheism was coupled with an expressly egalitarian social ethic. A similar trend was apparent in some seventeenth-century Protestant sects such as the Quakers and Levellers.

6. See Falla (1992) for a detailed account of scorched earth policies and wholesale massacres in the Ixcán region. This account has had tremendous impact in Guatemala. The military has publicly accused Falla of being a guerrilla, thus endangering his life. This is how the Guatemalan army declares a proverbial *fatwa* on writers who challenge its version of history.

7. Those destroyed included the villages of Chitú, Chituj, Tz'imahíl, Samác, Las Pacayas, Cruzmax, Sa'guachíl, Secaché, Xelabé, and Sa'chal.

8. Villages hard hit in this area included Cuzpeméch, San Lorenzo, Samocóch, Copalhá, Peñas Blancas, Nimlahacóc, Pasacúc, San José Río Negro, Chinajacóc, Rosario, Pakisil, and Satolohoox.

9. Other municipalities that suffered were Senahú, Cahabón, Panzós, El Estor, and communities along the Northern Transversal Strip. In Cahabón, the inhabitants of Pinares, Chiacté, Esquipulas, and Secuamó were massacred.

10. *Patrulla de Autodefensa Civil*. Manz (1988) includes sections on the operation of PACs in Huehuetenango (pp. 74–82) and the Ixil Triangle (pp. 101–103).

11. Villa-Rojas (1978:107) writes of how war and evangelization similarly ruptured pre-Hispanic pilgrimages in the Yucatan. Sallnow (1987:76) asserts that the Spanish invasion halted Andean pilgrimages until 1650, when events surrounding the Señor de Temblores shrine in Cuzco reinitiated pilgrimages to miraculous shrines.

12. Yet even in Quiché this military involvement in development was minimal, and it decreased significantly after 1986. This has led commentators such as Krueger and Enge (1985) and C. Smith (1990b) to question the premise that the military as a whole actually had a development plan for the highlands.

13. *Maquila* industries grew dramatically in Guatemala during the 1980s. They are labor-intensive enterprises owned by foreign multinationals that produce cheap goods for export. Working conditions are reported to be dire: most workers are poorly paid, female, and nonunionized. See Petersen (1992).

14. Sexton's (1992) *Ignacio: The Diary of a Maya Indian of Guatemala* is a vivid account of the distrust and paranoia generated by the war in one locale.

15. This house-construction ritual is quite common among Mayas; for example, among the Tzeltal a sheep's head is buried at the center post of the house (J. Nash 1970:12).

16. Silverblatt (1987) has similarly portrayed gender relations and foreign ideologies in sixteenth-century Peru.

17. For instance, C. Smith (1991:31) goes too far in writing, "Though always repressive and despotic, the Guatemalan state never controlled civil institutions in Maya communities."

18. CERJ is the acronym for "Council of Ethnic Communities 'We are all one.'"

19. As one of Kay Warren's (1993:32) informants told her, "The truth is that the violence always continues, is always a part of our lives."

CHAPTER EIGHT

1. For an analysis of state manipulation of the ideology of *indigenismo* in Peru, see Chevalier in Mörner (1970:184–96). Kantor (1953) sets out clearly the program of the Peruvian APRA party on the "Indian question." Collier (1975) and Warman (1982) assess the history of Mexican *indigenismo*.

2. Warren (1992:201) provides a similar description of the activities of Kaqchikel catechists of Catholic Action in San Andrés Semetabaj, who put on nostalgic *cofradía* rituals as community theater for their youth program in a local secular hall.

3. This experience differs from that described in Manning Nash's (1967) study of industrialization in a Maya community. He concluded that the Cantelese worldview was unaffected by people's transition from peasants to proletarians. Yet Cantel was a unique case in that the peasants retained their access to land, unlike most Q'eqchi' proletarians. New religious discourses did not accompany economic changes. The factory was located in a preexisting corporate community, the composition of which remained unchanged. In addition, the historical context of Nash's study is relevant in that neither widespread religious change nor grassroots economic development had yet made its full impact felt on the indigenous highlands.

4. IGER is the acronym for Instituto Guatemalteco de Educación Radiofónica.

5. One exception being the culture-and-personality school, e.g., Wallace (1961).

6. Watanabe (1992:155) describes the economic caution of inhabitants of Chimbal, who "decline to enter fully into the marketplace" and limit both consumption of Ladino luxuries and coffee production.

7. The quoted expression originally appeared not in Taussig's writings but in an earlier article by Scott (1977a:231).

8. Spalding (1982) shows that the peasant *ayllu* and capitalist/colonial sector have been dual aspects of one integrated system, and that Inkas and Spaniards were extracting labor power before fully fledged capitalism took root.

9. In his monograph, Roseberry (1983) demonstrated convincingly how a peasant region has had a variegated relationship with global capitalism. Instead of a continuous, steady expansion of capitalism in the area, peasantries have been "unconsciously" called into being and then destroyed in cycles of incorporation and disincorporation.

10. Burns (1977:260) writes of how "the rebel Maya of east central Quintana Roo are still involved in the Caste War." Over a hundred years after they were defeated by federal troops, these Yucatec Mayas still defiantly oppose the Ladinos, adhere to the ideal of a Mayan nation, and pay homage to the Talking Cross that incited them to revolt.

CHAPTER NINE

1. This seems to be a common feature of world religions, especially Islam and Christianity. See Peel (1989) for an African case of Christianity's encoding an ethnic (pan-Yoruba) identity through an indigenous intelligentsia.

2. Bricker (1979) has documented how the Tzeltal revolt of 1712 and the Chamula uprising of 1869 were sparked off by the efforts of Spanish and Ladino priests to prevent indigenous communities from expanding their festival cycle.

3. Note the commencing date in the title of C. Smith's edited collection, *Guatemalan Indians and the State, 1540–1988*.

4. Said (1978, 1993) and Prakash (1992) are just two examples.

GLOSSARY

(C) Castilian
(Q) Q'eqchi'
(Qu) Quechua

AAWK (Q). To plant.

AAWKLEB' (Q). Planting pole.

AJ (Q). Prefix denoting masculine and/or occupational status.

ATOL (C). Maize drink.

AWAS (Q). (1) Taboo; (2) result of breaking taboo; a calamity befalling maize crop or illness in children.

BALDÍO (C). Untitled lands, sometimes uncultivated and uninhabited.

BARRIO (C). Neighborhood.

(AJ) B'OQONEL (Q). She/he who calls the lost spirit.

B'OJ (Q). Alcoholic drink made from fermented maize and sugar cane.

CAMPESINO/A. Rural villager, peasant.

CATECHIST. Usually male indigenous lay activist who teaches the doctrine of the Catholic church and leads the weekly Bible reflection meetings in his community.

CHAK (Yucatec). Rain god.

CHAPOK K'AL (Q). Grab crop ritual on the morning of the planting.

CHINAM (Q). Traditional village leader, elder, mayordomo in cofradía.

CH'UTAM (Q). Weekly village meeting of the "Word of God" led by catechists.

(AJ) CH'UTAM (Q). Participant in the ch'utam, catechist.

COFRADÍA (C). Religious brotherhood, formed at the village level to celebrate the patron saint at the annual fiesta.

COMPADRAZGO (C). Spiritual coparenthood created through baptism or marriage.

COLONO (C). Serf on plantation.

EGP (C). Guerrilla Army of the Poor, one of four guerrilla organizations in the URNG.

ENCOMIENDA (C). Colonial commission of land and its indigenous inhabitants granted to a conquistador for personal exploitation.

FINCA (C). Plantation.

FINQUERO (C). Plantation owner.

HACIENDA (C). Plantation of agricultural export crops, more commonly called a *finca*.

HACENDADO (C). Owner of a plantation.

HERMANDAD (C). Catholic lay brotherhood organizing events of Easter week.

HERMITA (C). Catholic village chapel.

IGER (C). Guatemalan Institute of Radio Education.

(AJ) ILONEL (Q). Curer, shaman, health care provider.

INDÍGENA (C). Indigenous.

INDIGENIST. Ideology that exalts indigenous culture and the Mayan past.

INDIGENISMO (C). Ladino and state ideology that seeks to legitimate nationalism through the appropriation of what it considers to be traditional symbols of indigenous culture.

INDIO (C). Indian (pejorative).

IXIM (Q). Corn.

IXQ (Q). Woman.

IYAJ (Q). Seeds.

KAXLAN (Q). Chicken.

KAXLAN WA (Q). Bread, literally, "chicken tortilla."

KAXLAN WIING (Q). Ladinos, literally "chicken men."

KE (Q). Cold.

KRISTIAN (Q). Person, derived from Castilian *cristiano*, or "Christian."

(AJ) K'AMOL B'E (Q). Catechist, literally, "she/he who leads the way."

K'ALEK (Q). Clearing of fields.

K'ATOK (Q). Burning of fields.

K'IL (Q). Flat earthenware griddle on which tortillas are cooked; in Castilian, *comal*.

LADINO/A (C). Nonindigenous person according to criteria such as language ability, dress, occupation, and assumed descent; a mestizo who identifies with Hispanic culture.

LADINOIZATION. The process of becoming more Ladino/a.

LATIFUNDIO (C). Large agricultural estate, dependent on the labor of smallholders of *minifundios*.

LOQ' (Q). Sacred, holy.

LOQ'ONIINK (Q). To respect, praise, revere.

MAYEJAK (Q). To sacrifice.

MAYORDOMO/A (C). Office holder in *cofradía*.

MINIFUNDIO (C). Agricultural smallholding.

MOZO/A (C). Day wage laborer, servant, or serf.

MOZOS COLONOS (C). Serfs on agroexport plantations.

MU/MUHEL (Q). Spirit, shadow.

MUXUK (Q). To profane.

PACHA MAMA (Qu). Mother earth matrix, earth in its benevolent aspect.

PO (Q). The moon; Qana' Po is "our Mother the Moon."

POCH (Q). Same as *tamál*.

POM (Q). Incense from the resin of the copal tree.

QA (Q). Possessive prefix for first person singular, "our."

QAWA' QUK'A (Q). Our sustenance, literally, "our food our water."

QAAWA' (Q). Our father.

QANA' (Q). Our mother.

QUINTÁL (C). One hundredweight.

Q'IX (Q). Hot, referring to inherent heat value of food, illness, piece of clothing.

RAWASINKIL (Q). Rite performed to cure human *awas* illnesses.

REDUCCIONES (C). Spanish towns of the early colonial period, set out on a grid pattern around a church and plaza, where indigenous peoples were concentrated and controlled by crown ecclesiastical and military authorities.

SAQ'E (Q). The sun; Qaawa' saq'e is "our Father the Sun."

TAMÁL (C). Ground corn flour boiled in banana leaves.

TESTIIG (Q). Master of ceremonies at a celebration.

TIOX (Q). The Christian God.

TIOXILAL (Q). Godliness, holiness.

TIQ (Q). Hot, referring to thermal temperature and environment.

TORTILLA (C). Flat, circular corn dough cooked on flat earthenware dish over fire, a staple form of eating corn.

(AJ) TUUL (Q). Witch, *aj ilonel* who can also kill.

TZAAMAANK (Q). To petition.

TZUULTAQ'A (Q). Mountain spirit; literally, "mountain/valley."

TZ'U'UJ (Q). Tortilla filled with beans.

UQ'UN (Q). Corn gruel.

URNG (C). Guatemalan National Revolutionary Unity, umbrella organization of four constituent guerrilla groups.

UTZ'UJ (Q). Flower, candle, to kiss.

WA (Q). Tortilla, food.

WA' (Q). Imperative of verb "to eat"; means "Eat it!"

WA'AK (Q). To eat.

WA'TESIINK (Q). To feed something, house-feeding ritual.

WAMANI (Q). Andean mountain spirit, localized shrine place, also *apu*.

WANKILAL (Q). Power, strength.

WIINQ (Q). Man.

WIINQILAL (Q). Personhood.

(AJ) XOKONEL (Q). She/he who delivers children.

XUL (Q). Animal.

YO'LEK (Q). Vigil, wake.

YO'YO (Q). Alive, living.

REFERENCES CITED

Adams, Richard N.
1952   Creencias y prácticas del indígena. Guatemala: Instituto Indigenista
         Nacional.
1959   "La ladinización en Guatemala." Integración Social en Guatemala
         2(9):123–37. Guatemala: Seminario de Integración Social Guatemalteca.
1965   "Migraciones internas en Guatemala: Expansión agraria de los indí-
         genas Kekchies hacía el Petén." Guatemala: Seminario de Integración
         Social Guatemalteca.
1970   Crucifixion By Power. Austin: University of Texas Press.
1990   "Ethnic Images and Strategies in 1944." In Guatemalan Indians and the
         State, 1540–1988, C. Smith, ed. Austin: University of Texas Press.
Agency for International Development (USAID)
1982   Land and Labour in Guatemala: An Assessment. Guatemala: Ediciones
         Papiro.
Aguirre Beltrán, Gonzalo
1956   "Indigenismo y mestizaje." Cuadernos Americanos 78:35–51.
Albó, Xavier
1987   "From MNRistas to Kataristas to Katarí." In Resistance, Rebellion, and
         Consciousness in the Andean Peasant World, 18th to 20th Centuries, S. Stern,
         ed. Madison: University of Wisconsin Press.
Allen, Catherine
1988   The Hold Life Has: Coca and Cultural Identity in an Andean Community.
         Washington: Smithsonian Institution Press.

America's Watch

1986   Civil Patrols in Guatemala. New York: America's Watch.

1988   Closing the Space: Human Rights in Guatemala, May 1987–October 1988. New York: America's Watch.

Anderson, Benedict

1991   Imagined Communities: Reflections on the Origin and Spread of Nationalism. Second edition. London: Verso.

Anderson, Thomas

1992   Matanza. Second edition. Willimantic: Curbstone Press.

✗ Annis, Sheldon

1987   God and Production in a Guatemalan Town. Austin: University of Texas Press.

Anuario Estadístico

1986   Guatemala: Dirección General de Estadística.

Arce Canahuí, Angel

1983   Caracterización del sistema productivo de los caseríos del microparcelamiento Sacsuhá de la aldea la Tinta. Cobán: Centro Universitario del Norte.

Arias, Arturo

1990   "Changing Indian Identity: Guatemala's Violent Transition to Modernity." In Guatemalan Indians and the State, 1540–1988, C. Smith, ed. Austin: University of Texas Press.

AVANCSO

1990   Política institutional hacia el desplazado interno en Guatemala, no. 6. Guatemala: Inforpress.

1991   Vónos a la capital: Estudio sobre la emigración rural reciente en Guatemala, no. 7. Guatemala: Inforpress.

1992   Donde está el futuro? Procesos de reintegración en communidades de retornados, no. 8. Guatemala: Inforpress.

Aveni, Anthony F., ed.

1992   The Sky in Mayan Literature. New York: Oxford University Press.

Barry, Tom

1987   Roots of Rebellion: Land and Hunger in Central America. Boston: Southend Press.

Barth, Fredrik

✗ 1969   Ethnic Groups and Boundaries. Boston: Little, Brown.

1984   "Problems in Conceptualising Cultural Pluralism, with Illustrations from Somar, Oman." In The Prospects for Plural Societies, D. Maybury-Lewis, ed. Washington D.C.: American Ethnological Society.

Bastien, Joseph W.

1978 *Mountain of the Condor: Metaphor and Ritual in an Andean* ayllu. American Ethnological Society monograph 64. St. Paul: West Publishing.

Bendix, Reinhard
1960 *Max Weber: An Intellectual Portrait*. London: Methuen.

Benson Gyles, Anna, and Chloë Sayer
1980 *Of Gods and Men: Mexico and the Mexican Indian*. London: BBC.

Berger, John
1979 *Pig Earth*. London: Writers and Readers.

Berryman, Phillip
1980 "What Happened at Puebla." In *Churches and Politics in Latin America*, D. Levine, ed. London: Sage.
1984a *The Religious Roots of Rebellion: Christians in Central American Revolutions*. London: SCM Press.
1984b *Christians in Guatemala's Struggle*. London: Catholic Institute of International Relations.

Black, George
1984 *Garrison Guatemala*. London: Zed Books.

Bloch, Maurice
1986 *From Blessing to Violence: History and Ideology in the Circumcision Ritual of the Merina of Madagascar*. Cambridge: Cambridge University Press.

Bloch, Maurice, and J. Parry, eds.
1982 *Death and the Regeneration of Life*. Cambridge: Cambridge University Press.

Blom, Franz
1956 "La vida precortesiana del indio Chapaneco de hoy." *Estudios Antropológicos*, pp. 283–84.

Boff, Leonardo
1985 *Church Charisma and Power*. J. Diercksmeier, trans. London: SCM Press.

Bossú, Ennio María
1986 *Un manuscrito K'ekchi' del siglo XVI*. Guatemala: Universidad Francisco Marroquín.

Bourque, Susan, and Kay Warren
1989 "Democracy without Peace: The Cultural Politics of Terror in Peru." *Latin America Research Review* 24:7–34.

Bricker, Victoria
1973 *Ritual Humor in Highland Chiapas*. Austin: University of Texas Press.
1977 "The Caste War of Yucatán: The History of a Myth and the Myth of

History." In *Anthropology and History in Yucatán,* Grant Jones, ed. Austin: University of Texas Press.

⋊ 1979   "Movimientos religiosos indígenas en los altos de Chiapas." *América Indígena* 39:17–46.

1981   *The Indian Christ, The Indian King: The Historical Substrate of Mayan Myth and Ritual.* Austin: University of Texas Press.

Bringa, Tone
1993   "Exorcising the Bosnian Soul." Paper presented at a conference of the Association of Social Anthropologists of the Commonwealth, July.

Brintnall, Douglas E.
1979   *Revolt against the Dead: The Modernization of a Maya Community in the Highlands of Guatemala.* New York: Gordon And Breach.

Bruneau, Thomas
1980   "Basic Christian Communities in Latin America: Their Nature and Significance (Especially in Brazil)." In *Churches and Politics in Latin America,* D. Levine, ed. London: Sage.

1982   *The Church in Brazil: The Politics of Religion.* Austin: University of Texas Press.

Bruner, Edward
1984   "The Symbolics of Urban Migration." In *The Prospects for Plural Societies,* D. Maybury-Lewis, ed. Washington D.C.: American Ethnological Society.

Bunzel, Ruth
1952   *Chichicastenango: A Guatemalan Village.* American Ethnological Society. Locust Valley, New York: J. J. Augustin.

Burkitt, Robert J.
1918   "The Hils [sic] and the Corn." *The Museums Journal* 9(3–4). Philadelphia: Institute of Archaeology.

Burnett, Virginia A.
1989   "Protestantism in Rural Guatemala, 1872–1954." *Latin American Research Review* 24(2):127–42.

Burns, Allan F.
1977   "The Caste War in the 1970s: Present-Day Accounts from Village Quintana Roo." In *Anthropology and History in Yucatán.* Grant D. Jones, ed. Austin: University of Texas Press.

Cabarrús, Carlos
1979   *La cosmovisión K'ekchi' en proceso de cambio.* San Salvador: Universidad Centroamericana.

Cambranes, J. C.

1985 *Coffee and Peasants in Guatemala.* Stockholm: University of Stockholm.

Cancian, Frank
1965 *Economics and Prestige in a Maya Community: The Religious Cargo System in Zinacantán.* Stanford: Stanford University Press.

Cardona, Rokael
1983 "Caracterización del trabajo temporero la agricultura." *Perspectiva,* no. 1, August.

Carlsen, Robert, and Martin Prechtel
1991 "The Flowering of the Dead: An Interpretation of Highland Maya Culture. *Man* 26(1):23–42.

Carmack, Robert M.
1979 *Historia social de los Quiches.* Guatemala: Editorial José de Pineda Ibarra.
1988 (Ed.) *Harvest of Violence.* Norman: University of Oklahoma Press.
1990 "State and Community in Nineteenth-Century Guatemala: The Momostenango Case." In *Guatemalan Indians and the State, 1540–1988,* C. Smith, ed. Austin: University of Texas Press.

Carter, William E.
1969 *New Lands and Old Traditions: Kekchi Cultivators in the Guatemalan Lowlands.* Gainesville: University of Florida Press.

Casas, Bartolomé de las
1909 *Apologética historia de las Indias.* Madrid: Serrano y Ganz. Reprinted 1967. México, D.F.: Universidad Nacional Autónoma de México.

Censo nacional de la población
1981 Guatemala: Dirección General de Estadística.

Chevalier, François
1970 "Official *Indigenismo* in Peru in 1920: Origins, Significance, and Socioeconomic Scope." In *Race and Class in Latin America,* M. Mörner, ed. New York: Columbia University Press.

Christian, William A.
1981 *Local Religion in Sixteenth-Century Spain.* Princeton: Princeton University Press.

Cleary, Ed L.
1985 *Crisis and Change: The Church in Latin America Today.* Maryknoll, New York: Orbis Books.

Clifford, James
1988 *The Predicament of Culture: Twentieth-Century Ethnography, Literature, and Art.* Cambridge, Massachusetts: Harvard University Press.

Cohen, Anthony P.
1975   *The Management of Myths: The Politics of Legitimation in a Newfound-
land Community*. Manchester: Manchester University Press.
1985   "Symbolism and Social Change: Matters of Life and Death in Whalsay,
Shetland." *Man* 20(2):307–24.

Collier, George A.
1975   *Fields of the Tzotzil: The Ecological Bases of Tradition in Highland
Chiapas*. Austin: University of Texas Press.

Comaroff, John, and Jean Comaroff
1992   *Ethnography and the Historical Imagination*. Boulder, Colorado: Westview Press.

Contreras R., Daniel
1968   *Una rebelión indígena en el partido de Totonicapán en 1820: El indio y la
independencia*. Guatemala: Editorial Universitaria, USAC.

CUNOR (Centro Universitario del Norte)
1979   *La Verapaz: Estructura y procesos*. Guatemala: Universidad de San
Carlos.
1986   *Plan de desarrollo de CUNOR*. Cobán: CUNOR.

Davis, Shelton
1988   "Sowing the Seeds of Violence." In *Harvest of Violence,* R. Carmack, ed.
Norman: University of Oklahoma Press.

Deere, Carmen Diana
1990   *Household and Class Relations: Peasants and Landlords in Northern
Peru*. Berkeley: University of California Press.

Deleuze, Gilles, and Félix Guattari
1988   *A Thousand Plateaus: Capitalism and Schizophrenia*. London: Athlone
Press.

Diamond, Stanley
1974   *In Search of the Primitive: A Critique of Civilization*. New Brunswick,
New Jersey: E. P. Dutton.

Douglas, Mary
1966   *Purity and Danger: An Analysis of Concepts of Pollution and Taboo*.
London: Routledge and Kegan Paul.

Dunkerley, James
1988   *Power in the Isthmus: A Political History of Modern Central America*.
London: Verso.

Dussel, Enrique
1976   *History and the Theology of Liberation: A Latin American Perspective*.
John Drury, trans. Maryknoll, New York: Orbis Books.

Earls, John
1969 "The Organisation of Power in Quechua Mythology." *Journal of the Steward Anthropological Society 1.* (1):63–82.

Economist Intelligence Unit
1989a *Guatemala, El Salvador, Honduras: Country Profile 1989–90.* London: EIU.
1989b *Guatemala, El Salvador, Honduras: Country Report no. 4.* London: EIU.

Ehlers, Tracy Bachrach
1990 *Silent Looms: Women and Production in a Guatemalan Town.* Boulder, Colorado: Westview Press.

Emery, Gennet Maxon
1970 *Protestantism in Guatemala.* Cuernavaca: Centro Intercultural de Documentación, Sondeos no. 65.

Eriksen, Thomas Hylland
1991 "The Cultural Contexts of Ethnic Differences." *Man* 26(1):127–44.
1993 *Ethnicity and Nationalism: Anthropological Perspectives.* London: Pluto Press.

Estrada Monroy, Agustín
1974 *Datos para la historia de la iglesia en Guatemala.* Guatemala: Biblioteca Goathemala.
1979 *El mundo Kekchi de la Verapaz.* Guatemala: Editorial del Ejército.

Evans-Pritchard, E. E.
1940 *The Nuer.* Oxford: Oxford University Press.

Evers, Tilman
1985 "Identity: The Hidden Side of New Social Movements in Latin America." In *New Social Movements and the State in Latin America,* D. Slater, ed. Dordrecht, Holland: FORIS.

Falla, Ricardo
1978 *Quiché rebelde: Estudio de un movimiento de conversión religiosa, rebelde a las creencias tradicionales, en San Antonio Ilotenango, Quiché (1948–1970).* Guatemala: USAC.
1992 *Masacres de la selva: Ixcán, Guatemala (1975–1982).* Guatemala: USAC.

Fardon, Richard
1987 "African Ethnogenesis: Limits to the Comparability of Ethnic Phenomena." In *Comparative Anthropology,* L. Holy, ed. London: Basil Blackwell.

Favre, Henri
1973 *Cambio y continuidad entre los Mayas de México.* México, D.F.: Siglo XXI.

1984   "Sentier lumineux et horizons obscurs." *Problemes d'Amérique Latine.*
       Notes et Etudes Documentaires 72:3–27.

Figueroa Ibarra, Carlos
1980   *El proletariado rural en el agro Guatemalteco.* Guatemala: Editorial
       Universitaria.

Flores Alvarado, H.
1977   *Proletarización del campesino de Guatemala.* Guatemala: Piedra Santa.

Flores Reyes, Monsignor Gerardo
1985   *Primera carta pastoral.* Cobán: Diocesís de la Verapaz.

Foster, George
1953   "Relationships between Spanish and Spanish-American Folk Medi-
       cine." *Journal of American Folklore* 66:201–17.

Foucault, Michel
1977   *Discipline and Punish: The Birth of the Prison.* London: Penguin.
1980   *Michel Foucault: Power/Knowledge: Selected Interviews and Other
       Writings, 1972–1977.* C. Gordon, ed. Brighton: Harvester.

Friedlander, Judith
1975   *Being Indian in Hueyapan: A Study of Forced Identity in Contemporary
       Mexico.* New York: St. Martin's Press.

Galdamez, Pablo
1986   *Faith of a People: The Story of a Christian Community in El Salvador,
       1970–1980.* Translation by Robert Barr. Maryknoll, New York: Orbis Books.

Gates, William E.
1931   "A Lanquin Kekchi Calendar." *Maya Society Quarterly* 1:29–32.

Giddens, Anthony
1985   *The Nation-State and Violence.* Cambridge: Polity Press.
1991   *Modernity and Self-Identity: Self and Society in the Late Modern Age.*
       Cambridge: Polity Press.

Gismondi, Michael A.
1986   "Transformations in the Holy: Religious Resistance and Hegemonic
       Struggles in the Nicaraguan Revolution." *Latin American Perspectives*
       13(3):13–36.

Gómez Lanza, Helio
1983   *Desarrollo histórico de la Verapaz y la conquista pacífica.* Guatemala:
       Instituto Indigenista Nacional, Publicaciones Especiales Segunda Epoca, no. 1.

Gossen, Gary H.
1986   *Symbol and Meaning beyond the Closing Corporate Community: Essays
       in Mesoamerican Ideas.* Albany, New York: Institute for Mesoamerican
       Studies, SUNY.

Gow, David D.
1979 "Símbolo y protesta: Movimientos redentores en Chiapas y los Andes peruanos." *America Indígena* 39(1):47–80.

Gramsci, Antonio
1971 *Selections from the Prison Notebooks of Antonio Gramsci.* Q. Hoare and G. Nowell-Smith, eds. London: Lawrence and Wishart.

Guiteras Holmes, Calixta
1961 *Perils of the Soul: The World View of a Tzotzil Indian.* New York: Free Press of Glencoe.

Gutierrez, Gustavo
1974 *A Theology of Liberation: History, Politics and Salvation.* London: SCM Press.
1983 *The Power of the Poor in History.* Robert Barr, trans. Maryknoll, New York: Orbis Books.

Haeserijn, Stephen
1967 *Estudio sobre el estado religioso del indígena de Alta Verapaz (y Purulha), Guatemala.* Cobán: Biblioteca Monasterio de la Resurección.

Handy, Jim
1984 *Gift of the Devil.* Toronto: Between the Lines.

Harris, Olivia
1978 "Complementarity and Conflict: An Andean View of Women and Men." In *Sex and Age as Principles of Social Differentiation,* J. La Fontaine, ed. London: Academic Press.

Hawkins, John
1984 *Inverse Images: The Meaning of Culture, Ethnicity, and Family in Postcolonial Guatemala.* Albuquerque: University of New Mexico Press.

Hays, Terence E.
1990 "Pits of the Forest and Other Unwritten Papers." In *The Humbled Anthropologist: Tales from the Pacific,* P. DeVita, ed. Belmont, California: Wadsworth.

Hill, J. D. ed.
1988 *Rethinking History and Myth: Indigenous South American Perspectives on the Past.* Urbana: University of Illinois Press.

Hill, Robert M., and John Monaghan
1987 *Continuities in Highland Social Organization: Ethnohistory in Sacapulas, Guatemala.* Philadelphia: University of Pennsylvania Press.

Hobsbawm, Eric, and T. Ranger, eds.
1983 *The Invention of Tradition.* Cambridge: Cambridge University Press.

Hocart, A. M.
1970 *Kings and Councillors: An Essay in the Comparative Anatomy of Human Society*. R. Needham, ed. Chicago: University of Chicago Press.

Holy, Ladislav, ed.
1987 *Comparative Anthropology*. London: Basil Blackwell.

Hubert, Henri, and Marcel Mauss
1964 *Sacrifice: Its Nature and Function*. London: Cohen and West London.

Hugh-Jones, Stephen
1989 "Waribi and the White Man: History and Myth in Northwest Amazonia." In *History and Ethnicity*, E. Tonkin, M. McDonald and M. Chapman eds. London: Routledge.

Hunt, Eva
1977 *The Transformation of the Hummingbird: Cultural Roots of a Zinacantecan Mythical Poem*. Ithaca: Cornell University Press.

Ingham, John
1986 *Mary, Michael, and Lucifer: Folk Catholicism in Central Mexico*. Austin: University of Texas Press.

Ingold, T.
1986 *Evolution and Social Life*. Cambridge: Cambridge University Press.

Instituto Indigenista Nacional
1985 *Informe del Congreso Lingüístico Nacional*. Guatemala: Ministerio de Educación.

INTA (Instituto Nacional de Transformación Agraria)
1984 *Asentamientos agrarios localizados en el departamento de Alta Verapaz*. Guatemala: INTA.

Isbell, Billie Jean
1978 *To Defend Ourselves: Ecology and Ritual in an Andean Village*. Austin: University of Texas Press.

Jay, Alice
1993 *Persecution by Proxy: The Civil Patrols in Guatemala*. New York: Robert F. Kennedy Memorial Center for Human Rights.

Juarros, D. Domingo
1981 *Compendio de la historia del reino de Guatemala*. Guatemala: Piedra Santa.

Jung, Carl G.
1989 *Aspects of the Masculine*. John Beebe, ed. London: Ark.

Kantor, Harry
1953 *The Ideology and Program of the Peruvian Aprista Movement*. Berkeley: University of California Press.

King, Arden
1974   *Coban and the Verapaz: history and cultural process in northern Guatemala.* Middle American Research Institute, Publication 37. New Orleans: Tulane University.

Krueger, Chris, and Kjell Enge
1985   *Security and Development Conditions in the Guatemalan Highlands.* Washington, D.C.: Washington Office on Latin America.

Laclau, Ernesto
1985   "New Social Movements and the Plurality of the Social." In *New Social Movements and the State in Latin America,* D. Slater, ed. Dordrecht, Holland: FORIS.

La Farge, Oliver
1947   *Santa Eulalia: The Religion of a Cuchumatan Town.* Chicago: University of Chicago Press.

Lan, David
1985   *Guns and Rain: Guerrillas and Spirit Mediums in Zimbabwe.* Berkeley: University of California Press.

Lancaster, Roger N.
1988   *Thanks to God and the Revolution: Popular Religion and Class Consciousness in the New Nicaragua.* New York: Columbia University Press.

Landa, Fray Diego de
1975   *The Maya: Diego de Landa's Account of the Affairs of Yucatán.* A. R. Pagden, ed. and trans. Chicago: J. Philip O'Hara.

Lash, Scott, and Jonathan Friedman, eds.
1992   *Modernity and Identity.* Oxford: Blackwell.

Leach, Edmund
1954   *Political Systems of Highland Burma: A Study of Kachin Social Structure.* London: Bell/London School of Economics.
1972   "Melchisedech and the Emperor: Icons of Subversion and Orthodoxy." *Proceedings of the Royal Anthropological Institute.* London: RAI.
1989   "Tribal Ethnography: Past, Present, and Future." In *History and Ethnicity.* E. Tonkin, M. McDonald, and M. Chapman, eds. ASA Monographs 27. London: Routledge.

León-Portilla, Miguel
1988   *Time and Reality in Mayan Thought.* Second edition. Norman: University of Oklahoma Press.

Levine, Daniel, ed.
1980   *Churches and Politics in Latin America.* London: Sage.

1986   *Religion and Political Conflict in Latin America.* Chapel Hill: University of North Carolina Press.

Lévi-Strauss, C.

1968   *Structural Anthropology.* C. Jacobson and B. Grundfest Schoepf, trans. London: Penguin.

McClintock, Michael

1985   *The American Connection, Volume 2: State Terror and Popular Resistance in Guatemala.* London: Zed Books.

McCreery, David J.

1976   "Coffee and Class: The Structure of Development in Liberal Guatemala." *Hispanic American Historical Review* 56(3):438–60.

Malinowski, Bronislav

1967   *A Diary in the Strict Sense of the Term.* London: Routledge and Kegan Paul.

Mann, Michael

1986   *The Sources of Social Power: A History of Power from the Beginning to A.D. 1760.* Cambridge: Cambridge University Press.

Manz, Beatriz

1988   *Refugees of a Hidden War: Aftermath of Counter-insurgency in Guatemala.* Albany, New York: SUNY.

Mariátegui, José Carlos

1969   *Siete ensayos de interpretación de la realidad peruana.* México, D.F.: Ed. Solidaridad.

Martínez Pelaez, Severo

1971   *La patria del criollo.* Guatemala: Editorial Universitaria.

Menchú, Rigoberta

1984   *I, Rigoberta Menchú: An Indian Woman in Guatemala.* E. Burgos-Debray, ed. London: Verso Books.

Minority Rights Group

1989   *The Maya of Guatemala.* Report no. 62, by Phillip Wearne with Peter Calvert. London: MRG.

Morley, Sylvanus

1946   *The Ancient Maya.* Stanford: Stanford University Press.

1947   *La civilización Maya.* México, D.F.: Fundo de Cultura Económica.

Mörner, Magnus, ed.

1970   *Race and Class in Latin America.* New York: Columbia University Press.

Murra, John

1984   "The Cultural Future of the Andean Majority." In *The Prospects for Plural Societies,* D. Maybury-Lewis, ed. Washington D.C.: American Ethnological Society.

Nash, June

1970   *In the Eyes of the Ancestors: Belief and Behavior in a Maya Community.*
New Haven: Yale University Press.

1979   *We Eat the Mines and the Mines Eat Us: Dependency and Exploitation in
the Bolivian Tin Mines.* New York: Columbia University Press.

Nash, Manning

1967   *Machine Age Maya: The Industrialization of a Guatemalan Community.*
Chicago: University of Chicago Press.

1989   *The Cauldron of Ethnicity in the Modern World.* Chicago: University of
Chicago Press.

Neuenswander, Helen L., and Shirley Souder

1977   "El sindrome caliente-frío, húmedo-seco entre los Quiches de Joyabaj:
Dos modelos cognitivos." In *Estudios cognitivos del sur de Mesoamerica,* H.
Neuenswander and D. Arnold, eds. Dallas: SIL.

Oakes, Maud

1951   *The Two Crosses of Todos Santos: Survivals of Mayan Religious Ritual.*
New York: Bollingen Foundation.

O'Hanlon, Rosalind and David Washbrook

1992   "After Orientalism: Culture, Criticism, Politics." *Comparative Studies
in Society and History* 34(1).141–67.

Pacheco, Luís

1985   *La religiosidad Maya-Kekchi alrededor de maíz.* San José, Costa Rica:
Editorial Escuela para Todos.

1988   *Tradiciones y costumbres del pueblo Maya Kekchi: Noviazgo, matrimo-
nio, secretos, etc.* San José, Costa Rica: Editorial Ambar.

Paige, Jeffrey

1975   *Agrarian Revolution: Social Movements and Export Agriculture in the
Underdeveloped World.* New York: Free Press.

Painter, James

1987   *Guatemala: False Hope, False Freedom. The Rich, the Poor and the
Christian Democrats.* London: Latin America Bureau.

Payeras, Mario

1983   *Days of the Jungle: The Testimony of a Guatemalan Guerrillero 1972–
1976.* New York: Monthly Review.

Paz Cárcamo, Guillermo

1986   *Guatemala: Reforma Agraria.* Centroamérica: EDUCA.

Peel, J. D. Y.

1989   "The Cultural Work of Yoruba Ethnogenesis." In *History and Ethnicity,*
E. Tonkin, M. McDonald and M. Chapman, eds. London: Routledge.

Petersen, Kurt
1992   The Maquiladora Revolution in Guatemala. Occasional Papers, no. 2. Yale University: Orville H. Schell, Jr., Center for International Human Rights at Yale Law School.
Pitt-Rivers, Julian
1970   "Spiritual Power in Central America: The Naguals of Chiapas." In Witchcraft, Confessions and Accusations, M. Douglas, ed. London: Tavistock Publications.
1973   "Race in Latin America: The Concept of 'Raza'." Archives Européenes de Sociologie 14:3–31.
Plant, Roger
1977   Guatemala: Unnatural Disaster. London: Latin America Bureau.
Popkin, Samuel L.
1979   The Rational Peasant: The Political Economy of Rural Society in Vietnam. Berkeley: University of California Press.
Prakash, Gyan
1990   "Writing Post-Orientalist Histories of the Third World: Perspectives from Indian Historiography." Comparative Studies in Society and History 32(2):383–408.
1992   "Can the 'Subaltern' Ride? A Reply to O'Hanlon and Washbrook." Comparative Studies in Society and History 34(1):168–84.
Recinos, Adrian, trans.
1987   Popol Vuh: Las antiguas historias del Quiché. Versión de Adrián Recinos. Guatemala: Piedra Santa.
Redfield, Robert
1941   The Folk Culture of Yucatán. Chicago: University of Chicago Press.
1950   A Village that Chose Progress: Chan Kom Revisited. Chicago: University of Chicago Press.
Redfield, Robert, and Alfonso Villa-Rojas
1934   Chan Kom: A Maya Village. Washington, D.C.: Carnegie Institution of Washington.
Reed, N.
1964   The Caste War of Yucatán. Stanford: Stanford University Press.
Reina, Rubén
1966   The Law of the Saints: A Pokomam Pueblo and Its Community Culture. Indianapolis: Bobbs-Merrill.
Remesal, A. de
1932   Historia géneral de las Indias Occidentales y particular de la gobernación de Chiapas y Guatemala. Vols. 1–5. Guatemala: Biblioteca Goathemala.

Richards, Michael
1985 "Cosmopolitan World View and Counter-insurgency in Guatemala." *Anthropological Quarterly* 3:90–107.
Riches, David, ed.
1986 *The Anthropology of Violence.* London: Basil Blackwell.
Roseberry, William
1983 *Coffee and Capitalism in the Venezuelan Andes.* Austin: University of Texas Press.
Said, Edward
1978 *Orientalism.* New York: Pantheon Books.
1993 *Culture and Imperialism.* London: Chatto and Windus.
Saint-Lú, André
1968 *La Verapaz: Esprit evangelique et colonisation.* Ph.D. thesis, Université de Paris.
Sallnow, Michael J.
1987 *Pilgrims of the Andes: Regional Cults in Cusco.* Washington, D.C.: Smithsonian Institution Press.
1991 "Pilgrimage and Cultural Fracture in the Andes." In *Contesting the Sacred: The Anthropology of Christian Pilgrimage,* J. Eade and M. Sallnow, eds. London: Routledge.
Salvadó, Raul
1980 "La Verapaz: Estructura y procesos." Cobán: CUNOR.
Salomon, Frank
1981 "Killing the Yumbo: A Native Drama of Northern Quito." In *Cultural Transformations and Ethnicity in Modern Ecuador.* N. Whitten, ed. Urbana: University of Illinois Press.
1987 "Ancestor Cults and Resistance in the State of Arequipa, ca. 1748–1754." In *Resistance, Rebellion, and Consciousness in the Andean Peasant World, 18th to 20th Centuries,* S. Stern, ed. Madison: University of Wisconsin Press.
Samandú, Luís
1987 *La Iglesia del Nazareno en Alta Verapaz.* San José, Costa Rica: CSUCA.
Sapper, Karl
1897 *Das norliche Mittel-Amerika nebst einem Ausflug nach dem Hochland von Anahuac.* Brunsvic: Druck und Verlag von Friedrich und Sohn.
1985 *The Verapaz in the Sixteenth and Seventeenth Centuries: A Contribution to the Historical Geography and Ethnography of Northeastern Guatemala.* T. E. Gutman, trans. Institute of Archeology, University of California, Los Angeles, Occasional Paper 13.

Schackt, Jon
1984   "The Tzuultaq'a: Religious Lore and Cultural Processes among the Kekchi." *Belizean Studies* 12(5):16–29.
1986   *One God, Two Temples: Schismatic Process in a Kekchi Village.* Oslo: Department of Social Anthropology.

Scotchmer, David
1986   "Convergence of the Gods: Comparing Traditional Maya and Christian Maya Cosmologies." In *Symbol and Meaning Beyond the Closed Corporate Community: Essays in Mesoamerican Ideas,* G. H. Gossen, ed. Albany, New York: Institute for Mesoamerican Studies, SUNY.

Scott, James C.
1976   *The Moral Economy of the Peasant: Rebellion and Subsistence in Southeast Asia.* New Haven: Yale University Press.
1977a "Protest and Profanation: Agrarian Revolt and the Little Tradition." *Theory and Society* 4:1–38, 211–46.
1977b "Hegemony and the Peasantry." *Politics and Society* 7(3):267–96.
1985   *Weapons of the Weak: Everyday Forms of Peasant Resistance.* New Haven, Connecticut: Yale University Press.

Sexton, James, trans. and ed.
✕ 1992   *Ignacio: The Diary of a Maya Indian of Guatemala.* Philadelphia: University of Pennsylvania Press.

Siegel, Morris
1941   "Religion in Western Guatemala: A Product of Acculturation." *American Anthropologist* 43:62–76.

Silverblatt, Irene
1987   *Moon, Sun, and Witches: Gender Ideologies and Class in Inca and Colonial Peru.* Princeton: Princeton University Press.

Simon, Jean-Marie
1987   *Guatemala: Eternal Spring, Eternal Tyranny.* London: W. W. Norton.

Skinner-Klee, Jorge
1954   *Legislación indigenista de Guatemala.* México, D.F.: Instituto Indigenista Interamericano.

Skocpol, Theda
1979   *States and Social Revolutions: A Comparative Analysis of France, Russia, and China.* New York: Cambridge University Press.

Smith, Carol A.
1984   "Local History in Global Context: Social and Economic Transformations in Western Guatemala." *Contemporary Studies of Society and History* 26:193–227.

1988 "Destruction of the Material Bases for Indian Culture: Economic Changes in Totonicapán." In *Harvest of Violence*, R. Carmack, ed. Norman: University of Oklahoma Press.
1990a (Ed.) *Guatemalan Indians and the State, 1540–1988.* Austin: University of Texas Press.
1990b "The Militarization of Civil Society in Guatemala: Economic Reorganization as a Continuation of War." *Latin America Perspectives* 17(4):8–41.
1991 "Maya Nationalism." *Report on the Americas* 25(3):29–33.
Smith, Waldemar
1977 *The Fiesta System and Economic Change.* New York: Columbia University Press.
Sosa, John R.
1986 "Maya Concepts of Astronomical Order." In *Symbol and Meaning Beyond the Closed Corporate Community: Essays in Mesoamerican Ideas,* G.H. Gossen, ed. Albany, New York: Institute for Mesoamerican Studies, SUNY.
Spalding, Karen
1982 "Exploitation as an Economic System: The State and the Extraction of Surplus in Colonial Peru." In *The Inka and Aztec States 1400–1800,* G. Collier, R. Rosaldo, and J. Wirth, eds.
Sperber, Dan
1975 *Rethinking Symbolism.* Alice Morton, trans. Cambridge: Cambridge University Press.
Stern, Steve J., ed.
1987a *Resistance, Rebellion, and Consciousness in the Andean Peasant World, 18th to 20th Centuries.* Madison: University of Wisconsin Press.
1987b "The Struggle for Solidarity: Class, Culture and Community in Highland Indian America." In *Sociology of "Developing Societies," Latin America,* E. Archetti, P. Cammack, and B. Roberts, eds.
Stoll, David
1982 *Fishers of Men or Founders of Empire? The Wycliffe Bible Translators in Latin America.* London: Zed Press.
1988 "Evangelicals, Guerrillas, and the Army: The Ixil Triangle under Ríos Montt." In *Harvest of Violence,* R. Carmack, ed. Norman: University of Oklahoma Press.
1990 *Is Latin America Turning Protestant? The Politics of Evangelical Growth.* Berkeley: University of California Press.
1993 *Between Two Armies in the Ixil Towns of Guatemala.* New York: Columbia University Press.

Stutzman, Ronald
1981   "El Mestizaje: An All Inclusive Ideology of Exclusion." In Cultural Transformations and Ethnicity in Modern Ecuador, N. Whitten, ed. Urbana: University of Illinois Press.

Talmon, Yonina
1962   "Pursuit of the Millenium: The Relation between Religious and Social Change." European Journal of Sociology. 3:125–48.

Tannenbaum, Frank
1943   "Agrarismo, indianismo y nacionalismo." Hispanic American Historical Review 23:420–21.

Taussig, Michael
1980   The Devil and Commodity Fetishism in South America. Chapel Hill: University of North Carolina Press.
1986   Shamanism, Colonialism, and the Wild Man: A Study in Terror and Healing. Chicago: University of Chicago Press.
1990   "Terror as Usual: Walter Benjamin's Theory of History as a State of Siege." Social Text 28:3–20.

Tax, Sol
1963   Penny Capitalism: A Guatemalan Indian Economy. Chicago: University of Chicago Press.

Tedlock, Barbara
1992   "The Role of Dreams and Visionary Narratives in Mayan Cultural Survival." Ethnos 20(4):453–76.

Tedlock, Dennis, trans.
1985   Popol Vuh: The Mayan Book of the Dawn of Life. New York: Simon and Schuster.

Thompson, J. Eric S.
1932   "A Maya Calendar from the Alta Verapaz, Guatemala." American Anthropologist 34:449–54.
1938   "Sixteenth and Seventeenth Century Reports on the Chol Mayas." American Anthropologist 40:584–604.
1939   The Moon Goddess in Middle America, with Notes on Related Deities. Washington: Carnegie Institute of Washington pub. 509, contrib. 29.
1954   The Rise and Fall of Maya Civilization. Norman: University of Oklahoma Press.
1970   Maya History and Religion. Norman: University of Oklahoma Press.
1975   Historia y religión de los Mayas. México, D.F.: Siglo XXI.

Tonkin, Elizabeth, Maryon McDonald, and Malcolm Chapman, eds.
1989   History and Ethnicity. ASA Monographs 27. London: Routledge.

Tumin, Melvin M.
1952   Caste in a Peasant Society: A Case Study in the Dynamics of Caste. Princeton: Princeton University Press.
van den Berghe, Pierre L., and Benjamin Colby
1969   Ixil Country: A Plural Society in Highland Guatemala. Berkeley: University of California Press.
1977   Ixiles y Ladinos: El pluralismo en el altiplano de Guatemala. G. Li and F. Cruz, trans. Guatemala: Editorial José de Pineda Ibarra.
Villa-Rojas, Alfonso
1978   Los elegidos de Dios: Etnografía de los Mayas de Quintana Roo. México, D.F.: Instituto Nacional Indigenista.
Vogt, Evon.
1969   Zinacantán: A Maya Community in the Highlands of Chiapas. Cambridge, Massachusetts: Belknap Press of Harvard University Press.
1976   Tortillas for the Gods: A Symbolic Analysis of Zinacanteco Rituals. Cambridge, Massachusetts: Harvard University Press.
Wachtel, Nathan
1973   The Vision of the Vanquished: The Spanish Conquest of Peru through Indian Eyes. Ben and Siân Reynolds, trans. Hassocks, U.K.: Harvester Press.
Wade, Peter
1993   "Race, Nature and Culture." Man 28(1):17–34.
Wagley, Charles
1949   The Social and Religious Life of a Guatemalan Village. Menasha, Wisconsin: American Anthropological Association.
Wallace, Anthony F. C.
1956   "Revitalization Movements." American Anthropologist 58:264–81.
1961   Culture and Personality. New York: Random House.
1972   The Death and Rebirth of the Seneca. New York: Vintage Books.
Warman, Arturo
1982   "Indigenist Thought." In Indigenous Anthropology in Non-Western Countries, H. Fahim, ed., Durham, North Carolina: Carolina Academic Press.
Warren, Kay B.
1978   The Symbolism of Subordination: Indian Identity in a Guatemalan Community. Austin: University of Texas Press.
1992   "Transforming Memories and Histories: The Meanings of Ethnic Resurgence for Mayan Indians." In Americas: New Interpretative Essays, A. Stephan, ed. New York: Oxford University Press.

1993   "Interpreting *la Violencia* in Guatemala: Shapes of Mayan Silence and Resistance." In *The Violence Within: Cultural and Political Opposition in Divided Nations,* K. Warren, ed. Boulder: Westview Press.

Watanabe, John
1990   "Enduring but Ineffable Community in the Western Periphery of Guatemala." In *Guatemalan Indians and the State, 1540–1988,* C. Smith, ed. Austin: University of Texas Press.
1992   *Maya Saints and Souls in a Changing World.* Austin: University of Texas Press.
1995   "Unimagining the Maya: Anthropologists, Others, and the Inescapable Hubris of Authorship." *Bulletin of Latin American Research,* 14(1).

Weaver, Muriel Porter
1972   *The Aztecs, Maya, and Their Predecessors: Archeology of Mesoamerica.* New York: Seminar Press.

Weber, Max
1930   *The Protestant Ethic and the Spirit of Capitalism.* London: George Allen and Unwin.
1952   *Ancient Judaism.* Glencoe: Free Press.
1965   *The Sociology of Religion.* London: Methuen.

Whetten, Nathan
1961   *Guatemala: The Land and the People.* New Haven: Yale University Press.

Whitten, Norman
1976   *Sacha Runa: Ethnicity and Adaptation of Ecuadorian Jungle Quichua.* Urbana: University of Illinois Press.

Wilk, Richard R.
1991   *Household Economy: Economic Change and Domestic Life among the Kekchi Maya in Belize.* Tucson: University of Arizona Press.

Wilson, Bryan
1975   *Magic and the Millenium.* London: Paladin.

Wilson, Richard
1991   "Machine Guns and Mountain Spirits: The Cultural Effects of State Repression among the Q'eqchi' of Guatemala." *Critique of Anthropology* 11(1):33–61.
1993a   "Anchored Communities: Identity and History of the Maya-Q'eqchi'." *Man: Journal of the Royal Anthropological Institute.* 28(1):121–38.
1993b   "Ametralladoras y espíritus de la montaña: Los efectos culturales de la represión estatal entre los Q'eqchi'es de Guatemala." Con introducción por Dr. Demetrio Cojtí. Cobán: Textos Ak' Kutan.
1993c   "Continued Counterinsurgency: Civilian Rule in Guatemala." In *Low*

Intensity Democracy: Political Power in the New World Order. B. Gills, J.
Rocamora and R. Wilson, eds. London and Boulder, CO.: Pluto Press and
Westview Press.

1994   "Comunidades Ancladas: identidad e historia de los Maya-Q'eqchi'."
Cobán: Textos Ak' Kutan.

Wisdom, Charles

1940   *The Chorti Indians of Guatemala.* Chicago: University of Chicago
Press.

Witherspoon, Gary

1977   *Language and Art in the Navajo Universe.* Ann Arbor: University of
Michigan Press.

WOLA (Washington Office on Latin America)

1988   *Who Pays the Price? The Cost of War in the Guatemalan Highlands.*
Washington, D.C.: WOLA.

Wolf, Eric

1957   "Closed Corporate Communities in Mesoamerica and Central Java."
Southwestern Journal of Anthropology 13(1):1–18.

1966   *Peasants.* Englewood Cliffs, New Jersey: Prentice-Hall.

1967   'The closed corporate community in Mesoamerica and central Java,' in
Jack Potter, May Díaz and George Foster (eds.) *Peasant Society: a reader.*
Boston: Little, Brown and Co.

1969   *Peasant Wars of the Twentieth Century.* New York: Harper and Row.

1986   "The Vicissitudes of the Closed Corporate Community." *American
Ethnologist.* 13:325–29.

Worsley, Peter

1984   *The Three Worlds: Culture and World Development.* London: Weiden-
feld and Nicholson.

Zuidema, R. T.

1966   "Observaciones sobre el Taqui Onqoy." *Historia y Cultura* (Lima)
I(1):37.

INDEX

Reyes, Monsegnor Gerardo; Reducciones; Virgin icons

Sacrifice: attitudes of catechists, 194–95; in chapok k'al ritual, 100–108; and ethnicity, 86–89; indigenist attitudes towards, 264, 270; to mountain spirits, 57, 59–60, 68–77, 101–108, 270; as practical activity, 91, 99–100, 106; prayer in cave sacrifice, 73–74. See also Pom incense; Wa'tesiink, sacrificial ritual
Saint-Lú, André, 160
Salaquím, 208, 216, 221, 223
Sallnow, Michael: celestial markers and Inka empire, 104–105; cultural schizophrenia, 86; sacred landscapes and domination, 309; Spanish invasion and Andean pilgrimage, 225n; wayri chuncho dancers, 84; whitening of Señor de Temblores icon in Cusco, 278
Salomon, Frank, 86, 296–97
Salvadó, Raul, 36, 38, 237
Samandú, Luís, 168–71
San Cristóbal Verapaz, 209
San Juan Chamelco, 163
San Pedro Carchá, 163, 173, 180–81, 215
Sapper, Karl, 59
Saraxoch. See Model villages
Schackt, Jon, 78
Scott, James: isolated smallholders and rebellion, 216; millenialism, 214; weapons of weak, 300–301
Sexton, James, 240n. See also Bizarro Ujpán, Ignacio

Sexuality: guilt, 112; licentiousness, 111; of soldiers, 253
Silverblatt, Irene, 67, 81, 139n, 246n
Skocpol, Theda, 216
Smith, Carol: development of pan-Maya identity, 259; economic reorganization of war, 237–38; global factors and local economy, 33; Guatemalan state and community institutions, 251n; on Ladinoization in the western highlands, 27; materialist conception of identity, 312 & n; peasantry in Guatemala, 49
Smith, Waldemar, 26, 165–66, 182n, 306
Sosa, John, 105
Spirit loss: in corn, 151–53; in people, 4, 123–24, 143–51. See also Catechist program
Stern, Steve, 165, 255, 298, 301
Stoll, David, 169n, 210, 255–56
Sun: and agricultural fertility, 104–105; and mountain spirits, 327–28. See also Hunt, Eva

Taki Onqoy uprising, 198, 308
Tannenbaum, Frank, 304
Taussig, Michael: on Andean mountain spirits, 76, 81, 86; Bolivian tin miners' critique of wage labor, 78; economic dualism of Andes, 107, 291 & n.7; healing and violence, 246; resistance and ideological encroachment, 302; wildness in the Putumayo, 84; writing about terror, 256
Tecún Umán, 280